CW00549314

DOUBLE DECK TRAMS OF THE WORLD

beyond the British Isles

by Brian Patton

Published by Adam Gordon

Cover illustrations
Front Cover:
Top left:
A view of an open top d-d car in Hong Kong c.1912. It is in the rural setting of the junction of Murray Road and Queen's Road, and is working inbound to the General Post Office. That terminal was not used in normal service, but was used to reverse cars which from 1912 ran on summer evenings to the bathing beach at North Point. To encourage this traffic, the Company provided bathing tents and refreshments, and also arranged for naval or military bands to play on the beach. To-day Queen's Road is completely built up and no one would wish to go bathing at North Point, no matter the inducements offered! (Author's collection)
Top right:
Alexandria. Car 209 in 1996. (Kyle Hulme)
Bottom left:
Barcelona. Class A 180 at Plaza de Colon on 14 June 1957. (Raymond de Groote)
Bottom right:
Bombay. Rebuilt Pullman car 128 leaves the city terminus on a short working (5A) to King's Circle, in 1961. (Hugh Ballment)

Back Cover:
Top left:
LCC class car 82 on service 3 at Museum West, Bombay, in 1961. It is followed by one of the war-time or post-war cars, and on the right is one of BEST's Leyland Titan double-deck buses. (Hugh Ballment)
Top right:
Hong Kong's newest car 168 about to leave the depot for its first trip in passenger service, October 2000. (Malcolm King)
Bottom left:
The Cathay Pacific advertising tram as renumbered to 165, seen in March 1993. (Author)
Bottom right:
Johannesburg. Brush bogie car N39, its dash painted silver, working on 'native' service in the southern suburbs, at the intersection of Hay and Turf Club Streets in Turffontein on 14 Thursday. November 1948. The abandoned tracks of the Forest Hill route, converted to buses in 1935, can be seen crossing at right angles. (B. T. Cooke)

A catalogue entry for this book is available from the British Library.

ISBN : 1874422397

Publication no. 41

Published by
Adam Gordon
Kintradwell Farmhouse,
Brora,
Sutherland
KW9 6LU

Tel: 01408 622660
E-mail: adam@adamgordon.freewire.co.uk

Printed in 2002 by Launton Press, Bicester, Oxfordshire

Typesetting and design by Trevor Preece, trevor@epic.gb.com

CONTENTS

DOUBLE DECK TRAMS OF THE WORLD
beyond the British Isles

INTRODUCTION

The idea of double-decker trams operating in countries beyond the shores of the British Isles has always been an intriguing one but, although some of the individual systems which used them have been studied in detail, there has not been any attempt to consider the topic as a whole. This book is an attempt to fill that gap and to evaluate the place of the double-decker in the development of tramcar types.

Where the topic has been mentioned, as in "Great British Tramway Networks", there has been a general supposition that, where the double-decker has been used, it has been employed because of British influence. On the face of it, this seems reasonable. The British empire, after all, once included about a quarter of the earth's population and it would not have been surprising if British ideas had had the same predominance in the tramway field as they did in that of main line railways. On closer investigation, however, it seems that this was not the case. There were many other influences at work, influences generally emanating from other countries and these seem to have had as much, if not more, responsibility for the use of double-deckers as did British practice.

In this book, each continent is discussed separately, with sections devoted to each undertaking which used double-

deckers or, in a few cases, considered doing so. Horse, steam and cable tramways are considered briefly within the context of the overall story, but a complete record of these – particularly horse trams – would merit a book of its own, always supposing that extant records allowed the history to be written. However, the book does aim to be a complete account of double-deck electric trams and, while a few individual cars may have escaped mention, all systems which have used these have been considered and it is hoped that this will form as complete a record as sources will ever allow. Although most of the story relates to trams which have long passed into history, coverage of the new trams in Alexandria and in Hong Kong, where further new cars are expected, shows that the double-decker still has a place, albeit a very small one, to play in the development of the electric tram world-wide.

A word about certain terms used in the book may not be out of place. Imperial measurements have been used, since these were normally used in Britain at the time when the trams concerned were running. However, for European systems and also for the new cars built for Alexandria, both imperial and metric measurements are given. In dealing with trams provided in Johannesburg for African passengers, I have used the term "native cars" which was then

The world's most elusive double-deck tram. See page 48 for more details. (Author's collection)

employed by that city's transport department, purely as a matter of historical record and have put this, wherever it occurs, in quotation marks. I trust that in doing so, I will have shown that it is not intended to be any part of the general vocabulary of the book. In Bombay, many streets have been renamed since British days, but the original names, as used in tramway days, are used in the text. They are in fact in many cases still in everyday use, perhaps because they are somewhat shorter than the new names! Similarly, Lourenço Marques is now Maputo but the trams ran in the city under its former name and it has been used here.

The book is not intended to be a complete history of the tramways concerned. References to more general histories are given, where appropriate, at the end of each section and readers who wish to know more about the systems concerned are referred to these.

ACKNOWLEDGEMENTS

It would have been impossible to have prepared this book without the help of a great many people throughout the world who have very willingly given of their time, knowledge and experience. Many of these have also loaned photographs from their own collections or have kindly given permission for the use of these from my own collection. The list of those who have helped is such a long one that it seemed best to break it down into sections, to try to ensure that no one has been left out. If anyone's name has been omitted, I hope they will forgive me and accept that this was due simply to the total volume of material. In every case, however, final responsibility for text and for choice of illustrations rests with myself. As far as present-day references are concerned, the book is correct as of March 2002.

Acknowledgements are given under the section for which help was given:

General
Mrs Rosy Thacker, (Librarian), Glynn Wilton and Alan Brodie, Photographic Curators, National Tramway Museum, Crich. Ms Debra Brill, Shamong, New Jersey. Martin Jenkins, Walton-on-Thames. M. J. Lea, Chigwell, Essex. David Packer, Bromley, Kent. Keith Terry, Leeds. Alan W. Brotchie, Aberdour.
Translation: Dr Noel O'Regan, University of Edinburgh, translation from Italian. Dr Michel Byrne, University of Glasgow, resolving doubtful points in French texts. Marcelo Benoit, Montevideo, translation from Spanish.
Preparations of illustrations: Paul Martin of Fantasy Prints, Berwick-upon-Tweed. Alasdair Ross, formerly of Edinburgh Cameras, Edinburgh.

Europe
Henrik Effersøe, Copenhagen. Mme C. Coquelard and other staff, Agence AudioVisuelle, RATP. Paris. André Maire, Archives Municipales de Lyon. Archive staff of ATM, Milan. Claudia Gonnella, Servizio Informazione, ATAC, Rome. Marco Montanarini, Rome. Frau I. A. Grieger, BVG Archives, Berlin. Wiener Stadtwerke Verkehrsbetriebe, Vienna. Library staff, Swiss Transport Museum, Luzern. Raymond de Groote Jr, Chicago. Pam Eaton, London.

North Africa
Hugh Ballment, John Clarke, Carshalton, Surrey. Pam Eaton. Kyle Hume, Alfreton, Derbyshire. Dave Spencer, PMP Video.

South Africa
Ms E. Bevan and E. Itzkin, Greater Johannesburg Library Services. Ms Kathy Brookes, MuseuMAfricA, Johannesburg. Peter Coates, Cape Town. The late Brian Cooke and Alan Cooke, Isleworth. Pam Eaton. Kevan J. Marden, Durban. Dr B. S. Noruka, East London Municipal Library. Ms R. Omar, Durban Local History Museums. Brian Sharp, North Lanarkshire Libraries. Brian Spencer, (retd) Durban Municipal Library. Keith Terry, Leeds.

India
Hugh Ballment. Surrey Hills, Victoria, Australia. H. E. Jordan, Reading. The late Maurice O'Connor, Crich. Richard Wiseman, Richmond, Yorkshire.

Australia
Ian Cooper, Canberra. Peter Duckett, Caulfield, Victoria. Roger Greenwood, East Doncaster, Victoria. David Keenan and Vic Solomons, Sydney. G. C. Nowell, Ivanhoe, Victoria.

Hong Kong
Malcolm King, Leeds.

New Zealand
Pam Eaton. David Himan, Christchurch. Graham Stewart, Wellington.

North America
Colin Brown, Luton. Henry Elsner, Philadelphia. Jim Schantz and George Sanborn of the Seashore Trolley Museum, Kennebunkport, Maine. Ms E. Bellknap and C.Stein, Fenton History Center and Ms L. Teresi, James Prendergast Library Association, Jamestown NY. Aaron Isaacs, Minneapolis. Julie Johnston, Chicago. Steve McGee, Tampa. Mrs M. McLean, Boston Public Library. Kenneth Rucker, National Capitol Trolley Museum, Maryland. Ross Willson, Canberra.

South and Central America
Marcelo Benoit, Montevideo. Allen Morrison, New York. Alberto Centurion, Buenos Aires.

Brian Patton, Berwickshire, Scotland
March 2002

A front view of car 209, Alexandria. (Kyle Hulme)

EUROPE

AUSTRIA

VIENNA

A few double-deck trailers were operated as horse trams in Vienna from 1894. However, the spread of electrification on the overhead wire system put an end to their use by 1900.

Just before the First World War, the Wiener Stadtwerke, which had by then acquired the city's tramways from private operators, went through something of a double-deck phase. Its first 30 motor buses were a variety of such vehicles, most of which looked British and some of which were British. It should be mentioned that traffic in the Austro-Hungarian Empire drove on the left, a practice which continued until 1938.

There were also three double-deck electric trams at this time. The first of these, which was also of British appearance, entered service in 1913. Originally numbered 2545, it was very soon renumbered 452 and classed E. It was built by the undertaking in its own workshops and had the lower saloon of a K class car. It was a totally enclosed two-axle car, with a double-width rear entrance and a single-width front doorway. Length was 10.65m/35ft and the height of 4.9m/16ft prevented use of this tram on all but a few services. For most of its life it was based at Simmering depot and worked on lines 74 to Wollzeite and 59 to Hütteldorf. Seating capacity was 32/20, most of the seats in the lower saloon being longitudinal, with only four being transverse. Standing room for 20 passengers was available. There was only a single staircase, located in the middle of the car, this being of a two-section layout. The tram saw little service after the early 1920s and was scrapped about 1930.

Two years later, two further double-deckers, 453 and 454, of class F entered service. These were designed by the manager of the undertaking, Ludwig Spangler, who later patented the design. They were based closely on current North American practice, resembling Manhattan's "Broadway Battleship" (qv), though they were rather smaller. They followed that tram's layout, having centre doorways and staircases at the ends of the lower saloons, but they incorporated certain modifications to ease passenger flow. This form of construction allowed a step height of only 190mm/7.5 in. at the doorway, considerably lower than most "low floor" cars of today. Both cars seated 56

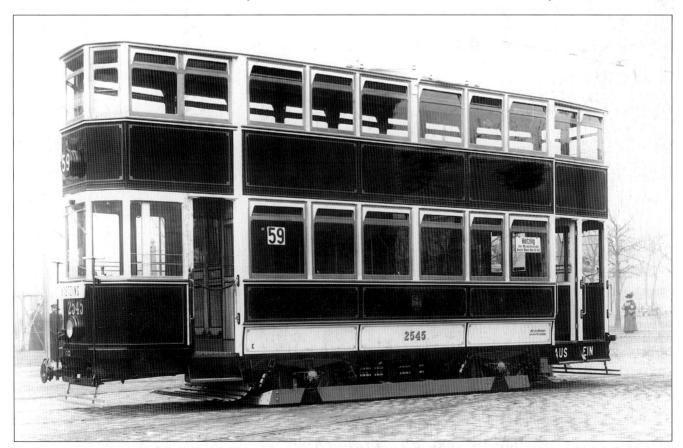

Car 2545 en route to Hietzing on service 59. The small window notice to the left of the platform reminds passengers that it is forbidden to board or alight while the tram is in motion. (Wiener Stadtwerke Verkehrsbetriebe)

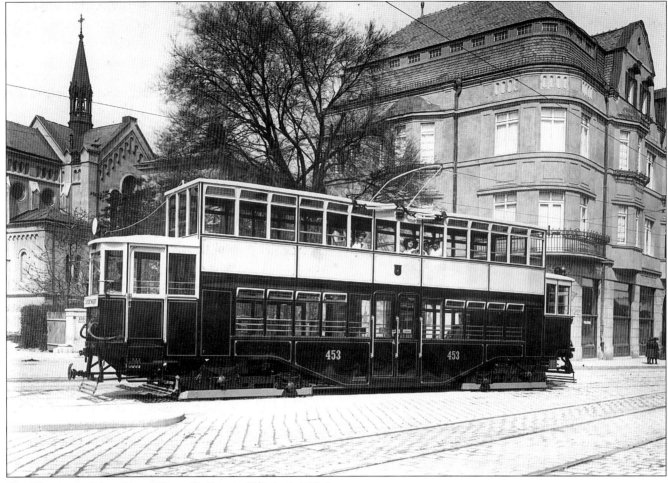

Car 453 on a special working. (Wiener Stadtwerke Verkehrsbetriebe)

passengers (32/24) and had room for 30 standees. The lower deck seats of 454 were a combination of transverse and semi-circular bays, the gangway being offset to the left in each saloon in the direction of travel, with the seating area to the right. With this layout, seated passengers were less likely to be jostled by those passing down the car to make for the upper deck. In car 453 seating was longitudinal. The cars were not quite "stepless" since there was a step halfway along the floor of the lower saloon and another at the foot of the stairs. The stairs themselves were a single straight flight, at right angles to the centre line of the body. Length overall was 14.4m/47ft 3in. and height 4.4m/14ft 5in., giving them a much wider route availability than car 452. To achieve this low height, the bow collector was mounted not on the roof but on the side pillars of the upper deck and the saloon was inset in the centre to make room for this. The upper saloons were also wider at floor level than the lower saloons, giving the cars something of a "concertina" appearance when viewed from the front. Unladen weight was 22,100kg/21 tons 14cwt. The two trams also differed in the external paint scheme, though in both cases this was the standard red and white. Later in its career, 453 was turned out in olive green. Reversed maximum traction bogies were fitted, in which the outer axles were driven, and the trams were the first in Vienna to have air brakes.

Although reported as being prone to derailment, these trams were quite successful in service and, but for the post-war troubles in Austria, there might have been more. They were laid up in 1931 but were not scrapped until 1938. The height of the roof of Rudolfsheim depot still testifies to the former operation of double-deck trams from it.

Total number of double-deckers operated in electric service:	3

Bibliography
Die alte Wiener Tramways. H. Lehnhart and C. Jeammaire. Verlag Eisenbahn, Wien, 1972
Osterreichs Strassenbahnen in Wort und Bild. W. Kramer et al. Zeitschriftenverlag Player & Co. Wien, 1951
Electric Railway Journal, 3 June 1916

BELGIUM

BRUSSELS

For the opening of the first line in Brussels in 1869, the English-owned company ordered 26 double-deck trams from Starbuck of Birkenhead. Thirteen of these were heavily rebuilt in 1876, when the eight side windows in the lower saloon were replaced by four large windows. It was found that it was difficult for the conductor to collect fares from the gentlemen seated on the upper deck – ladies were not allowed to use it – and the cars became single-deckers in 1881. One has been preserved in original condition and in running order and is housed in the museum in Woluwe depot.

Bibliography

Histoire des Transports Publiques à Bruxelles, tome 1. Société des Transports Intercommunaux de Bruxelles, Bruxelles, 1976

DENMARK

COPENHAGEN

The horse tramway system of the Danish capital was the second to open on the mainland of Europe, the concession being granted in 1862 and the first line opening for traffic on 22 October 1863. This was run initially by the Copenhagen Railway Company, registered in London, and standard gauge was used. The original rolling stock consisted of eight double-deck cars built by Starbuck. These were typical products of that firm, painted yellow and white and pulled by two horses. The next delivery was of five cars built locally, to a different design, which became standard for the remainder of the horse car era. This was also a double-decker but with straight-topped rather than arched windows and, latterly, with a canopy cover over the upper deck. The knifeboard remained standard on the upper deck, as did the rather primitive staircase; contemporary standards of decency dictated that ladies should not travel upstairs. Either eighteen or twenty passengers were carried on each deck. By 1898 the company, which had been domesticised as the Kjøbenhavns Sporvei-Selskab, owned 102 cars, 55 of which were double-deckers.

The next company to use double-deckers was the Nørrebroes Sporvejselskab (NS) which began operation in 1867 with eight open-top double-deckers, painted brown. Sixteen more were acquired later. It was soon followed by the Frederiksberg Sporvej-selskab (FS) and the Kjøbenhavens Forstaeders Sporveiselskab (KFS) (Copenhagen Suburban Tramway Company), both beginning service in 1872. The FS used 24 double-deck "tram buses" known as Keifler-omnibussar, which were in fact guided buses with two pony wheels which could be let down into the tram tracks; these were single-ended, open top and painted red, and in design they looked rather like the horse buses of Paris. These had the advantage that they could provide a through service to streets such as Strøget, a main shopping street where trams were not allowed to run. KFS trams were more conventional double-deckers, painted brown, and ultimately there was a total of 13 on its roster. An unknown number later served as trailers behind single-deck electric cars.

In 1884 the Falkoneralleens Sporvejsselskab began operations with single-deckers, but later acquired three double-deckers, which sported a light blue colour scheme. One of these was later modelled by a German manufacturer of tinplate toys.

Before this, in 1874 –75, there had been experiments with steam tram locomotives. The first of these pulled one double-deck trailer, while the second seems to have managed two. These experiments led KSS to form a subsidiary company, Strandvejens Dampsporvejs-Selskab (SDS) which opened a line northwards along the coast to Hellerup. Service began on 23 March 1884, using Rowan single-deck steam cars. These had limited success and the twelve cars were later converted to double-deck trailers, open on top, which were pulled by new and more powerful locomotives obtained from the local firm of Burmeister and Wain. This line carried heavy pleasure traffic and trains of several cars were operated, usually a mixture of single- and double-deckers.

Electric traction first appeared in the Copenhagen area on 4 March 1897, when the Nørrebros Elektriske Sporvei (NES) began a service of accumulator cars. This company was a subsidiary of Siemens and Halske. The line ran from Kongens Nytorv in the city – where the charging station was located – to Nørrebrogade. The first 18 cars were single-deckers and were known to the public as "acid wagons" because of the fumes given off by the batteries. There were also several fatal accidents.

All the undertakings in the Copenhagen area were combined on 22 April 1898 into two companies – A/S De Kjøbenhavnsk Sporveje (DKS) and Frederiksberg Sporvejs-og Elektricitets Aktie Selskab (FSEA). The NS line passed into control of the former.

Despite the public's view of the accumulator cars, traffic was increasing steadily and to cope with this DKS ordered four double-deckers. These were built by the local firm of F.C. Schultz in Nørrebro depot and were numbered 20-23. Electrical equipment for these cars was ordered on 19 April 1898 from the Union Elektrizitäts Gesellschaft and was intended to be compatible with that of the single-deckers as well as that on the new Frederiksberg double-deckers (qv). This order was later passed to Siemens and Halske, the idea then being that they would deliver six sets of equipment in all. The accumulators were of type GO 80, with two batteries of 87 cells. The electric brake was used for service stops. As the city magistrates would not agree to the proposed use of air hooters, the cars were fitted with the traditional gongs. In the lower saloon, the sets were originally upholstered in green cloth. The upper deck seating was still of the knifeboard pattern and was wooden. The upper decks were covered by a roof which ran the full length of the car but were open at the sides. Platforms were also open and the cars were double-ended. Car 20 was also fitted with sanding gear. They entered service on 2 March 1900.

These trams were very soon joined by a fifth double-decker, numbered 19. This had been built in 1898 by Larsen, another local firm, to allow the FSEA company to

One of the original accumulator double-deckers for the Nørrebro line, car 20 is seen in DKS colours, before rebuilding for trolley operation. (HT archives, courtesy Henrik Effersøe)

run trials with a compressed air car, but these had proved to be unsuccessful. It was then sold to DKS, fitted with accumulators and placed in service alongside 20-23 in March 1900. It differed from these in having D14/20 motors and a Siemens and Halske truck. Its length was 10.3m/33ft 9in. and width 2.1m/ 6ft 11in. and it originally seated 48 passengers, this figure being reduced in 1905 to 40.

Not long after a sixth double-decker of the same basic design appeared, car 24, the origins of which have puzzled historians over the years. It now seems possible to piece its story together, a story which provides another link between British tramways, double-deckers and Copenhagen. In 1898 both Manchester and Glasgow were planning the electrification of their tramway systems. Of these, Glasgow was in rather more of a hurry, since an international exhibition was planned for 1901 and it was hoped to have most

of the work completed by that year. Glasgow Corporation therefore invited tenders from a variety of builders for double-deckers to be built to its own very exacting specifications. In March 1899 Manchester invited tenders for five double-deckers from a variety of manufacturers, one of which was Hurst, Nelson of Motherwell in Scotland. In due course this firm supplied a two-axle double-decker which became Manchester 102 and whose lower saloon appears to be identical to that of Copenhagen 24. It also seated the same number of passengers, 43 (25/18). No order followed but the car remained in Manchester and in due course received a top cover.

It would appear that Hurst, Nelson built an identical second body in the hope of securing an order from Glasgow. There is no record of such a car ever having run in Glasgow and in the event Hurst, Nelson had to wait for almost thirty years before securing an order from that city.

However, a contemporary enthusiast many years later recollected seeing a derelict four-window double-deck body lying in Glasgow's permanent way yard. It was lettered "Mitchell Street and Springburn" – Glasgow's first electric service. On 2 November 1899 Hurst, Nelson invoiced DKS for the supply of one double-deck tram body, seating 43 passengers, at a price of £215 plus packing and carriage. This was probably something of a bargain since a comparable new tram, complete with truck, would have cost about £600. The body was duly shipped from Leith per Currie Line steamer and the builders were invoiced on 12 December for DKR841, about £84 at contemporary rates of exchange. But it is not recorded how Hurst, Nelson and DKS were put in touch with each other, though no doubt the builder was glad to be rid of the truckless body.

The car then received UEG electrical equipment and truck and the body was top covered to make it similar to the accumulator cars. Its dimensions were 9.3m by 2.1m/30ft 6in. by 6ft 11in. It entered service in September 1901 and was the first conventional double-decker to be owned by DKS. Like the others it received platform vestibules and enclosed upper deck canopies in 1912. When cut down to become a single-decker in 1924, it became a rail grinder and was scrapped in 1957.

Public dissatisfaction with the accumulator system

continued unabated and in 1900 a petition with 8,618 signatures called for its abandonment. It was decided in 1901 to convert the line to overhead current collection, with double overhead to guard against possible leakage of stray current. The new system went into operation on 15 March 1902, all the cars being rebuilt accordingly, and in July of the same year the double-deckers were transferred to operate alongside the other double-deckers of DKS on what had by then become line 3 (qv). In 1911 DKS passed into municipal control as Købehhavns Sporveje (KS) and in the following year cars 20-23 were again rebuilt, the platforms and upper deck balconies being enclosed. In 1915 new long wheelbase Scandia trucks replaced the original Berolina type. Car 19 was withdrawn from passenger service at this time and was cut down to single-deck form to serve as an office car in the workshops. It returned to passenger service about 1924 and ran until 1933, as a single-decker, before once again becoming a works car. In this form it lasted until 1963.

The others continued to run as double-deckers until 1924/25 when all were cut down to single-deck form, in which guise they ran until 1951. Two, 22 and 23, then became rail grinders S2 and S3 and worked until closure of the system in 1972. Both have been preserved by the Sporvejhistorsk Selskab at Skjoldenaesholm museum.

Chronologically the next double-deckers to be consid-

Bogie car 95 at Århusgade depot in 1913. The car has been rebuilt with vestibuled platforms and enclosed ends to the upper deck. The five window lower saloon has a distinctly 'Glasgow' appearance. This view was taken two years after DKS ceased to exist but the car still wears their livery – clearly KS saw no need to repaint the side panels when rebuilding took place! (HT archives, courtesy Henrik Effersøe)

After the fitting of a trolley and transfer to line 3, car 20 is seen at Enghavevej depot in 1909. (HT archives, courtesy Henrik Effersøe)

ered were those built for the Frederiksberg system of FSEA, which had decided on electrification on the overhead system immediately on its formation. The system comprised two lines, a cross-suburban line from Frederiksberg Runddel to Nørrebros Runddel, and a line from Frederiksvej running in a loop through the centre of Copenhagen and back to Frederiksberg. Trials on the former line began on 15 August 1899 and it opened for passenger traffic on 19 September 1899. The depot, which no longer exists, was situated in Allégade and originally had room for 50 cars. In 1915 a second depot was opened in a former horse bus depot in Manendalsvej.

Service was initially provided by 40 open-top two-axle double-deckers, numbered 1-40. These were built as follows:-

1-10 N Larsen, Frederiksberg
11-20 Falkenried, Hamburg
21-40 Vulkan, Maribo (built in the depot)

Two further cars, built by W. C. Hansen, followed almost immediately afterwards, in the early months of 1900.

These trams were single-ended and in service were turned on turntables at the termini. Dimensions were 9.0m/29ft 6in. by 2.1m/6ft 11in., and all were fitted with two GE52 motors by the Union Elektrizitäts Werk. Between 1901 and 1906 the driving positions on all cars were enclosed with glass vestibules and they received roofs over the front portion of the upper deck. This work was undertaken by different builders and some cars had much

flatter roofs that others. Until 1906 some were of canvas and could be opened on fine days, but after that date all had fixed roofs. Four further cars (43-46) were delivered from Larsen in 1908. These were built to the enclosed design and had GE58 motors. Finally in 1915 cars 47-52 arrived from the same builder, fitted with longer trucks and GE52g motors.

On 1 July 1919 the Frederiksberg company was merged with KS and the double-deckers were repainted from red and cream to the KS colours of yellow, grey and white. Services were integrated on 1 October of the same year and the double-deckers continued to run on what became KS lines 3, 8, 17 and 18, the last two being new services. The cars were renumbered 370-421 in sequence. Cars 370-374 became single-deckers in 1921 but the others survived the decapitation of other double-deckers in 1924, although they did not thereafter run on line 3, and line 17 was abandoned in 1931. Some withdrawals occurred after 1928 but the majority continued in service on line 18 until 10 June 1933. They usually pulled KS single-deck trailers. Most were scrapped but some became summerhouses and most fortunately 419 was set aside for preservation, as FSEA 50. It is normally housed in the HT museum at Rødovre but in 1999 celebrated its centenary by running at Skjoldenaesholm.

On 22 November 1901 DKS inaugurated electric service on the Christianshavn line from Højbro to Sundbyerne. To work this line, which used conventional single overhead

Near the end of double-decker operation in 1933, car 398 with trailer 1388 waits departure from Svanmøllen terminus on line 18. (HT archives, courtesy Henrik Effersøe)

An animated scene in Frederiksberg c.1910, taken from Gammel Kongevej. Facing the camera, car 45 – with the flatter type of top cover – has come from Frederiksvej and is leaving Smallegade en route for central Copenhagen. Allégade is on the left and Falkonér Allée on the right. (HT archives, courtesy Henrik Effersøe)

wire collection, 16 new bogie double-deckers were ordered from Larsen. All previous DKS conversions had used single-deckers, the result of a study visit to Frankfurt (M), but traffic was increasing and, following discussions with the municipality, it was decided to try double-deckers on this line. In design they were based closely on the ex-accumulator cars but, as there had been many complaints about the rough riding of these, it was decided to try bogie cars. Remscheid-type maximum traction bogies were supplied by UEG. These cars, numbered 90-104, remained on their original line only until 22 July 1902, when they were transferred en bloc to the Enghave line, which became line 3 when services were numbered on 27 November of that year. This line ran across the edge of the central area from Enghavevej to Strandboulvarden. From Trianglen a branch ran to Hellerup where it connected with the tracks of what was originally the A/S Tuborg – Klampenborg Elektriske Sporveje, a subsidiary of DKS. When the latter was municipalised in 1911, the TKES became independent as the Nordsjaellands Elektircitets og Sporveje A/S. Its line along the coast of the Øresund reached Charlottenlund in 1903 and Klampenborg on New Year's Day 1904. It carried heavy pleasure traffic in summer and the double-deckers of line 3 worked over it as far as Charlottenlund. In normal service they pulled single-deck trailers and for these workings an additional cross-bench trailer was often added.

The later history of these double-deckers is identical to that of the ex-accumulator cars. The ends of the upper deck and the platforms were enclosed in 1912. In the 1920s, a new bridge was constructed for a rail line which crossed the tracks of line 3 just before

The Frederiksberg cars had to be turned on manually-operated turntables at stub end termini. Here the crew seem to be putting quite some effort in turning 38 at Frederiksberg Runddel terminus of line 18. The date is 1919 or 1920, and the car is in the yellow and white KS livery but as yet has not been renumbered into the combined fleet. A small F has been placed before the number as a temporary measure. (HT archives, courtesy Henrik Effersøe)

Frederiksholm terminus, and it was not considered worth while making this high enough to allow double-deckers to pass under. They were therefore all withdrawn and cut down to single-deck form, in which condition they remained in passenger service until 1951. Fortunately car 100 is preserved, as a single-decker, in the HT museum.

On all DKS double-deckers the upper deck extended to a point over the middle of the platform and not to the end of the canopy, and seating capacity was therefore low in rela-

An upper saloon view of one of the ex-Frederiksberg cars taken in the 1920s, after they had passed into control of KS. (HT archives, courtesy Henrik Effersøe)

14

With a top cover but before fitting of a platform vestibule, car 19 heads for Copenhagen Radhuspladsen. On the pavement on the right is a car stop with plenty of information in its panels! (Colin Brown collection)

tion to the dimensions of the cars and also in comparison to that of similar cars used elsewhere. While LCC bogie double-deckers could carry 72 seated passengers, even the DKS bogie cars could seat only 40. However, as on the city's single-deckers, both front and rear platforms were used in service. The single-ended Frederiksberg cars were rather more capacious. Of course all cars ran in service with single-deck trailers to give added capacity.

The Copenhagen double-deckers could lay some claim to British ancestry and seem to have been quite popular in service. But while Frederiksberg is notable as being one of the few overseas systems whose fleet of motor cars was 100% double-deck, the type formed a small proportion of the city's fleet as a whole and a long-term future was therefore unlikely.

A visit to the HT museum is strongly recommended. Apart from a chance to see cars 50 and 100, the visitor can also enjoy a large display of photographs, many of which show double-deckers in service.

There are not many views of car 24 in service. In this postcard it is seen on line 3 at Enghaveplads in its original condition. (HT archives, courtesy Henrik Effersøe)

Bogie car 97, in original condition, is at the intersection of Frederiksberg Allée with Kingogade and Alhambravej, en route to Strandboulevarden on line 3. On the left, ex-accumulator car 20 is heading for Enghavevej. (HT archives, courtesy Henrik Effersøe)

Principal dimensions of DKS double-deck cars

19-23:
Length 9.7m/31ft 10in, width 2.1m/6ft 11in
Trucks 1: Tobler Berolina, 1700mm wheelbase, 2: Scandia 2200mm wheelbase
Wheel diameter 800mm
Two 16kW motors, later 2 x 23kW motors
Seating capacity 20/20 + 2, later (1921) + 8

90-104:
Length 9.7m/31ft 10in, width 2.1m/6ft 11in
Trucks "Remscheid" 9e UEG maximum traction
Wheel diameter 800mm/600mm
Distance between driving axles 1300mm
Two 16kW motors
Seating capacity 20/20 + 6, later (1921) + 8

Bibliography

Farvel Sporvogn. W. Christensen and J. Lundgren. Sporvejshistorik Selskab, second edition, 1980
Wonderful Copenhagen or from Starbuck to Düwag. Michael R. Taplin. Modern Tramway, nos 354-356, June-August 1967

Die Strassenbahnen in Kopenhagen. Ulrich Fröhberg. Baneforlaget, 1999
Unpublished material from HT Museum
The Manchester Tramways. I. Yearsley and P. Groves. Transport Publishing Company, Glossop, 1988

FRANCE

BAYONNE – BIARRITZ

This line, opened in 1877, was a steam tramway which used double-deck trailers of a design similar to those used by main line railways on some suburban lines around Paris. There were in all 16 of these. The locomotives had very tall chimneys to carry smoke and smuts clear of the passengers. They appear to have continued in service until the line was electrified in 1922.

BORDEAUX

This city operated open top double-deck horse trams, built for right hand running.

DUNKERQUE

The horse tramway system in this city was operated by a company which used British capital, although headed by one M. Spilliardaet, who hailed from Antwerp. The lines were of standard gauge and the first opened for traffic in June 1880. It had 14 double-deck cars, of two types, both being of British layout. Those of the first type were 6.25m/20ft 4in. long and had a seating capacity of 20/18, with standing room for ten. The upper deck seats were of the knifeboard pattern and the stairs projected beyond the edge of the platforms by 35cm/14in. Cars of the second type were slightly longer, at 7.5m/24ft 8in., and had a seating capacity of 20/20, again with standing room for ten. In these cars, the stairs did not project over the platforms. An additional double-decker was delivered in 1897. This tram originally had an open layout in the lower deck, with seven benches and a total seating capacity of 26/28. Length was 6.5m/21ft 2in. However, the authorities would not allow a car of this layout to run in urban service, and it had to be altered to have a gangway in the lower deck, with considerably reduced seating capacity of 47.

When electrification was discussed it was decided to use accumulator trams and the first ran on 25 July 1898, conversion of the rest of the system following in 1899. To work the new system, 14 double-deck cars were purchased, again of British layout. They had six side windows to the lower deck and knifeboard seats on the upper deck. The cars proved to have all the usual drawbacks of accumulator cars; they ran well enough when empty, but laboured when carrying any number of passengers, even although Dunkerque is a flat city. The batteries were located under the floor of the lower deck and were only 7cm/2.75in. above rail level. They were therefore inclined to "run aground" if there was any imperfection in the track. The batteries also gave off unpleasant sulphuric fumes and changing these was a time-consuming process. Former horse cars were towed as trailers.

One interesting incident illustrates the leisurely way of life on contemporary tramways – when a tram was descending the Rue de l'Eglise at the required 8km/hr, the driver found that his brakes had failed. He immediately jumped off and stopped the tram by the simple expedient of removing the battery! Probably as a result of this incident, the brakes on 13 trams were modified by August 1899. Problems increased as the batteries wore out and it became a common sight to see an accumulator car being rescued in service by two horses and towed back to the depot. Service was continued on six monthly periods, before being converted to the overhead system between July and September 1903. The two forms of operation seem to have co-existed during the changeover period. The accumulator cars were used as trailers behind the new single-deck trolley cars and in due course were also cut down to the same layout.

Livery of the trams in accumulator days was dark green. The double-deckers seem to have used the front platform for entry and exit, which must have made life inconvenient for the drivers.

Bibliography

Dunkerque à l'Heure des Trams, in Ch de Fer Régionaux et Urbains, no.279, March 2000

LYON

This city was rather late in adopting the tram, since the first line did not open until 1880.

It was operated by double-deck horse cars, known as "Impériales Buire" built by both Delettrez and the Société Dyle et Bacalan. In all there were 76 such cars. They had knifeboard seats on the upper deck, which could accommodate 24 passengers. Total capacity was 52 and the entrance was in the dash, rather than at the side of the platform. The lines were worked by the Compagnie des Omnibus et Tramways de Lyon, whose livery was green and cream with varnished window frames. Car 1 opened the first line of the system, Bellcour – Pont d'Écully, on 11 October 1880.

In 1899 38 of these cars, re-numbered 25-62, were converted for electric operation. It is not recorded if the numbers were in any kind of sequence, but it may be that car 25 was formerly 1. It was first tried on service 12, City – Vénissieux. However, they were actually placed in service on lines 1, 3, 8, 9, 10 and 11. In 1907 those from lines 3 and 11 were redeployed on line 12, as they were too high to pass below the railway bridges being constructed to serve the new station of Brotteaux. They were fitted with new trucks and top covers and were known as "belles mères" or mothers-in-law. The origin of the nickname is not known, but it was restricted to Lyon. Perhaps it was a commentary on the large size and rather unprepossessing appearance of these cars? Part of the lower deck was first class, the remainder and the upper deck being for those paying second class fares. Platform vestibules were fitted

En route to Monplaisir, 'Belle Mère' 37 crosses the Pont Tilsitt on mixed gauge tracks, at some date between 1898 and 1908. (Commercial postcard, Archives Municipales de Lyon)

by 1930. They lasted much longer than similar conversions elsewhere, suggesting that they had been strongly constructed, and the last was not withdrawn until 1936, just before the service was converted to trolleybus operation. They were scrapped in St Fons depot in 1939. Car 25 had become a works car in 1933, losing its upper deck in the process, and lasted rather longer.

Fortunately Lyon, almost alone among French cities, kept some of its trams for preservation, thanks mainly to the efforts of one of the engineers, Jean Arrivetz. Among those saved was one of the double-deckers, presumably 25. In 1958 this was restored to almost original condition, including replacement of the trucks fitted for electric service by the original type of running gear. It is in fact the only surviving French horse tram. To-day it may be seen, along with other preserved trams, in the Musée de l'Automobile Henri Malartre at Rochetaillée-sur-Saône, about 11km/7 miles north of the city and easily reached by local bus.

PARIS

There was a very long tradition of using double-deck trams in Paris, going back to the first line of 1855, very often known as the "American" line, since the inspiration for it came from the USA. The gauge was 1520mm/5ft and the line opened its first section in September 1855. Ultimately it ran from Concorde to Versailles and it was soon acquired by the Compagnie Générale des Omnibus. It appears that it was originally proposed to use on this line small single-deckers, with a capacity of only 24 passengers, but that

Alphonse Loubat, the promoter, realised that these would not significantly demonstrate the superiority of the tram over the horse bus and therefore had one of the cars modified by the fitting of an upper deck. It could then accommodate 50 passengers and was pulled by three horses. The company later added other double-deckers to its fleet and by 1861 had a total of fourteen, each seating 48 passengers. In 1864 a new design seating 50 appeared and ten of these were in service by 1867, to handle traffic to the exhibition of that year. For the line to Versailles, there were twelve long double-deckers, which were sold to den Haag in 1866/67. A line from Rueil to Marly, which was opened at a later date, had six double-deckers.

All the trams mentioned above were single-ended, with quarter-turn stairs and a knifeboard seat on the upper deck. The driver sat on the level of that deck. There was also one car of much more British appearance, double-ended and arranged for left hand traffic, but further details of it have not survived. In 1866 the service was extended inwards to Palais Royal, but rails were not laid on this section. Accounts written at a later date disagree as to whether the wheels of the cars were changed at Concorde or whether they simply ran on the ordinary road surface.

Despite the success of this pioneer operation, it was not until 1873 that Paris began to acquire a network of tramways.

Before considering details of vehicle design, it should be explained that until 1921, this network was worked by a variety of different companies. As in London, however, there was strong prejudice against the running of trams along the more elegant streets of the capital and, later, a complete ban on overhead wires in the central area.

Of these companies, by far the most important was the Compagnie Générale des Omnibus which, unlike its London counterpart, operated a large number of tram lines, mostly within the city area of Paris. In 1921 it had one third of the total number of cars in the area. Since the concession under which it operated in the 19th century was due to expire in 1914, it showed a distinct reluctance to contemplate electrification, either by conduit or overhead wire, during the first decade of the new century and instead turned to a variety of forms of mechanical traction, all of which were less capital-intensive.

Other large systems were those of the Tramways Nord and the Tramways Sud, both of which served from central termini areas lying outwith the municipal area of Paris, in what was throughout the tramway period the Département de la Seine. In 1884 both of these companies went into receivership and in 1890 they were reconstructed as the Tramways de Paris et du Département de la Seine (TPDS) and the Compagnie Générale Parisienne des Tramways (CGPT). From 1887, these were joined by the Chemins de Fer Nogentais, serving the affluent western suburbs from Vincennes with compressed air cars and enjoying a good deal of excursion traffic at week-ends. Later these operators were joined by other smaller companies, such as the Ouest Parisien and Est Parisien, while steam trams ran from Paris to Arpajon, and there was a cable line at Belleville which, confusingly, was always referred to as a funicular. Versailles was linked to Paris by a line operated by the CGO as successor to the "American", which it had taken over in 1875. The separate line from Rueil to Marly-le-Roi was worked at first by horse power and later by small fireless steam tram engines. It then expanded at both ends to link Paris with Saint-Germain and the fireless locomotives were replaced by conventional steam tram engines. In and after 1921 all these companies were merged, with others, to form the Société des Transports en Commun de la Région Parisienne (STCRP) which had no enthusiasm for double-deckers and fairly soon withdrew those which it had inherited, before going on to scrap the entire tramway network, a process completed in 1938.

It must be stressed that the above is a very abbreviated account of a complex history. With the exception of the Est Parisien and the Belleville cable line, all these companies used double-deck trams for part or all of their history, whether with horse, steam or compressed air power. Most took as standard the trams used on the "American" and most trams were therefore single-ended, the driver sitting on the level of the upper deck. Entry was by the rear, rather than the side of the single platform, and the upper deck was reached by a quarter turn staircase. There were, of course, detail differences, but all these trams resembled a horse bus much more closely than did their British and Irish counterparts.

In horse tram service, the CGO had three types of double-decker. The first, which entered service in 1874, had eight side windows and originally 47 seats, though this was increased to 51 from 1884. The second appeared in 1878, the year of another of the city's great exhibitions, one tram of this new class being on display and being awarded a gold medal. This class, with six side windows, seated 50 and after 1884, 51. There was later a much smaller design with only 30 seats. All trams confirmed to the basic design outlined above and all were built by the CGO in its own workshops. The last horse tram ran on 20 April 1913.

Most of the cars of the Tramways Sud resembled those of the CGO, but there were also some double-ended cars. The founder of the company, Harding, was British and its first cars were built in Greenwich. Later models were built in the company's own workshops or by the firm of Delettrez,

The cars of the Tramways Nord were much more like their British contemporaries, though of course arranged for right hand running. There were both open and closed double-deckers, some of the latter also having enclosed ends to the upper deck. These trams were very well-finished internally. All were double-ended with two stairs and side platforms. The cars were heated in winter, some by heaters filled with hot coals, some by containers of hot water which were changed at termini. The TN bought its cars from the Compagnie Francaise des Matériels de Chemin de Fer, the first car-building firm in the country.

No other company used double-deck horse trams. Given these beginnings, it is not surprising that double-deckers were adopted when mechanical traction came along.

The first form of such traction appeared in Paris in November 1876 when a Merryweather steam tram engine pulled a two-axle double-deck trailer of the Tramways Sud on a trial basis on the line Porte de Châtillon - Saint-Germain des Près. As the trials appeared to be successful, Harding, the engineer who had imported the locomotive, was given a concession for the Tramways Sud to operate with steam traction the line Gare Montparnasse - Place Valhubert, and on 9 August 1876 what is claimed to be the world's first urban steam tramway went into service, using double-deck trailers. However, though technically successful, the line proved to be unprofitable, as did that of the Tramways Nord. It had begun service in 1878 and its Swiss-built tram engines could pull two double-deck trailers. By 1882 the tram horse reigned supreme once again within the city. In the suburbs, the line Rueil-Marly was operated from August 1878 with fireless steam locomotives and it included in its rolling stock four two-axle double-deck trailers. This line proved to be much more successful.

It was in fact in Paris that the world's first double-deck electric tram ran in public service. In 1881 an exhibition was held to demonstrate the potential of electricity and a demonstration line, 493m/539yd long, was laid down by Siemens to link the Palais de l'Industrie with Place de la Concorde. On this ran a double-deck double-ended car rebuilt from one of the cars of the Tramways Nord. It could seat 50 passengers and had an unladen weight of 5,500kg/5 tons 8cwt. Overhead current collection was used, a cable connecting the car to two slotted overhead tubes, in which ran two small collectors for the supply and return of current. Service began on 10 August 1881 and ran successfully for the duration of the exhibition. However, many years were to elapse until this form of electric traction became common in Paris. Because of the above-mentioned unwillingness of the City of Paris to countenance overhead wires in its area, and the question of the expiry of the concession of the CGO, mechanical traction was instead developed in a wonderful variety of forms, quite unlike practice in any other capital.

Compressed Air Trams

A Les Chemins de Fer Nogentais
The first line to operate mechanically-propelled double-deck trams on a permanent basis was the Chemins de Fer Nogentais, which opened for traffic on 21 August 1887. In Nantes, a local engineer, Louis Mékarski, had been experimenting with compressed air as a motive power since 1875, and in 1879 the first tram line to use this form of traction was opened in that city. Mékarski had set his sights on Paris but wisely had no desire to enter into competition with the CGO, and so requested and was immediately granted a concession for a line from Vincennes to Ville-Everard, an area not previously served by trams. The cars used were 19 open-top, single-ended double-deckers on two-axle trucks of 1.90m//6ft 3in. wheelbase and in service they pulled one or two similar trailers. The motor trams, which were referred to at the time as "automobiles", were 7.53m/24ft 9in. long and had a seating capacity of 24/20, with six standing passengers being carried on the platform. Unladen weight was 10 tonnes. Some cars later received top covers. Under the floor were nine reservoirs which held 3,100 litres of air, compressed down to 45 atmospheres, which was further stepped down to six atmospheres for use in service. A controller on the platform allowed the driver to use between 0 and 6 atmospheres to regulate the speed of the car. Normally a single charge of air sufficed for a round trip. At first the reservoirs were recharged at the depot, which was located at La Maltournée, but charging points were later installed at the Vincennes terminus and at Bry-sur-Marne, one of the outer termini. The operation of recharging took about a quarter of an hour.

Despite some fairly severe gradients en route, the compressed air system worked well and lasted until electrification in 1900.

B Les Tramways de Saint-Maur
This operator opened four lines in the eastern suburbs between 1894 and 1899. It used ten cars similar to those of the CFN, but as the lines passed beneath several low bridges, top covers were not fitted. The company changed its title to the Compagnie des Tramways Est-Parisien in 1899 and proceeded to take over several other companies in the eastern suburbs. The compressed air lines were electrified in 1900.

C The Paris-Arpajon Line
The full title of this suburban roadside tramway, which operated for 32km/20 miles southwards from the centre of Paris to the town of its title, was the Société du Chemin de Fer sur Route de Paris à Arpajon. Its first section was opened in 1883, using steam power, soon supplemented by compressed air locomotives on the city section from Porte d'Orléans to Odéon. There were initially eleven double-deck trailers, with longitudinal seating downstairs and a knifeboard on the upper deck, which was open at the sides but roofed and enclosed at the ends. These cars were 8.43m/27ft 8in. long and rode on two-axle trucks; they could carry 20/20 seated passengers and had room for ten standing. Ten were composites, AB1-10, while BB1 was second class only.

The line was taken into the STCRP in November 1922. Between 1927 and 1929 twelve double-deck "74 seat" cars from the former CFN lines (qv) were transferred to the Arpajon line for use as trailers, to increase its capacity. They were given double doors to the end platforms and seating capacity was increased to 84. It was intended to work them in three car trains, but even after the removal of their motors, their unladen weight of 14 tonnes proved to be too much for the steam tram engines and they saw little use. The last part of the line closed on 25 January 1937. Although the inner part of the line as far as Antony was electrified in 1901, no double-deck electric cars were used.

D The CGO
Having studied compressed air traction for the above-named company, the CGO decided in 1893 to try it on its own account. The first units to be purchased were locomotives, but in 1894 it was decided to use compressed air trams in urban service on line TAD, Cours de Vincennes - Saint-Augustin. The vehicles used were two-axle single-ended cars, 8.1m/26ft 6in. long, 2.1m/6ft 11in. wide and weighing 11.5 tonnes empty. There was a roof over the upper deck with a flat windscreen at the front, but the sides were open. Seating was 24/20 and there was room on the platform for a further six seated and two standing passengers. Under the saloon floor were nine reservoirs, of which seven were used in normal service and two were a reserve. Two cylinders drove the rear axle through Walschaerts valve gear, and this was connected to the front axle by a rod, with an estimated horsepower of 35. All the motion was concealed. Air brakes were fitted, supplied by a reservoir. There were in all 31 of these cars, which in service pulled a former horse car as a trailer. As this weighed nine tonnes empty, and as there were also several hills en route, service speed could not have been very high, but nevertheless the experiment was judged to be a success.

In 1900 compressed air operation was greatly extended when six lines in the south and south-west of the city were

A lady in the height of hobble-skirt fashion studiously ignores both the photographer and a Mékarski compressed air car and trailer working on CGO line TJ at Place de la Concorde in 1913. (RATP)

converted from steam or horse power. These particular lines were chosen since the factory for the production of compressed air was located at Billancourt, and the conduits to carry the air to the charging points at the termini could thus be kept to a reasonable length. To work these lines a fleet of 148 new trams was built, numbered 1-148. These were 8.32m/27ft 3in. long, 2m/6ft 7in. wide, 4.80m/15ft 9in. high and weighed in running order 14 tonnes. Seating was now 28/20 but only four could be accommodated on the platform. The trucks had a wheelbase of 1.9m/6ft 3in. The first 88 cars, like those of the first series, had a boiler which was recharged by steam at each terminus, but on the second 60 the boiler was fired by coke during the journey and these cars therefore had a small chimney projecting through the top cover at the front. The earlier cars were converted to this system in 1904. This boiler also heated the lower saloon in winter. Apart from the chimney, the main external difference from the 1894 cars was that the dash and the windscreen on the upper deck were rounded. Mechanically the cars differed in having inside cylinders and Bonnefond valve gear, and there were only eight cylindrical reservoirs, although these had a slightly greater capacity than those fitted to the 1894 cars. Nominal horse power varied between 40 and 50, and again a double-deck trailer was attached in normal service; the lines in the area covered by these cars were fairly flat. A distance of 6-7 miles was normally covered between recharging if a trailer

were attached and 8-10 miles if the cars were running solo.

Two other lines were converted in 1902 and 1903 and the compressed air trams seem to have been generally satisfactory in service. The services worked included the busiest line of the entire Paris network, line TG (Montrouge - Gare de l'Est), which in 1909 carried 17.5 million passengers. In 1910 Paris suffered severe flooding and, despite precautions, the Billancourt factory was invaded by the waters when the Seine burst its banks on 26 January. Service TG was kept in operation using air from a small plant at Puebla, but all others were out of action until 4 February. But in the same year the vexed matter of the concession of the CGO was at last settled and the way was clear for electrification. The last Mékarski car ran on 2 August 1914.

Steam Trams

In 1876 the CGO tried out a self-contained double-deck steam car, built to the design of M. Bollée-Dalifol. This vehicle was single-ended and was probably a converted horse car. On trial it attained a speed of 27.5 mph, which so frightened the Company's engineers and managers that the experiments were abandoned forthwith.

A   Serpollet Cars of the TPDS
In December 1893 this company experimented with a Serpollet steam car between Saint-Ouen and Porte Maillot

21

and, as the results seemed promising, two lines were converted to this form of operation in 1895 and 1896. The Serpollet cars were fitted with a flash water tube boiler which could raise steam very quickly; this weighed 2.47 tonnes and as all this weight was carried by the front axle, it was necessary to counterbalance the body and the end result was a very heavy car, turning the scale at 13.3 tonnes. There were 23 such cars in all, numbered 1-23. Length was approximately 8.5m/27ft 9in., width 1.90m/6ft 3in. and capacity was 50 passengers. The lower saloon had six side windows and the upper deck provided a knifeboard seat; it was roofed and fitted with a windscreen but was open at the sides. The cars did not last very long in service, being replaced by electric trams in 1901. A few were then fitted with accumulators and used on the line from Saint-Denis to Porte Maillot from 1903.

B Serpollet Cars of the CGO

In the same year as the TPDS began regular service with Serpollet cars, the CGO experimented with one on line TIbis, Boulogne - Louvre. Again the trials were a success and more cars were ordered to allow the complete conversion of lines TI and TIbis in June 1897. In the next year, line TQ, Porte d'Ivry - Les Halles was similarly converted and in 1906 this was followed by line TE, Nation - La Villette. Finally from 1908 some of these cars were used on line TC to supplement the accumulator cars (qv) and in 1912, when line TE was converted to electric traction, the ex-Serpollet cars from it were transferred to replace the horse cars which still operated on line TH from Square Monge to La Chapelle. The last of these trams ran on line TQ on 12 November 1913.

The CGO Serpollet cars were 9.13m/30ft long by 2.10m/6ft 11in. wide and had a height of 4.62m/15ft 2in. They could carry 52 seated passengers, 26/20 plus six on the platform. The trucks had a wheelbase of 1.90m/6ft 3in. and air brakes were fitted. The interior was lit by petrol lamps, except for the cars on line TQ, whose passengers enjoyed the luxury of acetylene gas lights, while later some of those on line TI were fitted with electric lamps fed from batteries. These trams were just as heavy as those of the TPDS and therefore also had to be counterbalanced. In 1907, after the Purrey engine had proved itself to be superior, all the Serpollet cars were converted to that system, allowing the removal of the counterbalances, with a consequent saving in weight. There were 60 in all, numbered 401-460. In 1900 a prototype was built to test the use of diesel oil. This car was numbered 801 and seems to have been successful, particularly in reducing wear on the boiler tubes and having a wider range without refuelling, but no more were constructed. The earlier Serpollet cars were not really successful and two exploded fairly spectacularly, one on the Boulevard Saint-Michel, due to blockage of the tubes and safety valves, while a third disgraced itself by running away and colliding with a municipal dust cart, which stopped its headlong flight before it could do any greater damage.

C CFN Trials

In June 1895 the CFN tried two Serpollet cars, about which no details have survived. They may not have been double-deckers.

D Purrey Cars of the CGO

The Purrey design of steam tram was both lighter, at 9.7 tonnes unladen, and more powerful than the Serpollet model, and so slightly more economical. Externally they could be distinguished from their predecessors in that they did not have a separate motor compartment between the driving position and the saloon. They were also slightly smaller, and could accommodate only 48 seated passengers (24/20 + 4). They were considered to be the most serviceable model of mechanical traction of all the varied designs used by the CGO in this period, being almost silent in operation and producing very little vapour of any kind. The lower saloon was heated by steam from the engine and all the Purrey cars were lit by petrol lamps. Air brakes were fitted, with an axle-driven compressor.

Trials with a double-deck Purrey car were conducted between September 1897 and July 1899. The first production cars to this design entered service on line TL, Bastille – Porte Rapp, on 17 September 1900. Later lines TP and TD, from Trocadéro and Etoile respectively to La Villette also received Purrey cars on 20 December 1902 and they also performed some duties on line TK from March 1903. It had been intended to use them on line TM, Gare de Lyon - Avenue Henri Martin, but the cars intended for that line had to be hastily redeployed to line TC when the accumulator cars used on it had made the line into something of a disaster area. When these had been rebuilt, the Purrey cars went to join their colleagues on lines TP and TD, and it was not until additional cars had been delivered that line TM could be converted, on 18 July 1904. There were 40 cars in the first batch and ten in the second delivery, being numbered 701-750. There were also 36 single-deck Purrey cars. However, there is a conflict between records of the manufacturers, which show deliveries of a total of 98 Purrey cars, and those of the CGO, which show the totals mentioned above. No other operator in Paris used this type of steam car and the discrepancy cannot now be explained.

The last Purrey cars ran on lines TP and TD on 13 June 1914.

Accumulator cars

The first experiments with accumulator cars were made by the CGO in 1881, using a converted 50-seat horse car. Despite some success, particularly in the following year when the car ran to Versailles and back without recharging, the trials were discontinued. There were also experiments by the Tramways Nord in 1888/89, using an ex-horse car. These trials were successful and three other cars were similarly converted in 1890. It is not recorded if these trams were double-deckers, but it is likely that they were. The results were sufficiently positive to persuade the authorities

One of the Serpollet steam cars of the CGO poses in a depot yard. (RATP)

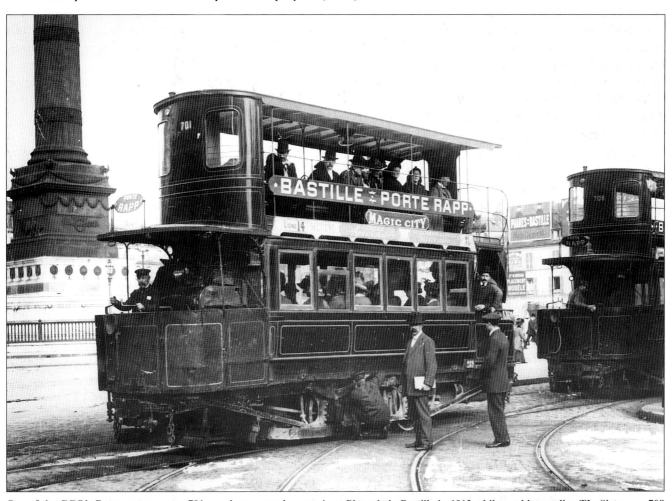
One of the CGO's Purrey steam cars, 701, receives a running repair at Place de la Bastille in 1913 while working on line TL. Sister car 708 has drawn up behind. (RATP)

was fitted which seems to have given quite good results on the hilly sections but was of little use on flat stretches of route.

The cars had a range of between 32 and 37 miles on one charge, this normally being sufficient for three round trips on one of the main lines, but to prevent embarrassing failure in service, cars returned to the depot for a new battery after each trip. Each tram made eight or nine round trips per day, as against five for horse cars, and, despite all its complications and also the fumes which permeated the saloons, the new system proved to be profitable.

A Purrey steam tram locomotive battles with the floods of February 1910 on the Quai de Passy, working inbound to Louvre. It is pulling two ex-horse cars of the type used by the CGO as trailers. (RATP)

that this form of traction should be generally permitted.

A   The Saint-Denis class of the TPDS

The first purpose-built accumulator cars entered service in 1892 when the TPDS converted its two main lines from the city to Saint-Denis to this form of operation, together with the shorter line from Saint-Denis to Porte Maillot. The cars used were two-axle single-ended double-deckers with a light awning over the otherwise open upper deck. They could carry 52 seated passengers. The trucks were rather unusual, since they consisted of two single-axle bogies linked to each other by a spring articulation on the Averley system. This radial arrangement allowed the axles to converge on curves. On straight track the wheelbase was 2.80m/9ft 2in. Each bogie was fitted with a single motor of 13hp. The cars were about 8m/26ft long and weighed 10.50 tonnes, of which the batteries accounted for about 4 tonnes.

These batteries were carried under the longitudinal seats of the lower saloon and could be removed from the exterior of the car. They consisted of twelve boxes, of nine elements each. They were known as "slow charge" batteries. Exchange of batteries was effected at the depot at Saint-Denis and this manoeuvre was carried out by small trains of seven wagons, of which the first was empty and numbers two to seven carried a recharged battery. This convoy gradually moved alongside the tram at the height of the storage space for the batteries and the exchange was effected, the first wagon receiving the first used battery, the recharged battery from the second wagon was fitted in its place, the second used battery was taken out, and so on until the entire process was complete. Recharging a battery required about six hours. Except in emergency, the two motors were permanently coupled in series and speed was controlled by using different couplages of batteries to give varying voltages. A kind of regenerative braking system

Complaints about those fumes soon led to the removal of the batteries from under the seats, to a position under the floor, from which they were suspended. Later, the upper decks were fitted with windscreens. The radial trucks gave much trouble and often the axles continued to converge when the car had regained straight track. They were therefore replaced in 1898 by ordinary two-axle trucks, with a wheelbase of 2.10m/6ft 10in. At this time, the power of the motors was increased to 20hp.

There were probably 30 of these cars, numbered 1-30. They lasted in service until 1913 and must be considered successful for pioneers.

B   The Heilmann cars of the TPDS

In 1897 the TPDS took delivery of additional accumulator cars to be used on the lines serving Courbevoie. They were similar to cars of the previous class as altered, but could be distinguished from them by the window in the upper deck windscreen. The trucks again had a wheelbase of 2.10m/6ft 10in. and the unladen weight was 11.3 tonnes, of which 3.6 tonnes was accounted for by the batteries. These were once again placed under the seats of the saloon. The batteries were of the Tudor "quick discharge" type and were recharged while the tram was standing at a terminus, the operation being under control of the driver and taking 10 to 15 minutes. Each terminus was now equipped with a charging point, to which current was supplied by underground cable from a power station at Puteaux. To prevent the car moving off while still connected to the supply line, the commutator which linked it to the cable also isolated the motors. A bell rang when the battery was fully recharged. The batteries contained 200 elements and supplied current to the two 20hp motors at 400V. These cars were fitted with normal controllers and resistances as it had been found that the practice of regulating speed by

24

One of the Heilmann cars of the TPDS, at an unknown location. (RATP)

altering the discharge from the batteries led to an imbalance in voltage.

It seems that trams from the various lines of the system were not interchanged, probably because of the different nature of the batteries used and these cars were numbered 1-35. They were 8.6m long and again passenger capacity was 52. They were all withdrawn in 1913.

C   The Aubervilliers Class
In 1898, for use on the lines serving Aubervilliers and Pantin, the TPDS acquired additional accumulator cars, of a different type to the earlier classes. Owing to lack of space at the suburban termini of the lines concerned, they were double-ended and they rode on maximum traction bogies, the first such to be used in Paris. But the greatest innovation with this class was that the motors were to be powered by both accumulators and conventional overhead current collection. The former method was used within the city area of Paris and the latter in the suburban area. As overall height was restricted by the bridges of the Petite Ceinture railway line, the trolley, when not in use, was stowed in a shallow trough in the roof. The batteries were suspended under the floor and were recharged when the car was taking current from the overhead. Unfortunately this apparently neat solution to the problem of recharging the batteries had its drawbacks, as the speed of the charging process made the batteries overheat and they then gave off even stronger fumes, which not only irritated passengers' noses and tempers, but also corroded the bodywork.

The trams of this class were 9.07m/29ft 9in. long and weighed 14.8 tonnes. There were two 25hp motors. Seating

capacity was for 56, at 28/24 + 4. Numbers ran again from 1-30. This class was withdrawn in 1914.

D   The Gennevilliers Class
Outwardly these trams were almost identical to their predecessors but they were slightly shorter and thus carried only 53 passengers. However, due to the problems mentioned above, they reverted to the "slow charge" type of battery, these being recharged in Asnières depot. The batteries were placed between the bogies and changing was carried out by a conveyor which moved under the car, at right angles to it, and automatically removed empty batteries and inserted the replacements. Again there were 30 trams in this class, again numbered 1-30, and they were also withdrawn in 1914.

In 1918, the administrator of the Ouest Parisien company, which was then under military control, following a complete collapse of the service, bought three redundant accumulator cars from the TPDS. A photograph shows a car corresponding to the Gennevilliers class but mounted on a two-axle truck. Two of these cars were still in service at the time of the formation of the STCRP and lasted until 1926.

E   The Motrices Impériales
The final class used by the TPDS was acquired in 1900 and 1902 for use on two new services and did not have a class name, being simply referred to by the above title, which is simply translated as "Double-deck motor trams". They saw a reversion to the two-axle type, with a 1.8m/5ft 11in. wheelbase truck. The batteries were once again of the

One of the Gennevilliers accumulator cars of the TPDS in 1899. Outwardly the Aubervillirs class were identical. (RATP)

"quick charge" variety and were suspended below the bodywork at the ends of the car, outside the axles. They also used trolley poles on a suburban section of one of the lines. There were 15 members of this class, numbered 31-45. They were 8.8m/28ft 11in. long and could accommodate 52 passengers. Unladen weight was only 10.80 tonnes.

These were the only TPDS double-deckers to pass directly to the STCRP, but all were withdrawn within two years of the merger.

Of all the operators in Paris, only the TPDS really perse-vered with accumulators and certainly had a measure of success with them. The total number of double-deck trams operated was 140, being made up of 80 two-axle and 60 bogie vehicles. All of the latter and 15 of the former could use both batteries and overhead current collection.

F CGO Experiment of 1893

Noting the success of the TPDS trials of 1892, the CGO decided to experiment with accumulator cars in the following year. However, probably to spread the weight of the battery, they opted for a three-axle car, the only one ever to

Everyone seems to be making for the upper deck on what was presumably a fine summer's day at Porte Maillot and the time taken to load the car must have been considerable. Car 45 is one of the double-ended cars of the TPDS, built for service Bb, Neuilly-Saint-Augustin. (RATP)

run in Paris; in fact, the car had three single-axle bogies, which could pivot on curves. The car used was converted from a horse car and was fitted with a roof over the upper deck.

Trials were conducted in the winter of 1893-94 on line TI, Porte de Clignancourt- Bastille. At first they went well, but one day the middle axle of the car broke in the very public surroundings of Place de la République and they were terminated forthwith. The cause of the accident is not known.

G Fives-Lille and SACM Cars of the CGO

In 1899 the CGO decided to try accumulator trams once again and this time chose two lines, TC and TF, which ran by different routes from Vincennes to Louvre. The first cars to enter service were those built by the Fives-Lille Company and these were placed on line TC in December 1899. They had radial axle trucks of 2.20m/7ft 3in. wheelbase, which were no more successful than similar trucks used elsewhere; the axles showed a distressing tendency to converge, even on straight track, and the trams were extremely noisy. They carried Blot batteries mounted under the floor of the car and a charging point, capable of dealing with several trams simultaneously, was set up at Château de Vincennes terminus. The batteries discharged too rapidly to give sufficient power for a round trip and the cars often had to suffer the ignominy of being rescued by

horse cars on the return trip. Between 13 July and 21 December 1900 all were taken out of service and line TCV was then worked by Purrey steam trams. The Blot batteries were replaced by Tudor batteries and the cars re-entered service between 3 November 1902 and 6 January 1903. Nevertheless some Purrey cars were retained on the line in case of further problems and it was not uncommon to see an accumulator car being pushed by one of these on the last lap of a return trip. In 1906 sixteen were taken for service on the Versailles line and were then fitted with trolley poles.

The other class, built by the Société Alsacienne de Constructions Méchaniques, entered service on line TF from April 1900. These were fitted with normal two-axle trucks of 1.80m/5ft 11in. wheelbase and had Tudor batteries, placed under the seats and weighing 4.8 tonnes. A further charging post was set up at Cours de Vincennes. These cars were rather more successful in service but were still not without problems. Power was often lost on the return journey and no driver dared to stop on the gradient of Boulevard Voltaire, no matter who wished to board or alight. This effectively excluded lady passengers and men who had to board or alight at the run were not best pleased either.

Both classes carried the standard CGO body, as fitted also to steam and compressed air trams. They were thus single-ended, with a capacity of 52 seated passengers

This view taken at Rond Point de la Vilette clearly shows the platform layout of CGO double-deck cars. Beyond the viaduct of the new Metro, on the other side of the road, a horse tram discharges its passengers into the roadway. (RATP)

A view of Vanves terminus, at a time when it was safe to stand and be photographed in the middle of the road! Car 239 is nearest the camera, with two others of the 200 class of the CGPT beyond. All are in original condition. (RATP)

(28/20 + 4) and were 8.42m/27ft 8in. long, 2m/6ft 7in. wide and 4.80m/15ft 9in. high. With the battery charged and in place, they weighed 19.5 tonnes. They were numbered 501-585, although it is not now possible to say which type carried which numbers. It is thought that there were 45 Fives-Lille cars and 40 SACM cars. By 1910 only 48 remained in service and the last ran in 1913.

Perhaps fortunately the CGO did not actually place in service a prototype Fives-Lille car, 586, which had a radial truck of 3.90m/12ft 9in. wheelbase. It was exhibited at the universal exhibition of 1900, along with Purrey steam car 722, Serpollet car 801 and Mekarski compressed air car 128. Overseas visitors, many already used to efficient electric trams in their own countries, may well have been puzzled at this display of unusual technology, and perhaps the kindest conclusion that they might have reached was that the CGO believed in keeping its options open!

H   The 200 Class of the CGPT
In 1901, after prolonged wrangling about the length of its concession, the CGPT took delivery of 60 bogie double-deckers equipped for both accumulator and trolley operation and based closely on the Aubervilliers class of the TPDS, having maximum traction bogies and two 43hp motors. They were double-ended and were totally enclosed on both decks, with a seating capacity of 26/28. At 15.6 tonnes, they were fairly heavy. At a later date, conduit operation was permitted in the city area and the accumulators were removed, plough carriers being fitted instead. This operation was completed by 1913.

The cars were numbered 201-260. Originally they were

9.14m/30ft long, but between 1911 and 1914 32 were lengthened, becoming 10.20m/33ft 6in. long and having a capacity for 61 passengers. Alterations were made to the suspension at the same time. A total of 49 survived to be taken over by the STCRP. Very shortly afterwards, one of this class ran away at Vanves terminus and overturned at the corner of Boulevard Voltaire in Issy-les-Moulineaux. Fortunately there were no passengers aboard at the time. This accident may have sealed the fate of double-deckers with the new organisation and all of this class had gone by 1926.

Surface Contact Cars

Only a few lines in the Paris area used this form of current collection, in various forms, and only one of these used double-deckers. Generally none of these systems was any more successful than those in Britain.

In 1895 a concession for a line from Place de la République to Romainville was given to one M. Claret, who had already experimented with the surface contact system in Lyon during the previous year. To exploit the line, he formed the Compagnie de Tramway Electrique de Paris à Romainville. The course of the new line involved some fairly steep gradients which precluded the use of horse cars. In the system used by Claret for the line, the contacts were coupled in pairs, which were then coupled in groups of twenty; current was collected by a skate which was 3.30m/10ft 10in. long and was suspended under the car. This skate also energised the next contact ahead and a second, smaller skate placed behind the first short-circuited any contact which had not returned to "dead" after the passage of the car. Each section was controlled by a box located on the pavement. An inconvenience was that it was not possible to have more than one car within the radius of action of one group of contacts and, as these were located 8ft 2in. apart, cars had to keep a distance of at least 100yd between each other. However, as the service was not frequent and the roads traversed not congested, this was not a great drawback, except when things went wrong. The main trouble was with the distributors in the section boxes which often did not turn as intended. In such a case, the driver of a tram had to perform the operation manually to allow current to flow into the contacts under his car.

There were twenty double-deck single-ended trams, numbered 1-20, very similar to those of the CGO. They were 8.85m/29ft long and weighed only 9.10 tonnes. Seating capacity was 26/20 + 6 on the platform.

The line was taken over by the Est Parisien company in 1900 and immediately electrified on the overhead line system. The double-deckers were scrapped.

Gas Power

Almost the only form of mechanical propulsion not used on tramways in or around Paris was the gas engine. However, in 1896 the TPDS borrowed car 4 of the Lytham St. Annes company and ran it briefly between the gas works at Landy and the Porte de Saint-Ouen. The car concerned was an open top double-decker with garden seats on the upper deck. It soon returned to England and no further experiments were conducted.

Conduit/Overhead Electric Traction

A   Les Chemins de Fer Nogentais

This company was by far the most conventional of all the systems which used double-deckers.

Electrification of the lines worked by compressed air trams was encouraged by the approach of yet another international exhibition, that of 1900, which, though based mainly in the area around Invalides, had an annexe in Vincennes. The existing line was converted to electric traction, using overhead in the suburbs and extended inwards, using conduit collection, from Porte de Vincennes to Place de la République. Unfortunately on the last section inwards from Père Lachaise to République, the CFN had to use tracks of the Est Parisien, which on this line used another system of surface contact. As it was impossible to equip the CFN trams with all three forms of current collection, it was necessary to fit accumulators, much to the annoyance of the company. These were removed in 1913. A temporary link was also constructed between the former terminus and Porte de Bercy and it was in fact on this line that electric service commenced in May 1900, using double-deck trams pulling single-deck trailers. In June 1900 a new line was opened to Villmomble and in August and September the existing compressed air lines were converted to electric traction.

Two types of double-decker were bought by the CFN. There were 51 "54 seat" cars, numbered 1-51, which were enclosed but open sided on the upper deck, short canopies over the platforms and quarter turn stairs. The cars rode on Brill or Brill-type trucks of 2.13m/7ft wheelbase and had

It is hard to believe that this rural area at Noisy now requires a frequent service of double-deck trains on line A of the RER to cope with its population! One of the two-axle cars of the CFN waits at the terminus. (Martin Jenkins collection)

Bogie car 89 of Les Chemins de Fer Nogentais traverses Place de la Nation when new in 1900. At this point, it would be using its accumulators to provide current and the trolley is down. (RATP)

CFN bogie car 77 as rebuilt in 1914 seen at La Maltournée in STCRP livery in 1925. (RATP)

two Thomson TH2 43hp motors. They were the first to enter service in May 1900. By 1910 the wheelbase had been lengthened to 2.70m/8ft 10in. to improve riding qualities, and by 1920 the sides of the upper deck had been enclosed. The entire class was taken over by the STCRP in 1921 and all were then repainted in the green and cream livery of that operator. They lasted in service until 1929, when all were withdrawn.

The second type of double-decker to be built for the CFN was the "74 seat" class, which first entered service in June 1900 on the new line to République. These were built by Brill. They took the numbers 52-93 and were 11.9m/39ft long, running on two equal wheel Brill bogies. They weighed 16.40 tonnes as against the 11.60 tonnes of the other class, but despite this had only the same two 43hp motors. Both classes were fitted with air brakes. Unusually for double-deckers in the Paris area, they had double-width side platforms and in all respects were thoroughly modern, state-of-the-art trams for 1900. The upper decks were enclosed by 1920.

In 1914 the CFN rebuilt car 77 to produce the tram with the highest seating capacity ever achieved in Paris. The upper deck was extended out over the platforms and was totally enclosed. Seating capacity was now for 83 passengers and the unladen weight was increased to 17 tonnes. Unfortunately the war put paid to any further experiments of this nature.

The bogie cars lasted slightly less well than their smaller contemporaries, the first being withdrawn in 1926. As mentioned elsewhere, twelve were de-motored and transferred as trailers to the Arpajon line. The others were withdrawn in 1929. The CFN cars were the last electric double-deckers to run in the Paris area.

B   The Versailles Line of the CGO

Following an extension for the concession for this line, the CGO decided in 1905 to electrify it, from Porte de Saint-Cloud to Versailles, on the overhead system. Service began on 17 August 1906 using 16 Fives-Lille cars suitably rebuilt and fitted with two 43hp motors and trolley poles. They were now a good deal lighter, weighing only 11.80 tonnes and they were also now double-ended. These trams were renumbered 601-616 and a further car, 618, was converted at a later date. From Porte de Saint-Cloud inwards to the terminus at Louvre the cars were pulled initially by Mékarski compressed air locomotives, but as the electric cars also pulled double-deck trailers, the combined weight was clearly too much for these and in 1907 they were replaced by Purrey steam locomotives. The double-deckers were withdrawn in 1917 and replaced by single-deckers of class B.

C   The Versailles – Saint-Cyr Line

No further double-deckers were built or rebuilt for service in Paris, since the various companies were convinced that the future lay with single-deckers. However, two double-

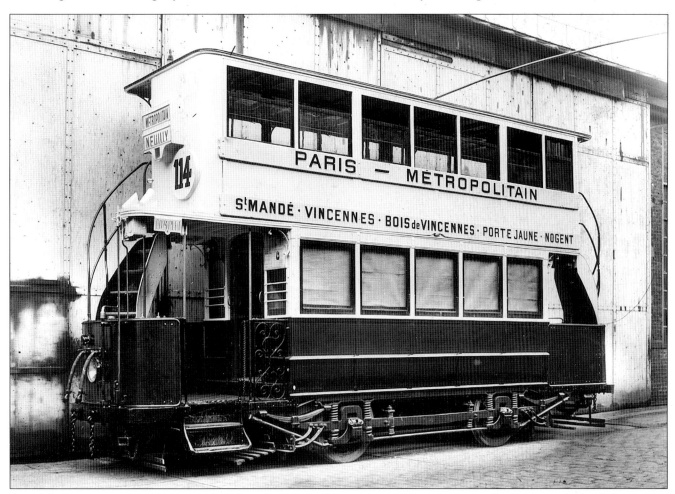

One of the 54-seat cars of the CFN as rebuilt and repainted in the livery of the STCRP, at the depot at La Maltournée in the 1920s. (RATP)

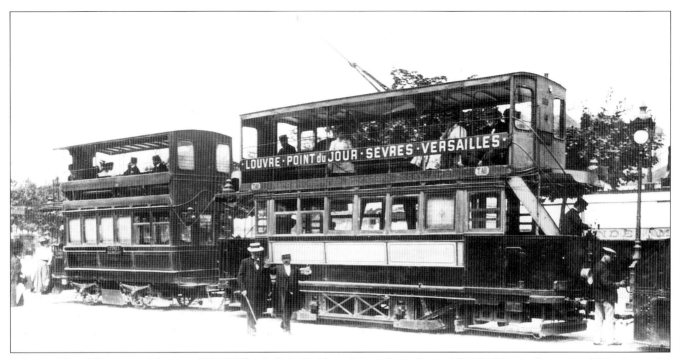

A former Fives-Lille accumulator car of the CGO rebuilt to double-ended configuration and fitted with a trolley, seen with trailer on the service to Versailles. (RATP)

deckers appeared on the neighbouring system in Versailles in 1908.

The local operator, the Société Versailleaise des Tramways Electriques, had a line, electrified on the overhead system in 1897, which linked the town to the military college at Saint-Cyr and on which traffic was subject to extreme fluctuations. At times the motor-trailer sets ran almost empty, while at others they scarcely sufficed for the traffic offering. The operator decided that double-deckers would be more economical and better adapted to the peaks and in 1908 took delivery of two double-ended cars not unlike the "54 seat" cars of the CFN, from the Etablissements Carde of Bordeaux. They ran on Brill trucks of 2.2m/7ft 4in. wheelbase and had two GE800 motors of 25hp, which in the event proved to be insufficient. Seating was 24/16, the lower saloon being first class and the upper deck, which was open at the sides, for passengers paying second-class fares. The cars were numbered 51 and 52 and entered service on 1 April 1908. They ran until 1927.

Trailers

The only line to use purpose-built double-deck trailers was the CFN during its period of compressed air operation. The cars were open top and, unlike the motors, double-ended.

The CGO used trailers behind its Mékarski cars and its Serpollet steam cars. The vehicles used were converted horse cars, fitted with a light roof and a windscreen to the upper deck. Most came from the 1878 design (qv) and had six side windows to the lower deck, but some of the 1874 design were also converted. It is not known how many there were in all, but as most Mékarski cars seem to have run with a trailer, there could have been 180 to work with these, plus 50 or 60 for the Serpollet cars.

Summary

Before the introduction of mechanical traction, CGO trams were painted in individual colours for each line. When the various forms of mechanical traction appeared, this scheme was changed to one in which cars of the same form of traction were painted in the same colour. In practice, this almost amounted to the previous practice, since so many trams were specific to one line or group of lines. The Mékarski compressed air cars and the Serpollet steam cars were painted a medium green and the Purrey steam cars were chocolate brown. The SACM accumulator cars were dark red with a black front, while the Fives-Lille cars were yellow. In every case, the lining was white. Later a universal green and cream paint scheme was applied but it is not known how many, if any, double-deckers received this livery.

The double-deck electric trams of the TPDS were dark green, while those of the CGPT were yellow with green ends and rocker panels. The CFN used an attractive yellow and cream livery. There is some debate about the colour scheme actually used by the Ouest Parisien, since its financial problems meant that cars were seldom repainted and the proper livery disappeared beneath a coat of grime. It seems likely however, that it was originally a dark brown.

In horse car days, service indication was given on a board carried on the level of the upper deck, its colour corresponding to the colour of the line. This practice was continued with mechanical traction, but the terminal information was supplemented by another board carried above the lower deck windows; this gave intermediate points and also, after 1910, the fare stages ("sections"). At night coloured lights provided identification. On CGO trams there were two lights, one placed at roof level on double-deckers and one by the driver. Thus line TK, Louvre -

Charenton, on which operated Purrey steam trams, had black route bands and at night was indicated by white and green lights. Until 1910 the CGO and the TPDS used letters to denote different services, while the CGPT had numbers running from 1 to 15. In 1910 this scheme was changed to one of numbers for the CGO and letters based on the name of the destination for the TPDS.

Although the tramways in the Paris area employed such a wide variety of forms of traction, air brakes were standardised by all companies at a very early date. The municipal authorities held very strictly for a long period to the "Three twenties" rule, which meant that a tram running at 20km/hr/12.5mph on a gradient of 20mm/m/1 in 50/m had to be able to stop in 20m/65 ft 6 in. They also took a very restrictive view of speed limits and mechanically powered trams were limited to a maximum of 12.5 mph in urban areas. There was therefore little incentive to fit trams with powerful motors and, as will have been noticed, those used were generally of low horse power in relation to weight. As speeds were so moderate, Parisiens continued to hop on and off trams wherever they pleased, although fixed stopping places had first been introduced by the TPDS when its first accumulator cars entered service. Platform entrances were narrow but congestion at busy stops was mitigated by the use of queue tickets, checked by the conductor. However, dwell time was often considerable.

All lines were standard gauge.

The double-deckers lent themselves to the two-class fare system which was in operation when they were in service, the upper deck being second class. Until 1910, the CGO flat fare within Paris was 30 centimes in first class and 15 in second, about 7d and 3½d in contemporary British terms. Other operators always had stage fares. From 1910 these applied also to the CGO services, when the fare for one section became 15 and 10 centimes respectively.

Commercial advertising was not carried on the outside of Paris trams in the double-deck period, but some cars did display a rather novel form of advertising. The CFN was electrified by the French Thomson-Houston company and the double-deck cars originally bore on the dash the legend "Traction Electrique - Système Thomson-Houston". Its Westinghouse rival replied with a similar message on some cars of the TPDS, but the practice was soon discontinued.

While the employment of so many different forms of traction in one city must have been a hindrance to the overall development of the network, it has to be said that it was also a tribute to the ingenuity of French engineers and to the management of the various companies, who refused to allow the particular political circumstances to act as a complete barrier to progress. What passengers thought of it all has not been recorded but it was certainly a delight to the few enthusiasts who were around at the time. It is however worth mentioning that the only double-deckers to enjoy anything like a normal life span were the fairly conventional cars of the CFN. It was

perhaps fitting that the last of the more unusual forms of traction went out of use in August 1914, co-incidentally with the first call-up of men for the front; nothing in Paris would ever be quite the same again.

Preservation

Very few Paris trams have survived and the last double-decker had gone long before preservation was considered. However, in 1961 the Association pour le Musée des Transports Urbains, Interurbains et Ruraux (AMTUIR) decided to preserve a Glasgow double-decker and obtained car 488 when it was finally taken out of traffic in the summer of that year. It has since formed part of the collection which was housed in a former bus garage at Saint-Mandé and was for many years under threat of closure. However, a new home has now been found for the collection in a new tram depot at Colombes, and at the time of writing preparations are being made for opening in 2002. The museum collection also has some excellent models and many photographs.

ROUEN

Rouen had similar horse trams to Bordeaux, but in this city a light roof was fitted, with windscreens at the end of the upper deck.

TOURS

The suburban line Tours-Vouvray was in 1889 worked by Rowan steam cars and had three double-deck trailers to run with these. They were unusual vehicles, having three axles and a seating capacity of 70. The line, which was built to standard gauge, was converted to metre gauge in 1911, by which date the double-deckers had gone.

Total number of double-deck electric trams operated:	
Overhead line:	38
Accumulator:	14
Total	52

Bibliography

Les Tramways Parisiens. J. Robert. Third Edition, 1992

The Continental Steam Tram. G.E. Baddeley. Light Rail Transit Association and Tramway and Light Railway Society, London, 1980

Dunkerque à l'Heure des Trams, in Ch de Fer Regionaux et Urbains, no. 279, March 2000

Histoire des Transports à Lyon. J. Arrivetz, 1966

Lyon du Tram au Tram. J. Arrivetz et al. La Régordane, Chansac, 2001.

Histoire des Transports dans les Villes de France, J. Robert, 1974

Modern Tramway, no.462, June 1976 and no.529, March 1982.

SUMMARY OF MECHANICALLY-POWERED DOUBLE-DECK TRAMS OPERATED IN THE PARIS AREA

	Fleet numbers	Total
1 Compressed Air		
CGO Mékarski	?	31
CGO Mékarski	1-148	148
CFN Mékarski	1-19	19
TSM Mékarski	1-10	10
Total		**208**
2 Steam		
1876 trial	?	1
TPDS Serpollet prototype	?	1
TPDS Serpollet prototype	1-23	23
CGO Serpollet prototype	?	1
CGO Serpollet prototype	401-460	60
CGO oil-engined car	801	1*
CGO Purrey Prototype	?	1
CGO Purrey Prototype	701-750	50
Total		**138**
3 Electric		
1881 Exhibition line	?	1 (overhead)
CGO Prototype 1881	?	1 (accumulator)
Nord Prototypes	?	4 (accumulator)
CGO F-L & SACM	501-585	85 (accumulator)
TPPDS Saint-Denis	1-30	?30 (accumulator)
TPDS Heilmann	1-35	35 (accumulator)
TPDS Aubervilliers	1-30	30 (acc, trolley, conduit)
TPDS Gennevilliers	1-30	30 (acc, trolley, conduit)
TPDS Impériales	?30-44	?15 (acc, trolley, conduit)
CCGPT 200 class	201-260	60 (acc, trolley, conduit)
CFN 54 seat	1-51	51 (acc, trolley, conduit)
CFN 74 seat	52-93	42 (acc, trolley, conduit)
TR	1-20	20 (surface contact)
STVE St-Cyr line	51-52	2 (trolley)
Total		**406**
4 Gas		
TPDS borrowed from Lytham	4	1
Total motor cars operated in service		**753***
5 Trailers		
	240* CGO + 38* CFN	
Grand total of double-deck cars		**1031***

Figure cannot be verified

GERMANY

BERLIN

Although no double-deck electric trams operated in Germany, the use of ex-horse double-deck cars as trailers was practised in Berlin for many years.

Berlin's first tram, of 1865, was a double-decker and many similar vehicles were built for the various companies which operated horse trams in the city. Most looked as though they were intended for use in left hand traffic, being of British layout, but in fact they always ran in right hand traffic. As there were openings on both sides of each platform, this may not have mattered too much. The last horse tram to operate was also a double-decker.

On electrification, the Grosse Berlin Strassenbahn, the largest company, decided to adapt many of its horse cars to run as trailers behind the new single-deck electric trams. A total of 99 were so converted. Most had been built by Herbrand of Köln, but a few were Stephenson cars, the oldest of these being car 217 of 1875. Most seated 18/18 but a few could accommodate 20/20. Length was generally 7.8m/25ft 7in.

Between 1914 and 1916, ten of these cars were given totally enclosed upper decks, though they retained their open stairs and short canopies over the platforms. Owing to their increased height, they were confined to line 25, Charlottenstrasse-Tegel.

All remained to be taken over by the Berliner Strassenbahn in 1919. They were then renumbered en bloc 469-567, their previous numbers having been scattered between 217 and 973. Under this scheme, the top covered cars were 558-567. Many were scrapped as new cars entered service in 1924, but 32 remained after that date and were further renumbered 2000, 2006 2008-33 and 2035-39. The last, some Herbrand cars of 1888, were not withdrawn until 1929 and just missed passing into the hands of the new BVG.

However, this was not to be the end of the story, since some became works cars and one of these, used as an overhead line car, managed to survive the Second World War and was used to repair damage to the overhead after 1945. It was then set aside for preservation and in due course went to the Transport Museum of the DDR in Dresden in 1959. It may still be seen there. Unfortunately it has been restored as 627, although no double-deckers bore that number, and its actual identity remains uncertain. It is most likely to have been car 2021 (1924 number) but this cannot be confirmed. Car 1 of 1865 is also preserved in Berlin.

Whatever questions remain about the accuracy of "627", its survival is a tribute to its original builders. The ex-horse trailers in Berlin survived not only the strains of electric operation over a period of more than twenty year but also the neglect of the world war and the time of the inflation.

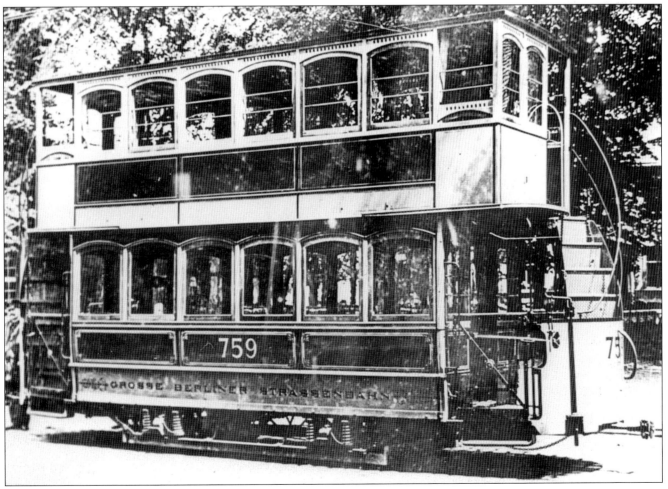

One of the ex-horse cars rebuilt as trailer 759. (BVG archives)

Yet photographs of them in service behind electric cars show them to be in good condition, with no sign of sagging bodywork or drooping platforms. The craftsmen who built them did a splendid job of work.

In 1908 one of the suburban companies, the Nord-Ostliche Berliner Vorortbahn, bought one short-canopy double-deck trailer from MAN. It had a seating capacity of 24/24. Presumably it was unsuccessful since it was rebuilt as a single-deck motor car only two years later.

DRESDEN

Dresden's two horse tramway companies, one of which was British-owned, used many double-deckers, again mostly of British layout, but none survived as such into the electric era, though many were then used as single-deck trailers.

HAMBURG

A suburban line in the Hamburg area, the Elektrische Kleinbahn Altrahlstedt-Volksdorf-Wohldorf, was opened for traffic in two stages in 1904 and 1907 and had a fleet of ten double-deck trailers. The line ran through pleasant woods to the west of the city, and carried a fair amount of pleasure traffic at weekends. The trams were two axle vehicles, with knifeboard seats on the upper deck, which was roofed but open at the sides and ends; the platforms had short canopies. The line was taken over by the Hamburger Hochbahn in 1924 and most of it was closed in 1934, when the double-deckers operated for the last time. Two, cut down to single-deck, ran on the remnant of the line until this was also closed in 1961. However, car 56 was then preserved privately and its top deck was restored. It is to-day part of the collection of the Museum of Hamburg History.

LEIPZIG

Projected Designs

Leipzig also had two similar trams, but these had only a very brief existence. Pleased with the success of their single-deck central-entrance motor and trailers cars, the Leipziger Verkehrsbetriebe proposed in 1929 to build some double-deck bogie trailers of a similar type. Plans and a small model show a car of only 4m/13ft 1.5in. height. The car would have been single-ended and two straight staircases would have risen from the offside of the platform. To keep the overall height within acceptable limits, these would have led into sunken side gangways, as in British and German lowbridge buses. It is not clear if there would have been a continuous floor on the upper deck or if the two saloons would have been quite separate, as in some earlier cars in the USA (qv). Unlike the handsome single-deckers, the double-deckers would have had a distinctly boxy appearance.

The entrances would have had a step height of only 425mm/16.75in. above rail level, though there would of course have been a further step into the saloon. The proposed length has not been recorded, but if the car had been built to conform with the single-deckers, the length would have been 11.6m/38ft. With 2+1 seating in the lower saloons and bench seats for four upstairs, seating capacity would probably have been 48/36. A sketch shows one single-decker pulling two such trailers, and such a combination would certainly have shifted rush-hour crowds, though it is not certain if the existing single-deckers would have been powerful enough to tow two loaded trailers without a reduction in average speed.

Discussions were first held with the Waggonfabrik Bautzen, and in May 1930 the LVB forwarded to them a sketch of a London car; the identity of this has not been recorded, but it could have been MET 331. However, with the onset of the economic depression, the City Council in November 1930 questioned the wisdom of proceeding with the idea and there were apparently also some problems with patents. Discussions with the manufacturers trailed on until 1932, but were ultimately without result.

It was a pity that this interesting concept was not followed through. If it had been, the later development of the German tram might have taken quite a different turn. Leipzig does not have many low bridges and the car would have had wide availability. When double-deck buses were used in the city in DDR times, they proved popular because of their high seating capacity and the trams might have been equally well received.

METZ

This city is the capital of Lorraine, which was from 1871 to 1919 part of Germany, and its tramway system was constructed and until 1919 worked as a German system. It had one double-deck trailer car, 28, built by van der Zypen in Köln, probably in 1906. It appears to have been of very British appearance, with five side windows in the lower saloon, a knifeboard seat on the upper deck, full canopies and a light roof over the upper deck, which was, however, open at the sides and ends. Platforms and stairs seem to have been arranged for left hand running, but this may have been to bring the entrance next to the rear entrance of a motor car. There was no truck, the axles being mounted directly onto the body frame. It was later converted to a single-decker and the reason for its construction is unknown.

Bibliography
Von Zweispanner zur Stadtbahn. Leipziger Verkehrsbetriebe, Leipzig, 1996
Strassenbahn Archiv 5, Berlin und Umgebung. G. Bauer et al. VEB Transpress, Berlin, 1987
Modern Tramway no.312, December 1963 and no.432, December 1973
Strassenbahn Magazin no.65, August 1987

POST-WAR DDR DESIGNS

The state railways of the DDR, Deutsche Reichsbahn, were in the forefront of developing the concept of the double-deck railway carriage for both suburban and (with less success) long distance traffic, and it is to these pioneering efforts that most of the present designs of this type of rolling stock on European railways owe their origins. Less well known, however, are the proposals made to develop double-deck trams for use in the cities of the DDR.

In fact, the first such proposal pre-dates the creation of that country by two years. As early as 1947 the outline of such a design was prepared for the Dresden undertaking by its technical department under the leadership of Professor Alfred Bockemühl, who had been responsible for the very advanced "Hechtwagen" design in 1929. Dresden had also in the immediate pre-war years experimented with a double-deck tractor-trailer bus with a very low floor height. The aim was to develop a tram with a much lower floor height than any existing design. This was conceived not in the interests of passengers with reduced mobility – though there must have been plenty of those around in Dresden in 1947 – but to decrease dwell time at stops. To allow a low floor height for as much of the length of the tram as possible, it was intended to displace the bogies to the extreme ends of the car. This would have given a length of 13m/42ft 8in. between the bogie centre lines and it was planned to widen the track spacing on certain tight curves to allow such a car to operate freely. The overall height of a single-deck version would have been only 2.50m/8ft 4in. above rail level, and it would therefore have been possible to have added an upper deck, without exceeding clearances. The double-decker would in fact have been only slightly higher than contemporary single-deckers and would still have had a headroom of 1.85m/6ft 1in. in the lower saloon.

The proposals suggest that there would have been both motor and trailer versions, and in the motor car the raised sections over the bogies would have incorporated the driving position, with a post for a seated driver. The trams would have been no less than 18m/59ft long and 2.2m/7ft 4in. wide, and current collection would have been by a bow collector placed over the driving position.

It was unfortunate that this interesting, though problematic, design had no chance to prove itself in service. The economy of what was still the SBZ (Soviet Occupation Zone) was in 1947 in no position to supply components for such a project, and in 1950 Professor Bockemühl went to the Federal Republic, where he became manager of the Stuttgarter Strassenbahn. His energies were thereafter devoted to the development of single-deck articulated trams of the very successful GT4 design, and he showed no further interest in the double-deck principle.

However, the idea was not forgotten in Dresden and in the early 1960s was revived by Dr-Ing Georg Kochan who was then teaching at the Dresden Hochschule für Verkehrswesen (College of Transport Science) and was also from 1964 to 1965 a member of the city's transport committee. His ideas stemmed from two quite separate concepts. The first was the 1½-decker bus (anderthalbdecker), a design which was then enjoying much popularity in the Federal Republic, and the second was the design of articulated trams which were then being placed in service in Bremen and München. In this design there were only two bogies and the articulation was supported by the frame. Kochan saw that this type of construction, unlike the traditional Jacobs bogie, could easily be used as the basis for a double-decker. Although this would not be a low floor car in the present-day sense, the entrances at the ends would have had the benefit of a fairly low step height.

From his report on the proposal, it would seem that Kochan was concerned that the design then being developed by the VEB Waggonfabrik Gotha – a design which in the event did not go into production – would provide a very low seating capacity, this being only 16% of the total complement. Track spacing in most undertakings in the DDR limited the operation of wide cars and therefore the only way in which additional seating capacity could be provided was by operating double-deckers. However, as a double-decker of conventional design, based on current Gotha trams, would have had an overall height of 4.385m/14ft 4.5in., it was proposed to build a car with double-deck sections at the ends only. In this design, it would have been possible to have a gangway between the axles and steps to the upper levels which would have been placed between the bogies. Using wheels of 500mm/19.66in. diameter, the overall height would have been 3.70m/12ft 2in, rather lower than a Berlin double-deck bus and in fact almost identical to the height of most 1½-deckers. Kochan did mention the possibility of using lighter wheels of smaller diameter or single steerable wheels, but doubted the ability of the former to withstand the strain of carrying a double-deck body and admitted that the latter would have been beyond contemporary technology.

In 1963 Kochan produced and circulated to some colleagues a design for such a car. It was based closely on the Bremen type, but was slightly longer, at 18m/59ft, and the width of 2.3m/7ft 7in. would certainly have required considerable alterations to track spacing in most undertakings. However, the height would have caused few problems and would have required alterations to only a few bridges in some cities. There would still have been clearance of 250m/10in. between the roof and the overhead. As the design was based so closely on existing technology, there would have been little risk in its construction. In appearance the cars would have looked rather like the later Tatra KT4D design, but with lower end platforms and above these upper saloons of somewhat limited headroom.

It was proposed to offer three variants. The first was a car with all axles motored and motors of 320kW, to allow trailer operation. The second used only two motored axles, precluding such operation, while the third was a trailer itself. It would also have been possible to have fitted an upper deck at one end of the car only for single-ended

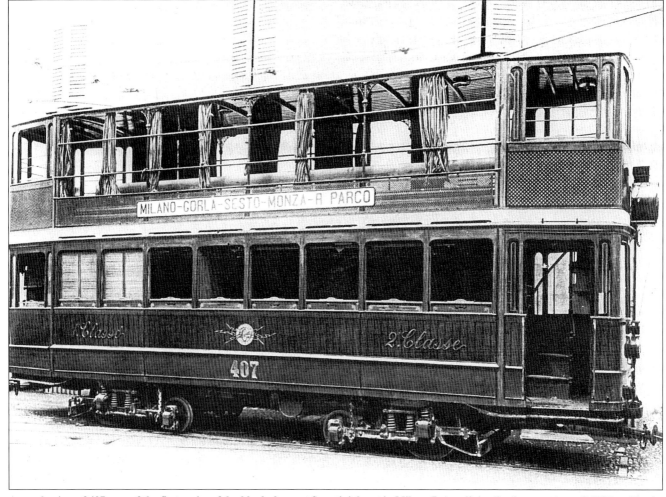

An early view of 407, one of the first series of double-deckers, at Spontini depot in Milan. (I. Angelini collection, courtesy of ATM archives)

operation, which seems to have been envisaged as the norm on most systems. The cars would have offered total capacities of 357 or 341 passengers, of whom 163 and 139 respectively would have been seated. There would have been more economical use of road space than with single-deckers.

Sadly, this innovative and potentially useful design had also come at the wrong time. Very shortly afterwards it was decided under the Rat für gegenseitige Wirtschaft (RGW) (Law for economic Co-operation) that tramcar production for the Comecon countries should be concentrated at the Tatra factory in what was then Czecho-slovakia. Any further development in the DDR ceased forthwith and with it went any further thought of double-deckers.

Bibliography
Strassenbahn Magazin no.108, April 1997.

ITALY

MILAN

In 1876 a radial line was opened from Milan to Monza and on it operated ten double-deck horse trams, four of which had been built in Belgium. There were also two open-sided

double-deckers. Electric service on this line began on 31 December 1900.

To work the new service, ten double-deck bogie cars were delivered by the Officina Societa Edison, Milan, which had built most of the single-deckers used on the city system. These trams, numbered 405-414, were mounted on Brill 22E maximum traction bogies and had two 50hp GEC motors. Overall length was 10.5m/34ft 6in., width 2.1m/6ft 11in. and height was 4.8m/15ft 9in. Unladen weight was 19,000kg/18 tons 14cwt. Maximum speed was 18.75mph.

The lower saloon was divided into first and second class compartments, seating nine and seventeen passengers respectively, while there were 32 second class places on the upper deck, 24 on knifeboard seats in the open central portion and four on each of the enclosed end balconies. The open sides could be enclosed by curtains in wet weather. Reversed stairs rose from the rather narrow end platforms and there were two trolley poles, fitted with retrievers. The top decks could be removed for winter service, in which condition the cars became clerestory roofed single-deckers. This provision was made partly on grounds of safety and partly because it was expected that traffic would diminish considerably during the winter. However, either the winters proved to be milder than expected or the attractions of the new line were greater than hoped, since large numbers of passengers were carried throughout the year. The trams also proved to be totally safe in operation.

Very soon they began to run as double-deckers all the year round and in fact there are photographs of only two (408 and 413) in single-deck form. Possibly only a few were ever actually decapitated for winter service. The cars could work in multiple unit formation and also pulled trailers, some of which were ex-horse double-deckers.

Evidently these trailers proved to be inadequate for the traffic, since ten double-deck trailers were soon acquired, numbered 424-433. They were similar to the motor cars in general appearance but had a single off-centre doorway and a single staircase. They did not run for long as trailers and all received motors between 1913 and 1919. The first four conversions had GEC motors and Thomson-Houston controllers, while the later ones had Brown Boveri motors and Westinghouse equipment. The original livery of all cars was varnished teak.

On 31 December 1916 the line passed under local government control (STEL) and the cars were repainted cream. After 1919, the original motor cars were renumbered 10-19 and the converted trailers 20-29. Of the latter batch, cars 24 and 28 had been scrapped by 1939 and the remainder had gone by 1948. Nine of the original motors were still in service in 1947 and were in that year cut down to single-deck form, to allow them to run on other lines in the suburban network.

The double-deck trams of Milan proved to be successful and popular, with both summer excursionists and with small boys who devised a game of marbles using the slatted floors of the upper decks! One also had the distinction of appearing in a painting of a street scene by A. Bonzagnai, a local impressionist painter.

ROME

THE CASTELLI ROMANI LINES

To the south of Rome lies the very attractive area of small towns and villages known as the Castelli Romani. Its attractions are not lessened by the presence of numerous vineyards, producing well-known wines such as Frascati. It is not surprising that this area should have attracted the attention of promoters of electric tramways.

It has not been possible to compile an exact account of the rolling stock of the lines built to serve the area, since records were not kept with any degree of regularity and many of those which did exist were destroyed in the second world war. Nor do photographs greatly help, since the cars did not carry prominent fleet numbers and identification can be difficult.

The first line of the network was built by the Societa Thomson-Houston de la Mediterrane. It was opened for traffic on 9 November 1903, running from Rome to Via della Cave and was extended onwards to Frascati on 19 February 1906. The promoters had noticed the success of the Monza line and their first rolling stock was based closely on that line's double-deckers. Use of such cars would give the necessary capacity on a single track line which, it was hoped, might be carrying up to 3,000 passengers per day when the weather was fine. The views available to passengers from the upper deck would be an added attraction.

For the opening of the line, twelve double-deck trams were delivered. They were a mixture of motors and trailers

A double-deck tram/trailer set on the Viale per Vedano in Monza. (Alan W. Brotchie collection)

and it is not known how many there were of each. They were numbered in one series from 10 to 21. It is known that 10, 12, 19 and 21were motors while 15 was definitely a trailer. In 1906 it was stated that there were eight Thomson-Houston equipped cars on the property and it is possible that there were eight motors and four trailers. The cars were fitted with Thomson-Houston train control, allowing one or two trailers to run between two motor cars. Photographs of the opening day show both M-T-M and

One of the double-deckers of STEFER seen about 1949 in the city, just outside the city walls. (A. Mayou, courtesy of Martin Jenkins)

M-M-T formations. The trams were similar to the cars in Milan but were slightly larger, having an overall length of 11.8m/38ft 9in. and a capacity of 82 passengers. The lower deck was reserved entirely for passengers paying first class fares. On the upper deck there were again knifeboard seats in an open centre section and enclosed end balconies. The best materials were used for the coachwork; the frame was of steel and there were mahogany cornices in the lower saloon. The seats (presumably in second class) were of pitch pine. There were two trolley poles and reversed stairs. Unladen weight was 23,000kg/22 tons 11cwt for a motor and 18,000kg/17 tons 14cwt for a trailer. All rode on Böcker bogies built under licence from Brill and had air brakes. Motor cars had two Thomson-Houston 60hp motors, giving a maximum speed of 14.37mph and so allowing the through journey from the city to Frascati to be completed in 75 minutes. As most of the track was single with passing loops, this represented a creditable average of 11mph.

The line proved to be extremely popular right from the opening day, when would-be passengers got in through the windows as well as by the platforms. Even the derailment of car 10 at Grottaferrata junction and the cancellation of one working did not dampen the public's enthusiasm. The line was used not only by day trippers but also by many who wished to escape from the city for an hour or two in the evening, to sip a glass of wine and enjoy a meal in a trattoria in Frascati. However, in 1906 a serious accident cast doubt on both the T-H train control system and the wisdom of working a trailer sandwiched between two heavier motor cars. There are varying accounts of this accident and that which follows seems to be the most consistent with the evidence.

On 22 July 1906 a three-car train was returning to the city, running in M-T-M formation. The trailer was crowded with a party of gypsies, most of whom had crowded on to the upper deck, where they were singing, carousing, hanging over the sides and generally having a good time. Near

Torlonia di Frascati, the trailer appears to have derailed and plunged down an embankment, turning in the process at right angles to the track. The second motor, still under power, rammed it and the projecting coupling penetrated the middle of the lower saloon. The unfortunate gypsies were flung in all directions and there was at least one and possibly more deaths. While some newspaper accounts blamed the gypsies for having overcrowded the upper deck, the real cause of the accident was found to lie with the control system, exacerbated by the running of a lighter trailer between two heavy motor cars. The use of the train control system was discontinued immediately and only single cars were run thereafter. The trailers were motorised in 1910 and the couplings were removed from the earlier motor cars at a later date, probably around 1920.

In 1927 the entire class was renumbered to either 40-51 or 41-52. Trailer operation was resumed after 1930 to increase capacity, but only with single-deckers. In the 1930s they were re-equipped with GE motors and electro-magnetic controllers and it was probably at this time that they received pantographs in place of the trolley poles. Eleven remained in service in 1935 and the original varnished teak finish was replaced by a blue and cream colour scheme. At least one car was substantially rebuilt with a three-window lower saloon. The double-deckers were last used in 1955 and were replaced by articulated single-deckers. The last was not broken up in San Guiseppe depot until 1958, some having been converted to works cars after the first withdrawals in 1954. They did not operate at any time on any other line in what had become the STEFER network.

ATAC

Although the only two-level tram to have operated on the city system in Rome lasted as a single-decker, until recently, surprisingly little about it has appeared in print.

In 1936 the ATAG, forerunner of to-day's ATAC, placed in service an experimental bi-level car, numbered 2P1 (Due

A view of 2P1 at a depot in pre-war days. (Centro di Documentazione Multimediale, ATAC, S.p.A Roma

piani = two storeys). Double-deck motor buses had recently been introduced on the Rome-Tivoli line to provide extra capacity, as it had been found that the single-deckers which had replaced steam trams could not cope with the numbers travelling at peak periods and it seems that, from these, there was developed the idea of using double-deck trams in city service. This car was based closely on the standard bogie trams of class MRS, to which it was mechanically and electrically identical. However, the layout of the body was totally different. Transverse seats, in facing pairs, were fitted in the lower saloon and between the backs of each pair of seats, a short flight of steps led to another pair of seats at an upper level. There was no upper deck as such and it would be incorrect to refer to this tram as a double-decker. It was very similar in conception to some coaches which operated in the UK in the 1950s, before maximum permitted length was increased. There were large panoramic windows for passengers seated at the upper level and the roof sloped down at the front, rather in the style of the Coronation observation cars on the LNER. There was no front window at the upper level. This car represented an attempt to increase total capacity and the proportion of seated passengers to total capacity without incurring increased personnel costs, but the doorways remained exactly as on the standard single-deckers, with rear entrance and front exit, and this no doubt prolonged dwell time at stops.

Car 2P1 was nicknamed the "Vienna" tram, although it had nothing in common with the double-deckers which had operated there (qv). It was used on line 7 in 1937/38, where its nominal capacity was not in any case needed, but proved to be unsuited to city traffic and was very soon put in storage. In late 1942 or early 1943, when extra capacity was needed for wartime traffic, it was rebuilt as a single-decker, numbered 2265. After the war, it saw infrequent

service, as crews disliked the driving cab, which was smaller than those on standard trams. In 1975 it was rebuilt with new ends and from then on was a regular performer until 1998, when it was withdrawn. It is now stored and it is likely that it will be preserved.

TURIN

Two double-deck Rowan steam trams were acquired in 1897. Their later history has not been recorded.

The two lines which operated double-deckers in Italy had much in common. Both were constructed to link villages with a nearby city and both had heavy pleasure traffic, especially in the early years. Later this was overtaken by increased commuter traffic and ultimately both lines were replaced by a combination of bus and metro. All the lines mentioned in this section were of standard gauge and it should be noted that, until 1 March 1925, Italy drove on the left. The attempt to use a single bi-level car in Rome was an interesting experiment, but suffered from lack of attention to passenger flow in a car which would carry about 50% more than a standard tram. It also suffered from the usual fate of any odd car in a very large fleet.

> **Total number of double-deckers operated in electric service: 33, all bogie cars.**

Bibliography
Fuori Porti in Tram. G. Comoio. E. Albertalli, Parma, 1980
Le Tramvie del Lazio. V. Fromigari and P. Muscolino. Calosi, Cortona, 1982
Binari sulla Strade Interno a Roma. G. Angeleri, A. Curci, U. Bianchi. Edizioni Abete, Rome, 1982
Moderne Trams. F. van der Gragt. Wyt, Rotterdam, 1972
Modern Tramway, no.375, March 1969

MALTA

No horse trams operated on Malta. The electric tramway system operated by the Malta Tramways Company consisted of three routes radiating in a south-westerly direction from the edge of the city of Valetta. The system was built by the contractors Macartney, McElroy and Company Ltd under a concession obtained in 1903 from the Maltese government and was of metre gauge. The first tram ran on 23 February 1905 and the contractors operated the lines after completion. They had previously constructed the electric tramways of Durban and Lourenço Marques (qv), and the first superintendent and engineer and de facto manager in Malta was Mr W.D. Jeffs, who had previously served in a similar capacity in Durban. This may explain the choice of double-deckers for Malta, although local politics also had something to do with it. It had in fact been originally intended to use single-deckers, of both saloon and cross-bench designs, and also to have a two-class fare structure, which did operate for the first few months of service. However, the Governor, Sir Charles Mansfield Clark, had insisted that the two-class cars should be of the open type, in view of the island's climate, and had also hinted that double-deckers could be used if permission were obtained from the commanding officer, Royal Engineers, to demolish the inner arches of the Porte des Bombes city gateway in Valetta.

This permission was granted in December 1903 and the Company decided to opt for double-deckers, which would provide a convenient way of operating a two-class fare structure. There seems later to have been some confusion about what Sir Charles actually said, since in the autumn of 1905, the Crown Advocate, Dr V. Azzopardi, claimed that operation of open cars, which were not expressly approved by the government, was in breach of the concession. He went on to add, rather despairingly, that it was now too late to do anything about this, the line having opened in the meantime, but the government did insist that the two-class fare system be retained, by the expedient of reserving certain seats for passengers paying first class fares.

The system was opened by Sir Charles and Lady Mansfield Clark on 23 February 1905. The initial fleet consisted of 16 cars of two designs. All were built in 1904 by the British Electric Car Company and all were mounted on Brill 21E trucks of 6ft 6in. wheelbase, with Westinghouse controllers and motors. Cars 1-6 had enclosed lower saloons, with six full-drop windows on either side and seating for 30/22, with longitudinal seats in the saloon. The upper decks were surrounded by wire netting and lacked decency panels; tough advertisements were fitted soon after the opening of the system and helped to preserve the modesty of any lady passenger brave enough to attempt to ride on top. Cars 7-16 had cross-bench seating on the lower deck and, save for the lack of decency boards, were identical to the cars supplied by BEC to Lourenço Marques (qv). They were intended for use on workmen's services and seated 30/28. It was these cars

All three routes of the Malta Tramways terminated in a loop in Floriana, outside the city of Valetta. In the early days of the tramway, car 10 leaves St Anne Square, Floriana for Cospicua. The conductor is collecting fares from the running board, apparently unaware of the small boy who seems to be hitching a lift on the rear fender. Behind is one of the cars with enclosed lower saloon. (National Tramway Museum)

A builder's view of car 26 (UEC courtesy A. K. Terry)

which were used briefly as two-class trams, until November 1905.

On 30 September 1905 car 4 ran away and derailed at the foot of Ghajn Dwieli hill when en route to Cospicua. It was running behind schedule, was very overcrowded and was being driven under supervision by a trainee motorman. There were four fatalities and four cases of serious injury, the motorman in charge having to have a leg amputated. The subsequent enquiry found that some of the wiring had short circuited due to inadequate insulation and that in consequence the magnetic track brake had become unusable. Mr Jeffs was held responsible but left Malta before he could be prosecuted. The tram was towed to the depot by a traction engine belonging to the Royal Engineers. It is not clear what happened to it, but a later photograph shows a car 4 with a cross-bench lower deck and, as no single trams were ordered at any time, it must be presumed that this was a rebuild of the car involved in the accident.

In November 1905 five more cross-bench cars, 17-21, were ordered from Brush and these were delivered in 1906. These were slightly wider than the cars of the first batch and could seat five people abreast on the cross-bench seats, but were otherwise identical to these.

Finally in 1909 the last purchase of cars was made when 22-26 arrived from the works of the United Electric Car Company of Preston. These were saloon cars, 27ft 6in. long and 6ft 6in. wide at roof level. There were full-drop windows in the lower saloon and when open the window spaces could be covered by louvres. These cars rode on Preston Patent Compensating trucks of 6ft 6in. wheelbase and Westinghouse equipment was again fitted.

There were complaints about the use of cross-bench cars on winter service, when passengers were exposed to mud and rain, and in 1910-11 they were fitted with canvas awnings on the upper deck. Although these were light in weight, they seem to have imposed some strain on the bodywork and they were removed again in 1914. The BEC cars were cheaply constructed and in later years showed considerable weakening of the bodywork, with drooping platforms. Examination of some car bodies which survived closure suggested that some of these cars had been rebuilt by the company, with the window next to the platform becoming a doorway to the lower saloon and a solid bulkhead separating the saloon from the platform. Presumably this was done to strengthen the bodies. It is not known when this work was done or how many cars were so treated. Photographic evidence also indicates that some cars were fitted with Dick, Kerr controllers at a later date but no order for these has been traced and they may have been bought second-hand. Following many complaints from passengers who had received electric shocks from the trolley masts, these were encased in protective wooden casings from 1919 onwards.

The only rebuilding which took place was that of car 6. In 1926 drawings were prepared for rebuilding this car with a six-window upper saloon, a full-length roof, open balconies and a separate entrance to the lower saloon, as described above. However, the car which emerged and was proudly displayed to members of the island's legislature in June 1927 had a short upper saloon of four windows only, long balconies and the normal platform arrangement. It had now been renumbered 16 and had a capacity of 70 passengers. It may have been intended as the first of a new fleet but by this date the financial position of the tramway was precarious and no more cars were so treated.

The last tram ran on 15 December 1929 and the cars, which then became the property of the government, were taken to Hamrun railway station. Some equipment may have been sold to Tunis but many trams ended up as beach huts at St. Thomas Bay. Until at least 1991 there was one unusual survivor, a BEC saloon mounted on top of a UEC lower deck behind the Fisherman's Rest restaurant.

The livery of the Malta Tramways was green and white and the cars displayed the title on the cant rail, in the case of the cross-bench cars, and on the rocker panel in the case of the saloons. In deference to contemporary practice, they were originally fitted with spittoons, but these were frequently stolen and there were complaints about the state of the floors of the cars. Only one conductor was carried per car, and on the open cars fares had to be collected from the running board while the car was in motion.

The total number of double-deckers, and of passenger trams operated, was 26.

Bibliography
The Malta Tramway and the Barracca Lift. J. Bonnici and M. Cassar, Malta, 1991.

NETHERLANDS

AMSTERDAM

Proposal

In 1931 the municipal tramways (GVBA) engaged a consultant to report on the transport undertaking, which, due to the onset of the economic depression, was suffering a decline in traffic and so in receipts. One of the comments made in the report was the low productivity of individual members of the platform staff, owing to the use of tram-

trailer sets. The average loading was given as 22 passengers per three-crew train, compared to 28 passengers on contemporary British double-deckers. The management of the system seem to have taken this point on board, since they then engaged the firm of Werkspoor of Utrecht to prepare a design for a double-deck tram suitable for use on the lines serving the Leidsestraat, where the length of the passing loops on the canal bridges limited the scope for trailer operation in any case.

It would seem that the Werkspoor staff took as their inspiration MET car 331, since the plans which were produced showed a centre-entrance bogie double-decker with projecting cabs. The car would have been 12m/39ft 4in. long overall and 4.75m/15ft 7in. high. The triple width central doorway would have had a clear opening of 2.4m/7ft 10in. and the first step would have been 36.5cm/14in. above road level. A separate single-width exit, with a sliding door, would have been located immediately behind the driver's cab. Both double- and single-ended designs were prepared, the rear driving cab in the latter case being fitted with two extra seats for passengers. This version would have seated 33/24 passengers and there would have been standing space for an additional 20. Given the habits of the travelling public in Amsterdam, this figure would almost certainly have been exceeded. There would have been two centrally located straight stairs, one for ascent and one for descent. The car is shown with a domed roof and a pantograph, rather than the then-standard bow collector. There would have been two equal wheel bogies.

In the event the GVBA decided to improve its services by using solo operation of single-deckers at slack hours, and to improve service speeds by fitting motors of higher horse power to existing stock. The double-deck project was shelved until more new cars were needed and when these were ordered in 1947, the choice fell on single-deckers with three-axle trucks.

Bibliography
The Felthams. M.Dryhurst. Dryhurst Publications, London, 1962.

DEN HAAG

This city operated some double-deck horse trams, the only such ever to have run in the Netherlands. These were acquired from the original line in Paris (qv).

RUSSIA

SANKT PETERSBURG

The first horse tram ran on 27 August 1863. There were ultimately two main operating companies, with some minor ones in the suburbs. The first double-decker entered service in 1864 and many others followed in later years. These were operated on a two-class system and ladies were forbidden to use the upper deck.

In August 1880 trials were made of a double-decker powered by an electric motor. The idea was the invention of Fyodor Pirotsky, an artillery officer who had previously experimented with a small electric locomotive. For the trials, a 3kW motor was mounted on the underframe of double-deck horse car 114, owned by the Second Tramway Company. The motor was linked by gears to both axles and switches to control the speed were mounted on each platform. A similar 3kW motor served as a generator. Firotsky used the running rails for both collection and return of current and these were therefore insulated from the sleepers by canvas. Trials began on 22 August and lasted for several days, 400 volunteer passengers being carried on certain runs. These trials were conducted on a 60m length of track within Rozhdestvensky (now Smirnov) depot. The car ran smoothly but at very low speed, and the motor and generator were therefore replaced by 4.5kW versions, which gave better results. However, the operating company baulked at the expense of insulating 90km of track and the experiment was quietly dropped. Car 114 therefore has some claim to fame as a pioneer but it did not operate outside the depot and it did not carry fare paying passengers.

Electrification did not reach Sankt Petersburg until 1907 and some of the double-deck horse cars were then cut down to single-deck and used as trailers. During the first world war some were also used as flat trucks for goods traffic.

For the fiftieth anniversary of the October revolution in 1967, a replica of a double-deck horse car was constructed on the frame of a railway flat wagon. The car was used in several films and was then set aside for ten years until given to the city museum in 1977. In 1989 it was taken out again and made several trips through the central area of the city. It still exists and there are plans to include it in a future transport museum, but to date no funds have been made available for this purpose.

There were also two suburban tramways in the area and one of these, the Nevsky line, used two axle double-deck trailers, seating 22/18. It is thought that the other line, the Poutilov line, had some rather larger Rowan self-propelled steam cars built by Kitson of Leeds. These seated 38/32 and cost £1,480 each.

OTHER CITIES

Double-deck two axle trailers built by Ringhoffer of Prag operated behind steam tram engines in Odessa.

A replica of a horse drawn double-decker is preserved in the transport museum in Moscow. It is of car 35 of 1899 and has seven side windows to the saloon and a knifeboard seat on the upper deck. It was built for the centenary of the tramways in 1999.

Bibliography
Light Rail and Modern Tramway, no.707 November 1996 and no.709 January 1997
The Continental Steam Tram, op cit.

SPAIN

BARCELONA

The Catalan capital was the only city in Spain to operate double-deck electric trams.

Like those of Madrid, its first horse trams were double-deckers. The first line was opened in 1872 and the cars used on it were British-built double-deckers of typically Starbuck appearance, though it is not recorded if they were actually built by that firm. Other similar cars were acquired later, some of these being built in Belgium. Until 1904 the network was operated by eight different companies, of which three, including the largest, were British owned. In that year, these three were bought by another, new Belgian company, but the British influence remained and double-deck vehicles, buses and trolleybuses as well as trams, could be seen on the city's streets until the 1960s.

Very soon after electric operation was begun in 1899, ten double-deck horse cars were rebuilt for this service. These were numbered 133-139 and 166-168. They were given Brill 21E trucks and extended platforms and canopies. The upper deck seating did not extend over the canopy, but transverse seats replaced the original knifeboard. New reversed stairs were fitted and the conversions had a rather square appearance. They had two motors and were 8.60m/28ft 2.5in. long by 2.37m/7ft 8in. wide. The conversion was carried out by the local firm of Girona. These cars were later cut down to single-deck form.

The first purpose-built double-decker, 169, arrived in 1908 from the United Electric Car Company of Preston and was followed in the next year by 24 identical cars from Girona, 170-193. These cars, known as class A, were of distinctly British appearance, having four side windows to the lower saloon, open tops, reversed stairs and drivers' windscreens. Seating capacity was 38/30 and ten passengers could be carried on the platform, presumably as standees. Brill/Preston 21E trucks were fitted and there were two 28hp motors of type V104. The original livery was dark yellow and the side panels of the lower deck could be removed in summer to give the type of tram known locally as "jardinera", though after a few years this practice was given up and the panels remained fixed throughout the year.

Between 1933 and 1942 this class was rebuilt. Air brakes were fitted to some (at least 176/7and 180/1) and the top decks were enclosed with a rounded roof and a large number of small windows. Further rebuilding took place in 1946-47, when, along with most of the Barcelona fleet, the class was altered for single-ended operation, with passen-

A builder's view of car 169 0f 1908. The trolley still has to be fitted – this is not a trailer! (UEC courtesy A. K. Terry)

ger flow from rear to front. Both stairs were replaced by a single stair on the offside of the lower saloon, towards the rear. Alighting passengers from the upper deck were supposed to leave by the lower saloon and front exit but in practice not all did make this lengthy detour. The original 38 seats remained on the upper deck but were now fixed in the direction of travel. There were now 15 seats in the lower saloon, four double transverse seats on the left and seven single seats on the right. The seats themselves were of dark stained wood. In this condition, external livery was dark red and cream with a grey roof.

By 1963 only five cars of this class remained in commission, employed on circular services 60 and 62. It was said that the added weight of the upper decks caused damage to the tracks and all were withdrawn later in that year.

The second series of new double-deckers, class B, 194-208, came into service in 1914/5 and all were built by Girona. However, with seven narrow side windows to the lower deck, these cars had something of a North American appearance. Again drivers' windscreens and reversed stairs were fitted and they rode on Böcker 21E trucks. Rebuilding with an enclosed upper deck began in 1933 but because of the problems caused by the civil war, was not completed until 1942. After 1950 this class was also converted for passenger flow, as with the previous batch. As converted cars of class B had a much flatter roof than those of class A and all had air brakes, but the internal layout was identical. The rebuilding was undertaken by the local firm of Molosa. Thirteen cars were still in service in 1963, also on services 60 and 62 and the last, 205, was not withdrawn until 1967, though latterly it had not seen much use. It was the

Car 171 shows its British ancestry in the lower saloon. It is working on service 60 at Easter 1958. (Pam Eaton)

Car 207 on service 62 exactly a year later is followed by single-decker 265. (Pam Eaton)

last double-deck tram to run in normal service on mainland Europe.

During their last years, the Barcelona double-deckers attracted much interest from tramway enthusiasts, especially those from Britain. One visitor in 1962 commented on the mixture of "elegance and clumsiness in riding, vaguely reminiscent of Dublin". Some mentioned that they ran steadily and evenly and could still, when necessary, display a good turn of speed. Others said that they rattled and were rather dirty, with a tendency to lurch in and out of points. The controllers were noted as being manufactured by AEG Thomson Iberica, though it is not recorded if this was the original equipment.

Although several Barcelona trams have been saved for preservation, no double-decker has survived.

VALENCIA

Some double-deck trailers built by Milnes were used behind steam tram engines in this city. These had enclosed upper decks but open canopies and were of very British appearance.

Bibliography
Tranvies de Barcelona. F. Zurita. Barcelona, 1988
Tramvias de Barcelona. A. G. Massip. Colleccio Cami Ral, no.10, Barcelona, 1997
Strassenbahn Magazin nos.41/2
Modern Tramway, no.191, November 1953 and nos.303/4, March and April 1963

SWITZERLAND

INTERLAKEN

Prior to the extension of the main line railway from the West to the East stations in this resort, these were linked by a steam tramway. The trailers were double-deck bogie vehicles, of fairly British appearance.

VEVEY – MONTREUX – CHILLON

Proposals to link these three towns on the shore of Lake Léman by an electric tramway using hydro-electric power were first made in the early 1880s, but the promoters had difficulty raising capital and this pioneer line had a prolonged gestation period. In the end, it was only because E.L. Roussy of the Nestlé firm provided backing that it was possible to proceed. The Société Electrique Vevey-Montreux was granted permission to build and operate the line, with the necessary power station, in August 1886 and it was formally opened on 1 May 1888, though full service did not begin until 4 June. It was the first practical electric street tramway not only in Switzerland but also in Europe.

Although the overhead wire system was already a practical proposition by this time, the company was not allowed

The preserved car 4 in the transport museum in Luzern. (Author)

to use it, since the Federal government feared that an earth return would cause severe disruption to the local telephone system. Instead a version of the system demonstrated by Siemens in Paris in 1881 (qv) was used. The overhead consisted of two slotted copper tubes, in which ran a small "chariot capteur" or wheeled collector. This was linked to the tram by flexible steel-covered copper cables. Originally a crew member, known as a "tubier" (trolley boy) travelled on the upper deck to guide the cables as necessary, but in 1890 he was replaced by an automatic guiding system. The line voltage was 450-480V. The system required complicated pointwork in the overhead and was not particularly flexible in service; nonetheless it worked well enough for over 25 years. Tracks were laid to metre gauge.

As there was already a good main line railway connexion between the towns concerned, it would seem that the tram line was intended to cater primarily for tourist traffic and for that reason it was decided to use double-deck cars. For the opening twelve cars were built with mechanical units by SIG and electrical components by the SEVM. The bodies were constructed by the Société Industrielle Suisse at Neuhausen. The cars measured 5.6m/18ft 4in. by 1.7m/5ft 7in. and weighed 3.5 tonnes. There was one 15hp motor mounted between the wheels, which drove one of the axles through a system of toothed gears, propelling the car at a maximum speed of 16km/hr. In the early days there were complaints from local residents about the excessive speed of 9km/hr in the towns! A six-notch controller was located under one of the bench seats in the lower saloon and was operated by a handle on each platform, to which it was linked by a chain. The resistances were mounted on the roof. Braking was by hand, originally on one axle only.

Seating capacity was 8/12, only part of the upper deck being available for passengers because of the need to accommodate the resistances and the current collector. Fifteen standing passengers could be carried. Longitudinal wooden seats were fitted on both decks, those in the lower saloon being covered by cushions in winter. Although the cars were double-ended, only one staircase was fitted and in one direction passengers intending to use the upper deck had first to pass through the lower saloon, since only the rear platform was used in

service. Originally cars 1-11 were illuminated by petrol lamps, since it was feared that electric lamps would not withstand fluctuations in the line voltage. However, car 12, which did not enter service until February 1889, had electric lamps fed by a battery and this proved to be so successful that the other cars were similarly equipped. Heating was originally by a small stove-type heater located under one of the seats.

The little cars proved to be very popular with tourists and to cope with the growth of traffic, three more cars were bought in 1890. These were almost identical to those of the first batch but were slightly heavier, weighing 4.1 tonnes. These had electric heating and the earlier cars were similarly converted. Their brakes acted on both axles and, due to alterations in the suspension, they were quieter when running than the first cars. They took the numbers 13-15. In an attempt to improve adhesion, car 10 was altered to allow each axle to be driven, but this overloaded the motor and, instead, sanding gear was fitted to all cars.

Despite their pioneering nature these cars worked well for 25 years and deserve an honoured place in history as the predecessors of thousands of double-deck electric trams which have since operated around the world. However, by 1905 it was clear that the line would have to be modernised to cope with the increased passenger loadings. Local authorities tried to use this modernisation as a means of having road improvements made, at the tramway's expense, and it was not until the ensuing disputes were resolved that modernisation work could actually begin. The work was finally completed on 8 June 1913, when the original system was converted to normal overhead current collection and the pioneer cars were retired.

Fortunately car 4 was saved and briefly returned to service in 1950 when, fitted with a bow collector, it toured the system again. The line itself was converted to trolleybus operation in 1958 and no further outings were possible. Car 4 may now be seen, with a section of the original style of overhead, in the Swiss Transport Museum in Luzern. Car 10 also exists but has been cut down to single-deck to represent Zürich horse tram 27.

No other double-deckers ever operated on an electric tramway in Switzerland, although on 1 April 1912 the citizens of Zürich were surprised to find in their daily newspaper a photograph of a double-deck car which had entered service on line 7. It was a totally enclosed two-axle tram, being a double-deck version of the class constructed from 1909, beginning with car 144. It had the briefest career of any tram anywhere, so brief that no one ever actually saw it in service!

Total number of double-deckers operated in electric service: 15

Bibliography
Les Tramways Vaudois. Grandguillaume et al. Lausanne, 1979

AFRICA

EGYPT

ALEXANDRIA AND RAMLEH

Apart from Hong Kong, this is the only electric system to operate double-deckers in normal service outwith the British Isles and it is also the only other system which has put such trams into service in recent years. It has in fact the longest history of double-deck operation, although this has not been unbroken, since only single-deckers ran for about eight years between 1988 and 1996. However, the arrival of the new cars has allowed it to resume the tradition.

The Alexandria and Ramleh Railway Company began operation in 1869 with horse trams. These ran between the city and San Stefano with a branch to Zinzinia. The main line was later worked by steam tram engines pulling double-deck trailers rather like those used on suburban lines in the Paris area. The company was sold to British owners in 1890, when the concession was also extended. Plans were then made for electrification and this was inaugurated in December 1903, when the system assumed its present form, running from Place Zaghoul in Alexandria to Victoria (later renamed El Nasr), with two long loops on

both eastern and western sections, which allow a total of four through services to be operated. There are also short workings, and in recent years a connexion to the city system has run as service 12. The line was incorporated into the Alexandria Transport Authority in 1973 when the old company was finally wound up, after having been in Egyptian hands for some years. It is of standard gauge throughout and the present overhead line voltage is 600V DC.

The first electric trams to be used were double-deckers built by the British Electric Car Company. These were open top double-deckers running on Maguire or Brill two-axle trucks with British Westinghouse equipment. The bodies had four window saloons, full length upper decks and reversed stairs. These trams ran initially as two car sets, one being first and one second class, although at times they seem to have worked with a two axle single-deck trailer. The first class cars had detachable canvas awnings over the full length of the upper deck. There were 30 or (more probably) 32 of these cars, numbered at one time 1-32, though at a later date they were renumbered into the 100s, possibly to match the numbers of the new single-deckers with which they then worked. Some at least were converted to control trailers at this time. It is not known how long they lasted in service but they would seem to have been still running in the 1920s. Two may have been converted to works cars, 301 and 402 which were still operating in the early 1970s, but this cannot be proven.

An early view of Place Zaghoul with car 44 and a cross-bench trailer bound for Bacos. (Alan W. Brotchie collection)

Balcony double-decker 59 and matching single-deck motor car 209, seen in 1962. Hugh Ballment)

However, the first of these had a distinctly "double-deck" outline, while 402 was in 1982 recorded as having a BEC truck, the last example known anywhere. It is not known if these cars still exist.

Traffic grew at a very satisfactory rate and there was soon a need for additional cars, of higher capacity. The next double-deckers to arrive came between 1908 and 1914 from the United Electric Car Company of Preston. They formed part of an order for 25 motor trams and (probably) 16 trailers, and about half of the motor cars were double-deckers. The motor cars were numbered 39-63 and it is known that 40, 42-44, 47 and 57-63 (12 in total) were double-deckers, the last batch having reversed stairs. They rode on Brill 27G bogies and were open balcony cars of

A builder's view of bogie car 43. (UEC courtesy A. K. Terry)

The city terminus in 1962. Balcony double-decker 59 and matching motor are on the left while rebuilt car 531 and a more modern motor wait to depart on a short working to Bacos. (Hugh Ballment)

typical British appearance, although the seating capacity of 106 was greater than that of most British cars. They ran semi-permanently coupled to single-deck control trailers. Each deck was divided by a central bulkhead into first and second class sections, the former having leather, and the latter wooden seats. The side panels of the lower deck were detachable for summer use and to allow this to be done, the cars had ribbed sides. Later these panels were fixed in place all year round. As it was found that there was a greater demand for second class travel, the double-deckers later became all second class.

From about 1952, these trams were gradually converted to control trailers to work with the newer 500 class single-deck motor trams. In most cases the upper deck was totally enclosed with a domed roof and on some cars the ribbed panels were sheeted over to give a smooth outline. By 1962 the only two known to be still running as balcony cars were 58 and 59, and these were the last cars to operate in this condition in normal service anywhere. They were converted to enclosed condition soon afterwards. There also appears to have been some renumbering between 1973 and 1976, probably to align the cars' numbers with those of the single-deck cars with which they were then working. It will be noticed that latterly the double-deckers carried odd numbers only. The exact situation will probably never be fully known but several lists allow an estimate of the position.

An undated list gives the following as double-deckers: 51, 53, 55, 57, 59, 61, 65, 77, 81, 83, 85, 87, 89 (Total 13)

This is in part corroborated by information supplied to visiting members of the (then) Light Railway Transport League in March 1973. According to this information, the double-deckers were numbered 40, 42-44, 47, 51, 53, 55, 57-63 (15 in total). A further list of 1976 gives the numbers of the double-deckers as 51, 53, 55, 57, 61, 65, 69, 77, 83, 85, 87, 89 (12). To these should be added car 81, which had been reported as a double-decker in 1975, converted to a single-decker by the simple expedient of removing the upper deck.

The most likely position is that, in the 1970s, the following were double-deckers: 51, 53, 55, 57, 59, 61, 65, 69, 77, 81, 83, 85, 87, 89 (14).

The line experienced a great increase in traffic during the Second World War, when new cars were unobtainable. To cope with the situation, the management decided to convert some single-deckers to double-deckers in the workshops at Mustafa Paça. This programme began in 1944 and was continued until the early 1960s, to provide two car sets of a double-deck control trailer coupled to a single-deck motor car. These sets were numbered 516/517 to at least 538/539, the double-deckers carrying the odd numbers. However, a list of 1976 suggests that between 503 and 527 every third car was a double-decker, a total of nine, and 518 was certainly in service as a double-decker in the late 1970s, while 525 had become a single-decker. The same list states that between 528 and 539 the cars carrying odd numbers were double-deckers, a total of six, and this is in part borne out by contemporary photographs showing 531, 533 and 537 as double-deckers. However, there is also a photograph of 502 in service as a double-decker in 1961.

A depot view with a line of the new double-deckers waiting to enter service in 1995. (John Clarke)

There could therefore have been fifteen conversions in all. These cars were noticeably lower than the earlier batch and had wooden seats on both decks, straight stairs and unlined ceilings. The later rebuilds had a slightly different arrangement of upper deck windows and some, such as 537, were given a separate cab for the driver, which required them to be fitted with new windscreens of extremely sloping outline.

With the transfer of PCC cars from the city system and the arrival of new Japanese-built single-deckers from 1975 onwards, the need for the double-deckers was reduced and the last was scheduled to run in April 1982. However, at least four were still available for service in 1984 and were occasionally used on shuttle line 12. The actual date of their final withdrawal is not known. Two still survived in 1996 outside the gate of the city zoo, but it is unclear whether they are officially preserved or simply being used as stores.

However, the departure of these cars did not mean the end of the double-deck story in Alexandria, and in fact it is clear that the operator did not intend to be without such cars for very long, since an order was placed with Kinki Shanyo for delivery of six double-deckers in 1986. Due to problems with foreign exchange, delivery was somewhat protracted and the cars did not finally arrive in Egypt until early 1995. They entered service in the summer of that year. Considerable track relaying and realignment was undertaken before they were placed in traffic.

These are the world's newest double-deck trams and are impressive vehicles. They are single ended, double-sided

The upper saloon of one of the new double-deckers. (Kyle Hulme)

driving motor cars and work as part of three car sets, in which the other vehicles are a single-deck driving motor and a non-driving motor, which is reserved for women passengers. The double-deckers are incapable of independent movement, since they are not fitted with a pantograph, and an emergency pantograph has been fitted to the single-deck driving car for use in emergency. Dimensions of these large cars are 16.45m by 2.60m, identical to those of the single-deckers with which they work. Height is 4.8m but the cars have been constructed to have a low centre of gravity. Unladen weight is 30 tonnes. There are four 52.5kW motors per car, giving a maximum speed of 62/5km/hr, though of course nothing like this is attained in ordinary service. Normal acceleration is 2.16km/hr/second and deceleration is 2.29km/hr/second, though with emergency braking this can be increased to 3.29km/hr/second. Air brakes are fitted. The cars ride on equal wheelbase swing bolster trucks of a wheelbase of 1.9m, wheel diameter being 660mm.

Three doors are fitted on each side, one at each end and one centrally. Passengers can enter and leave from any door on the nearside. Two straight staircases are provided, one to the rear of the front nearside door and one on the offside by the rear nearside door, both rising towards the centre of the upper deck. Seating capacity is 64/28, on hard seats made from orange plastic material. Most of these are arranged back to back. There is a seat for the conductor at the outer end of the lower deck behind the stair, but this is for his use only when not collecting fares. It seems likely that, in view of the total number of passengers carried, an additional conductor is used at peak periods. Total capacity is given as 340! At a crush loading of six passengers per square metre, this would indicate that approximately 74 stand on the upper deck, 70 in the lower deck gangway, 30 in designated standing spaces and 54 around the doorways. Exactly where the remaining 20 are expected to go is not clear – perhaps the crush load is calculated at 6.5 passengers per square metre or perhaps standing is permitted on the stairs. At all events, there would seem to be, to European eyes, some degree of overcrowding, and the cars must hold the world record for passenger load on a bogie tram!

Given the loads carried and the local climate, it is perhaps surprising that air conditioning is not fitted, though this would have added to the cost. Ventilation is provided by full drop windows in the lower saloon and half drop windows in the upper saloon, the end windows being fixed. There are no roof ventilators.

The cars are numbered 209,212,215,218, 221 and 224. In November 1995 they were working at the city end of three car sets as follows:

209 108 109
215 186 187
218 159 160
221 147 148
224 138 139

Car 212 seems to have been a spare. The sets worked on two short workings from the city terminus at Place Zaghoul to Sidi Gaber station (service 6, two sets) and to San Stefano via Sidi Gaber Mosque (service 8, three sets).

These trams seem to be a successful attempt to combine the traditional British high seating capacity with the high standing capacity universal elsewhere, and it will be interesting to see if the example of Alexandria is followed by other cities.

The original livery of the Ramleh line cars is not known, but for many years a blue and cream colour scheme has been in use. The present cars have much larger areas of cream paint than did earlier double-deckers. For many years, destinations were carried on boards, in French and Arabic, and colour coded according to route. Nowadays destinations are given in Arabic only. Fleet numbers are carried in both scripts.

Estimated total number of double-deck trams in Alexandria:	
Original two axle cars	32
UEC balcony cars	14
Conversions from single-deck	15
Kinki Shanyo cars	6
Total	67

Bibliography

Modern Tramway/Tramways and Urban Transit, various issues to date, but particularly no.298, July 1962, no.434, February 1974 and no.698, February 1996

Pabst M. Tram and Trolley in Africa, Röhr Verlag, Krefeld, 1989

Information Sheet, Kinki Shanyo, 1995

Mediterranean Trams and Alexandria 1997. PMP Transport Videos.

SOUTHERN AFRICA

CAPE TOWN

This city was early in the field of tramway development and the first line was opened on 1 May 1863 by the Cape Town and Green Point Tramways Company. The line prospered and was soon carrying 128,000 passengers per annum. Two of the original cars were double-deckers, named VICTORIA and ALBERT, but these were cut down to single-deck form after a short period in service. The company also built a small double-decker in its own works when it opened a line to Gardens in 1885. A second company, the City Tramways Company Ltd, was founded in 1878 and began service in 1879. This company used single-deckers only at first, but some of these had upper decks added in 1885 "for the convenience of smokers".

In 1895 both these companies were taken over by a new concern, the Metropolitan Tramway Company Ltd, formed with a view to electrifying the network. This was rapidly accomplished – possibly too rapidly – and the first electric car ran on 6 August 1896. Henry A. Butters, a national of the USA, was the driving force behind the scheme and capital provided by the Parrish brothers, tramway contractors from Britain, formed a link between the electric trams in Cape Town, Chile, Mexico City and other places.

The administrative history of the early days of the Cape Town system and its various constituent companies is complicated and ultimately the trams were operated under the name of "Cape Town Tramway Companies", although this in itself was not a registered title. The history of the early rolling stock is equally complex and it is not now possible to compile a full and accurate record. There are few primary sources other than the Brill order book and it is not always totally accurate for early deliveries of cars. Printed sources often differ significantly one from another in many respects. A large collection of official photographs was unfortunately destroyed when the photographer died. It does not help historians that it was the practice in Cape Town, until about 1914, to paint fleet numbers at first in the middle of the waist panel then later on the rocker panels only, rather than in the more usual position on the dash,

which was in the early days occupied by an oil lamp. Even with a good photograph – and there are not many of these – it is not always possible to identify a tram.

The main original printed sources are a list compiled in 1904 by the City Engineer and further lists compiled by council staff between 1919 and 1928. These seem to be generally supported by photographic evidence. Other information was set down by a retired employee of the tramways many years later, but this evidence is not always borne out by photographs. It seems certain that renumbering of at least part of the fleet took place, but exactly when this occurred and which trams were affected is not now clear. It must be emphasised that, due to this absence of detailed records and the unreliability of these which do exist, much of what follows is speculative and should not be taken as a definitive account but rather a best estimate.

The first trams to operate were two series of double-deckers built by Brill in Philadelphia. Some sources give the first batch as 1-11, but two (Gill and Howarth) state that service began with ten cars, some of which (possibly 1-10) were single-deckers. However, the fleet list of 1904 gives 1-11 as double-deckers. These were two-axle cars riding on Brill 21 trucks. The lower decks had five windows per side, while the upper decks were roofed but open at the sides and ends. These could be enclosed by blinds in

A demonstration trip of the new trams to Members of Parliament and city councillors on 13 July 1896, a few weeks before the official opening on 13 August. W. B. Rommel, Chief Engineer, is at the controls of the first car, one of the five-window design, while one of the larger six-window cars follows behind. (National Archives of South Africa)

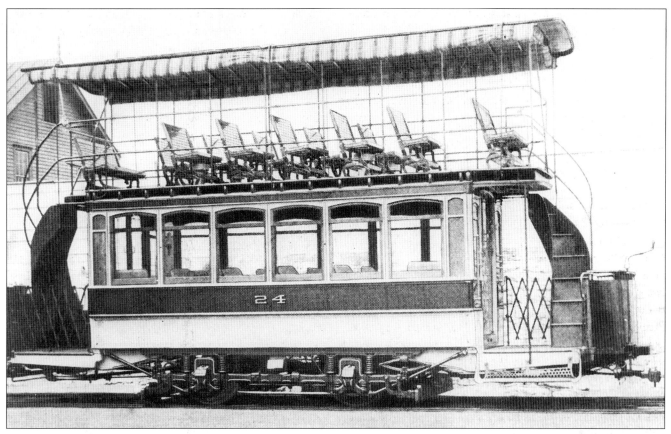

Six-window car 24, photographed at a later date, probably at Tollgate depot. (Author's collection)

inclement weather, the blinds being provided with celluloid peep holes to allow passengers to ascertain their whereabouts. There were short canopies and the rather tight quarter-turn stairs rose directly to the bulkheads. As the saloon length was only 14ft 5in, these were clearly not part of the order mentioned below. On examination of the first few trams to be assembled, it transpired that there was insufficient headroom in the lower saloon to allow an average-sized man to stand upright with his hat on and they were placed in secure storage until Brill could send replacement ceilings. These trams had longitudinal rattan seating in the lower saloon and wooden transverse seats upstairs. Seating capacity is given as 24/20 in the 1904 list though some sources give the total capacity as 40. They continued to be listed as double-deckers until the 1930s.

Brill order 6553 was placed by H. Parrish and called for 16 trams with 18ft bodies for delivery in June 1895. Numerically the next batch of double-deckers, 16-24, formed part of this order as they had 18ft bodies, having six side windows and a seating capacity given as 50 (1904 list) and later 28/24. Seating in the lower saloon was transverse, except for bench seats at each end. These trams also rode on 21E trucks and were similar to the cars mentioned above. It is not clear when they entered service, but a photograph shows a six-window car on a pre-opening trial run and another shows a similar car decorated for the Diamond Jubilee celebrations of 1897. However, this order number covered in all a total of 16 cars, leaving a balance of seven cars unaccounted.

Not long after the trams began running to Mowbray, on 13 November 1896, the Company become embroiled in a dispute with the Eastern and South African Telegraph Company. Return current was not flowing by the tram tracks as intended but was leaking off into the earth and interfering to a serious extent with telegraph messages. Although the tramway electricians did their utmost to find the cause of the problem, the Company was ultimately sued for £50,000 by the E & SATC, who lost the case both in the Cape Town court and again on appeal to the Privy Council in London. However, the evidence presented at the hearings throws considerable light on the problems faced by early promoters of electric tramways. It was also revealed that the Cape Town double-deckers then in service were fitted with either K2 or K10 controllers and either GE800 or GE1000 motors.

Eight cars with double-deck bodies were ordered from Brill in February 1900 (order 9952) for delivery in May. A builder's photograph of car 32 shows it with six side windows to the saloon, a roof over the upper deck and a short canopy and the typically Brill design with a small landing at the top of the stairs, which were thus displaced out to the edge of the dash and came down to the edge of the platform. Trams to this design had been delivered to several US systems in the 1890s. Unfortunately the number cannot be guaranteed to be that carried by the car in service, as it was a fairly common practice for car builders to give a car a suitable number for the purpose of an official photograph. A postcard also shows a car of this type, but unfortunately the number is not visible. However, it may be that these Brill cars were numbered 25-32 or 32-39. Dimensions were 27ft by 7ft 4in, with a saloon length of 17ft and, as was usual with Brill double-deckers by this

A scene in Adderley Street taken in or soon after 1905. On the right car 41 is outbound for Wynberg, while on the left car 5 is bound for Gardens via Plein Street. As yet no motor traffic is in evidence, but some competition to the trams is offered by numerous hansom cabs, of which no. 159 waits outside Cleghorn and Harris's store on the right, while another is parked between the tram tracks behind the centre pole. (Cape Town Archives, courtesy P.R. Coates)

A view from a point slightly further down the street, outside the railway station, taken about 1920. Car 62 picks up passengers outside the Grand Hotel, with a single-truck car behind. The latter carries a board to indicate that it is working an express service with a minimum fare of 2d. (National Tramway Museum)

date, headroom in the lower saloon was over 6ft. Seating was 24/24, all seats in the saloon being transverse. The cars may indeed have reached Cape Town in May 1900 but were not placed in service until later in the year. The Anglo-Boer war was by this time in progress and press reports mention that the unloading of these cars was being delayed by pressure of wartime activity in the docks. The Company was experiencing something of a boom in passenger numbers, due to the increase in the city's population and the number of people passing through en route to the war zone, and complaints of overcrowding of the trams were made in parliament. The managers must have been glad when they could at last take delivery of the Brill cars, which were in service by the end of the year. By 1919 these cars had 28/24 seats and a view of car 33, taken about 1914, shows it to have been rebuilt to be very similar to the early classes of double-decker. By this date also cars 37-39 were shown as single-deckers. The other cars of this class then remained unaltered until the 1930s, when they were scrapped.

At the same time as these cars were ordered, Cape Tramways also ordered four bogie cars from Brill numbered 41-43 and (probably) 40. Delivery was intended for May 1900 but these cars were probably also delayed at the docks. They had GE equipment, Brill "Eureka" 22 maximum traction bogies and 66 or 68 seats, arranged 36/32, these being rattan in the lower saloon and wooden upstairs. The lower saloon had eight windows per side and these trams were basically an enlarged version of the standard two-axle cars, with short canopies and open stairs. Between 1925 and 1928 the upper decks were extended and in some or all cases enclosed and in this form the trams seated 54/36.

However, at the time these Brill cars were finally entering service, opinion in Cape Colony was turning away from things American because of US support for the South African Republic, and this probably accounted for the ordering of the next two batches of cars from Dick, Kerr and Company in Preston. In July 1901 an order (C116) was placed for ten double-deck two-axle cars on Brill 21E trucks and six bogie cars on Brill maximum traction bogies. A repeat order was placed in August 1902 (again C116) for seven two-axle cars and three bogie cars, the only difference being that the 21E trucks for the former were to be supplied by Brill, rather than being Preston built as in the first batch. Both types of car had a full-length upper deck which was roofed but open at the sides and ends. They had reversed stairs and a headlight on the canopy.

The two-axle cars had six side windows to the lower saloon, Dick,Kerr 25A motors and DE1B controllers. The original fleet numbers are not known, but the builder's photograph shows a car numbered 61, and 13 are shown in the 1904 list as 57-66 and 76-78. The numbers of the other four cannot at that stage be traced. Their career in their original form seems to have been brief. A commercial postcard, helpfully dated 1906 by the sender, shows a similar

car in service, but there are no later views of cars of this design. The lower saloon was identical to that of the cars supplied to East London in 1904 by what had by then become the United Electric Car Company. In 1910, the manager of East London Municipal Tramways, when under criticism from councillors concerning the troubles of that undertaking's UEC cars (qv), stated that Cape Town had had a batch of twelve similar cars which had had to be rebuilt as bogie cars after a few years. In the relatively confined world of tramways in the colony, he would certainly have been broadly aware of what another undertaking was doing. It may be therefore that these cars were indeed rebuilt and renumbered soon after 1904 and that they are the cars which appear in the 1926 list as 66 and 76-91. They are then given as being mounted on Brill 21 trucks. The discrepancy could be explained if either the East London manager was incorrect in detail of the rebuilding or if the compiler of the list worked from original records. Whatever the actual truth, it is clear that in their original form, these English cars proved to be less satisfactory than the earlier imports from the USA and had to undergo some fairly extensive rebuilding. There was probably also some renumbering.

There is no problem with the next numerical series, nos 44-51, Brill bogie cars of 1913, Brill order 1891. These trams were ordered in March 1913 for delivery in the following July and took the numbers of an earlier batch of single-deck cars. They had a full-length upper deck which was, however, still open at the sides and ends, canvas blinds allowing some protection in inclement weather. Once again Brill "Eureka" maximum traction bogies were used but these were reversed with the pony wheels pointing outwards. Seating capacity was originally 46/32. In the lower saloon, most of the seating was transverse 2x2, with bench seats for two at each side of each end and all seats were covered in rattan. Wooden seats were fitted on the upper deck. The lower part of the saloon windows could drop down into the waist panel and this part could also be covered by curtains, while the upper part could open inwards. Spring bolts were fitted to prevent rattling when these were open. Overall length was 34ft 9in. and height to trolley base was 14ft 5in. All cars had their top decks enclosed between 1926 and 1928 and some also received drivers' windscreens. Both this class and the previous one were used on the trunk service to Sea Point and all seem to have survived until final closure in 1939.

The next delivery of double-deckers was of cars 52-63, which were Brill bogie cars of 1919. They had enclosed upper decks, though originally the balconies were open. Sliding double sash lower windows were fitted on both decks, with upper opening windows as before, and there were reversed stairs. Seating capacity was 48/32, the seating arrangement in the lower saloon being identical to that of the earlier cars. In what was now the upper saloon, however, the 36 seats were upholstered in rattan and were of the Brill "Waylo" design; this had the particularly light weight of 30lb and was in fact the type of seat fitted to that

A builder's photo of two-axle car 61, taken probably early in1902 before the car was shipped to Cape Town. (National Tramway Museum)

manufacturer's Birney cars. The sliding door which gave access to this saloon was fitted into the nearside edge of the bulkhead and this allowed the fitting of a bench seat for three and three single seats on each balcony. These seats were wooden and two of the single seats on each balcony could be folded up if necessary. This gave a maximum seating capacity on the upper deck of 48. The cars were 33ft 4in. long, 7ft 6in. wide and 14ft 5in. high. Unladen weight was just over 13 tons. This class formed Brill order 20800 and took the fleet numbers of earlier single- and double-deck cars. Again Brill maximum traction bogies were fitted but with the pony wheels in the normal position. From 1925 the balconies were enclosed and some cars also received drivers' windscreens; in this condition the upper deck seated 48. This class was normally used on the Hanover Street service and survived until 1938/39.

Numerically but not chronologically the next class to be considered are 67-75. These were the bogie cars ordered from Dick, Kerr in 1901 and 1902. Length was 33ft and the lower saloons had eight windows per side. English Electric equipment was fitted and seating capacity was 44/32. These cars had full length upper decks, roofed but open at the sides and ends and reversed stairs were fitted. This class also had Brill 22 bogies, in the normal position. The upper decks were enclosed in the 1930s. Exact date of withdrawal has not been recorded, but from photographic evidence it would appear that all survived until 1939.

The next trams to appear in numerical order are again something of a puzzle to the historian. The 1904 fleet list shows cars 76-78 as two-axle double-deckers with English Electric equipment and 60 seats. They continue to appear

as such in later lists, with seating capacity of 36/24, until 1928, after which date these numbers seem to have been taken by new single-deck cars. Numbers from 79-90 are not shown in the 1904 list and are given as single-deckers in 1919, but from 1923 to 1928 they appear, along with car 91, as double-deckers seating 36/24, which would suggest that they were two-axle cars. They could possibly be those trams previously shown as nos 57-66 plus some rebuilds of Brill cars. This latter point would be confirmed by a mention in the 1926 list which says that these formed Brill order 6553 of 1895. These trams also seem to have been replaced by new single-deckers after 1928. The 1926 list goes into more detail on these trams and gives a length of 18ft (presumably for the saloon), a six-window lower deck and Brill 21E trucks.

As the 1919 and 1920 lists show overlapping sequences for nos 78-82, giving these as both double- and single-deck cars, there seems to have been some confusion and it is unlikely that the exact history of the trams with the numbers 76-91 can now be ascertained.

The final batch of double-deckers for Cape Town consisted of six large cars obtained from Brush in 1924, nos 101-106. Originally these had open balconies but these were enclosed in the 1930s. Drivers' windscreens are not shown in the works photograph but seem to have been fitted on or soon after arrival in Cape Town, as all views of the cars in service show these. Full depth sliding windows were provided on both decks and seating capacity was 56/48, with an official standing number of 16. These trams had equal wheel bogies, air and electric brakes and in view of their great length, two trolleys were

Car 69 posed against a background of Table Mountain. (Author's collection)

fitted. They were the only double-deckers in the fleet to be thus equipped. They were fast cars and could reach 30mph. Car 102 was the last tram to run in Cape Town and closed the service in the early hours of 29 January 1939, to the strains of "Old Soldiers never Die", "Sarie Marais" and the horns of 200 motor cars. All had survived until the final closure, but attempts to sell these still modern cars to other undertakings were frustrated by the unusual track gauge of 4ft 9in., since no prospective purchaser was willing to go to the expense of regauging them.

No further double-deckers were purchased, all later new cars being single-deckers.

It is thus very difficult to give final totals for double-deckers used in Cape Town and the list given overleaf should be considered only an estimate.

A builder's photograph of car 101. (Author's collection)

Original short Brill two-axle cars 1-11	**Total 11**
Longer Brill two-axle cars 16-24	**Total 9**
Brill two-axle cars of 1900 32-39	**Total 8**
Brill bogie cars of 1900 40-43	**Total 4**
Dick, Kerr two-axle cars of 1901/2 57-66	
7 others	**Total 17**
(later renumbered, ?76-91)	
Dick, Kerr bogie cars of 1901/02 67-75	**Total 9**
Brill bogie cars of 1913 44-51	**Total 8**
Brill bogie cars of 1919 52-63	**Total 12**
Brush bogie cars of 1924 101-106	**Total 6**
Fleet totals : Two-axle cars	**52**
Bogie cars	**39**
Total	**91**

It should also be mentioned that the modernisation of the double-deckers which took place in the 1920s seems not to have followed any very definite system. Some cars became totally enclosed, some had drivers' windscreens fitted but retained open balcony upper decks, while yet others had the balconies enclosed but retained open platforms. A film made c1936 shows cars in service in all the above conditions. It should also be noted that there were always a substantial number of single-deckers in service and that this was at no time a 100% double-decker tram system.

The livery used was green and cream.

No trams were preserved when the system finally closed, but some bodies were sold off to be used as garden sheds and at least one body, of a single-decker, was still extant in 1990.

DURBAN

The first horse tramway in this city opened in 1881 and was operated by the Durban Tramways Company Ltd. It used four double-deck cars built by Starbuck in Birkenhead. These had seating for 40 passengers on longitudinal seats on both decks and had closed sides with a light awning over the upper deck. In 1885 a second company, the Suburban Tramway Company, began service but used only single-deckers. The two companies amalgamated in 1889 and some further double-deckers were obtained from Brill in the early 1890s. The system was taken over by the municipality on 1 August 1899. Although electrification was already being discussed, some additional horse cars were bought, including at least one from Milnes. This had garden seats on the upper deck and the manufacturer featured it in advertisements, as Brill had also done some years earlier. The city's electrical engineer and assistant borough engineer were then dispatched on a study tour to Britain, Europe and the USA, and on their return reported favourably on the overhead line system of electric traction. Work was put in hand immediately and, despite the pressures of the Anglo-Boer War, went ahead rapidly. The first electric car was driven by the Mayor to inaugurate the system on 1 May 1902.

The first electric cars were obtained from Milnes (1-22) and Brill (23-30). The former cost £1,198 each and the latter £1,106. There are no details for the Milnes cars but the Brill cars were to be "as open as possible" and had open mesh waist panels. From photographs, it would seem that both batches were almost identical as delivered. There were transverse rattan seats in the lower saloon and wooden seats upstairs; seating capacity was originally given as 50 but by 1930 both classes seated 58. These cars were 26ft long by 7ft 2in. wide. Car 1 was used to inaugurate the electric system in 1902. The Brill cars had suffered fire damage on board ship and were not ready for service until July 1902. A third batch of similar cars, numbered 31-46, came from Hurst, Nelson of Motherwell and entered service in 1903. These trams were rather cheaper, costing £1,006 each and rode on the builder's own design of cantilever truck. Seating was originally for 54, later for 58 passengers.

In 1905 six trailers originally built by Milnes were motored and took the

This view was probably taken on the opening of the first electric line, 1 May 1902. (Alan W. Brotchie collection)

"Something between a large bathing machine and a very small second class carriage". Perhaps W. S. Gilbert had had a vision of this tram of the future when he put those words into the Lord Chancellor's nightmare song in 'Iolanthe'? One of Durban's Hurst, Nelson built trams, its canvas blinds drawn, prepares to cope with the worst weather the Indian Ocean could throw at it. (North Lanarkshire Libraries)

Car 6 at Stamford Hill Road, Sutton Park between 1908 and 1912. Standing in front of the car are (left to right) F. Chalsty, Assistant Manager, E. Corlett, Traffic Inspector and E. C. Harkins, Cashier. The driver's name was Blackmore. (Durban Local History Museums)

One of the two-axle cars was used as an illuminated tram during the visit of Prince George in 1934. (Kevan J. Marden collection).

of £1,207.10s. each presumably included the original cost of the trailer body; if not, this was an extremely expensive way of acquiring new cars!

In the following year, ten sets of equipment were ordered from the British Westinghouse Company and these were fitted to ten more cars, which were numbered 53-62. They are referred to as having been built by Milnes-Voss, but by 1906 this would have meant cars built by the United Electric Car Company to a basic Milnes design. These again seated 58. They had Mountain and Gibson radial trucks and Westinghouse Newell magnetic track brakes. They were much cheaper than all earlier cars, costing only £870.6s. each. Clearly UEC were now anxious for business, the boom of the early years of the century having passed. At the same time, one tram was bought from James

numbers 47-52. It is not certain if these had been built new as single-deckers for electric service or whether they were conversions of the horse cars bought on municipalisation. They were now rebuilt as 58-seat double-deckers. The cost

One of the two-axle cars as rebuilt waits outside the Post Office in West Street in August 1939. (Kevan J. Marden collection)

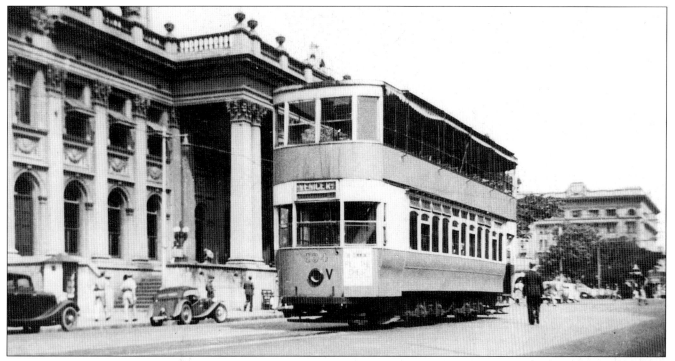

Bogie car 104 as rebuilt outside the GPO in Gardiner Street. (Alan W. Brotchie collection)

Brown Ltd, a local firm of engineers and ship-repairers, with premises at The Point. This became car 63, although it is reported that it was originally numbered 58. Two further cars, 64 and 65, followed in 1909, built this time by the Natal Government Railways using Brill trucks. All three cars seated 58 and were expensive, the first costing £1,107 and the two NGR-built cars £1,207.10s. each.

There were no more local orders! This was the only instance in southern Africa of electric trams being built by local firms, all others being either imported complete or built by the operators using imported components.

Two further cars followed from Brill in 1910, at a more modest cost of £1,006 each, although they seated only 50 passengers (30/20). A Brill photograph shows one of these

A view of West Street about the time of the first world war. Bogie car 95 on the right is still in its original condition. (National Tramway Museum)

By about 1930 car 89, the class leader, had been rebuilt and waits in Gardiner Street, with the city's handsome railway station in the background. A centrally-placed 'robot' (traffic light) has been installed and motor traffic, consisting mainly of British-built cars, has greatly increased. (National Tramway Museum)

cars as numbered 64, but it would seem that they later took the numbers 66 and 67. There may have been some renumbering of the fleet around this time. These trams had a length of 26ft 6in. over platforms, a width of 7ft 4in., and weighed 9.8 tons. Brill publicity emphasised the low weight per passenger, this being, at 440lb, well below the lowest figure for a single-deck car in the USA. All seats in the lower saloon were transverse and were upholstered in rattan, while those on the upper deck were of hardwood. The cars were constructed on a teak frame and were finished internally in oak with a ceiling of alternate poplar and bass boards. All windows in the saloon were fitted with spring roller curtains and the two in the centre were full drop. The upper deck could be enclosed by canvas drop curtains.

Thereafter Durban took to building its own cars, using Brill trucks, and turned out ten cars, 68-77, in 1910/11, at an average cost of £856.6s. per car. Most seem to have seated 54, though four seated 58. Cars 78-85 followed in 1912, at virtually the same cost, but seating only 54. The final two-axle trams, 86-90, arrived in 1914. These were rather larger, since two seated 64, and three 66 passengers. By now prices seem to have risen but since the figures quoted do not tally exactly, it is not possible to give an exact cost for this batch.

Although coming from various builders, the design of Durban's two-axle cars was highly standardised. All original batches had short canopies, enclosed lower saloons with (apart from 22-30) full drop windows and open-sided upper decks with a light roof. From car 78 of the 1912 build, this design was modified to have an extended (but

not full) canopy and a unique design of stair, with two straight flights of steps being linked at right angles. Apart from the exceptions mentioned above, all cars rode on Brill 21E trucks, of 7ft wheelbase, with wheels of 33in. diameter. Unladen weight was 9 tons. Until about 1920 Providence type lifeguards were fitted but these were then replaced by the standard British design. All had transverse seats on both decks and could carry 20 standing passengers. All except cars 53-62 had two GE58 motors of 37hp, B13 controllers and GE electric brakes. Some cars of later deliveries had two trolleys. The original livery was cream with light blue lining. Canvas waterproof curtains could be pulled down in wet weather to enclose each deck, when the cars took on the appearance of a mobile beach tent and must have been distinctly claustrophobic.

For the visit of the Prince of Wales in 1925 one car was decorated and illuminated, with a large Union Jack on each side. It toured the system at night and attracted much attention. A car was similarly decorated for the visit of Prince George in 1934, carrying the message "Welcome to Durban". Durban and Johannesburg were the only systems to use double-deckers as illuminated cars in southern Africa, as Cape Town used single-deckers for this purpose.

During their careers most if not all of the earlier batches of two-axle cars were rebuilt to conform with those built from 1911 onwards, receiving extended canopies and straight stairs. Some were also given flush side panels instead of separate waist and rocker panels. These rebuildings probably account for the different seating capacities cited for different cars and at different dates. At some date between 1931 and 1935, one car was cut down to single-deck form and used as a one-man car, but its number has not been recorded.

The first withdrawals, of cars 1-30, took place in 1935 on the arrival of the first trolleybuses. The remaining two-axle cars were scrapped between 1939 and 1941.

In 1914 the first of 30 very large bogie cars was built by the undertaking on Brill trucks (car 91). This particular car was simply an enlarged version of the earlier standard two-axle car, with short canopies, quarter turn stairs and eleven side windows in the lower saloon and consequently looked rather old-fashioned for its period. It would seem to have had accommodation for 100 passengers. It was followed in 1918/19 by ten cars of similar design. Costs had risen appreciably as a result of the war and these cost up to £4,016 each. These trams were numbered 92-101. Further bogie trams appeared as follows:

1922:102-106, 1924:107-110, 1925:111-114, 1927:115-118.

All were built by the undertaking and were large trams, seating over 90 passengers on transverse seats, though the exact figure varied from batch to batch. The highest seating capacity, of 98 passengers, was that of the 1918 series. All bogie cars had standing room for a further 25, though they are credited with carrying 150 passengers at times of peak traffic. They had four 25hp motors and Brill equal-wheel bogies, with a wheelbase of 7ft. It may be thought

that, when fully loaded on Durban's hills, they might have been rather slow, but as seen on film, they seem to have had a fair turn of speed.

Cars of later deliveries, probably from car 102, had extended canopies, straight stairs and standard lifeguards from new, and the earlier bogie cars had by about 1930 been rebuilt to match. Many of these trams later received platform vestibules, though on some protection for the driver was limited to a deep valance under the canopy. Some, such as cars 91 and 104, also had the ends of the upper deck enclosed. Another, possibly 105, had the sides of the upper deck enclosed with full-depth sliding windows.

Finally in 1928 Durban's last two trams appeared. These were numbered 119 and 120 and had platform vestibules and enclosed ends to the upper deck and could carry 104 seated passengers. These two trams had straight stairs, which intruded into the lower saloon. These cost only £2,794.10s. each.

The bogie cars worked what was left of the system after 1941 and the first two to be built were withdrawn in 1945. Those which remained after that date were renumbered 6993-7020, not necessarily in order of building. These new numbers were affixed to the dashes on neat metal plates, as with railway locomotives. Cars 6993-7004 were withdrawn in 1948 and the last went in 1949. Car 7015 closed

In 1948 an unidentified (renumbered) bogie car passes the commodious waiting shelter at Grayville Junction, where the lines to Marriot Road and North Ridge Road diverged. The tram is on the former service. Just to the left of the car an old-style British road sign and a Belisha beacon complete the vintage scene. The car disappearing towards the city has been fitted with a platform vestibule but retains its open-ended upper deck. (L.A. Woodroffe, courtesy Kevan J. Marden)

The final development of the Durban tram, car 120, outside the car sheds in Alice Street in 1940. (Durban Local History Museums)

the system with a ceremonial run on 2 August 1949, two days after the last service car had run.

No Durban tram has been preserved, though some bodies are thought to exist in the Natal countryside.

The livery used latterly was green and cream, with the title "Durban Municipal Tramways" on the rocker panels until the 1930s. Latterly the trams were liberally covered with advertisements, even the dashes and entire side panels being thus adorned.

In the early days of the electric trams, only Europeans were allowed to travel inside, unless the car had been reserved for "coloured" passengers. By 1930 a special service was operating for such passengers, using ten of the two-axle cars, whose numbers have not been recorded. Latterly seats at the rear of the upper deck were reserved for African and Asian passengers. The municipality was just beginning a conflict with the Nationalist government on the carriage of such passengers when the last car ran.

It should be noted that little has hitherto appeared in print concerning Durban rolling stock and few records have survived. The above account is based as closely as possible on original source material, including photographs and film, but it is subject to correction and revision.

Total number of double-deck electric trams operated:	
Two-axle	90
Bogie	30
Total	120

EAST LONDON

The tramway history of East London began with the electric era, internal transport in the city being provided by horse buses only until the end of the 19th century.

The municipally owned system began operation on 25 January 1900. It was constructed by the Electric Construction Company of Wolverhampton and was of standard gauge. It was a small system, consisting initially of one main line and a short branch, but as the city was a holiday resort for the industrial population of the Witwatersrand, there was always a certain amount of pleasure riding. To cater for this, the main line was extended in 1923 to form a circular drive through a wild and beautiful (but uninhabited) area to the east of the city. This route proved to be popular with holidaymakers. The entire system was replaced by motor buses in 1935.

The history of the rolling stock is again incomplete, due to absence of records. The first trams to be delivered were nine cars built by G.F. Milnes, numbered appropriately. The first three arrived in 1900 and were uncanopied, two-axle double-deckers with four round topped windows to the lower saloon. The upper deck was roofed but open at the sides and fitted with canvas blinds to give protection when necessary. The cars rode on Peckham cantilever trucks and electrical equipment was supplied by the manufacturers, though it is not clear if they manufactured this themselves or imported it from General Electric in the USA. Seating capacity was probably 24/18. These trams, though partially rebuilt about 1910, remained basically

One of the original three cars, 2, liberally adorned with advertisements, at an unknown location, which could possibly have been the depot entrance. The crew do not appear to be wearing any uniforms. (East London Municipal Library, Denfield Africana and Local History Collection)

At the hotel, car 4, also in as-built condition, turns inland from the beach and prepares to attack the gradient into the city centre. (East London Municipal Library, Denfield Africana and Local History Collection)

A scene at the Beach terminus between 1904 and 1912. On the left is one of the Preston built cars while beyond it is car 7, both being in original condition. The tent city which sprang up each year during the holiday season can be clearly seen, while the large Beach Hotel can just be discerned in the background. (East London Municipal Library, Denfield Africana and Local History Collection)

unaltered throughout their lives. In 1935 car 1 posed for a newspaper photograph alongside bus no 1, one of the new AEC Ranger single-deckers which were bought to replace the trams.

The second batch of the initial order, nos 4-9, were rather different and it may be that the first cars had proved to be unsuitable for the local climate, or were simply not big enough.

These cars had six full drop windows to the lower saloon, with toplights, and the decency boards were carried round the ends of the upper deck. The platforms were fitted with openings on both sides. The seating capacity has not been recorded but as these trams were larger than the first delivery, it would probably have been about 28/24. The very small headlamps were mounted on the roof. These trams entered service in late 1900 and 1901.

The third batch of trams was built by the Electric Railway and Tramway Carriage Works of Preston and arrived in 1904. There were six trams, numbered 10-15, and were quite different from the initial fleet. The lower saloons had six full drop windows and transverse rattan seats. There was a full length, totally enclosed upper deck which had full drop side windows and enclosed balconies, which had solid panels at the sides and single windows at the ends. This feature gave the cars a unique appearance. They were fitted with reversed stairs and had Brill 21E trucks with a wheelbase of 7ft and two DK 25A 25hp

motors. All cars in the East London fleet had trolley poles with fixed heads.

The municipal tramways were beset in their early years by chronic financial troubles – they did not cover working expenses until 1911 and did not make a profit until the 1920s – and in consequence little maintenance was undertaken. By 1909 the second batch of trams were in a bad state, suffering from both wet and dry rot. The Preston cars also had their problems, since the short wheelbase and long overhang made them hard on the track, while the condition of the track in turn damaged the bodywork. As a result, they spent much time in the depot, emerging only to deal with holiday crowds or sudden heavy showers. In 1909 a crisis developed when cars 4 and 8 had to be taken out of service simultaneously and virtually dismantled. It was clear that drastic rebuilding was required.

This could have been a daunting task for a small undertaking, but fortunately the shed foreman, Mr Douglas, had had experience of car building in Britain, where he had been employed by Leyton Council Tramways. Together with the General Manager, Mr Lambe, he was able to cope with the situation. Car 4 was rebuilt with a completely new lower saloon, in which the Milnes monitor ceiling was replaced by a plain arched design. New and rather straighter stairs were fitted, along with a new roof, deeper and flatter than the previous one, and fitted with a dwarf trolley base. The car now looked like those of Cape Town and Durban and appeared to be successful in traffic. In February 1910, after some debate, the city council agreed to spend £1,800 in similarly rebuilding cars 5, 6, 8 and 9.

Mr Lambe would have liked to rebuild the Preston cars as well, but the council would not contemplate such heavy expenditure on cars which were used only at peak periods. To support his case, the Manager mentioned that the similar Cape Town cars had had to be rebuilt after only two years service, but this did not cut any ice with the members. However, the success of the rebuilds concentrated the civic mind wonderfully and, probably

A view of the interior of the lower saloon of car 10 when new, showing the relatively high standard of comfort offered by these trams. (UEC, courtesy A.K. Terry)

between 1912 and 1914, these trams were similarly treated. In a fairly drastic operation they lost their end balconies and reversed stairs and emerged in a form identical to the earlier rebuilds. All these rebuilt trams seated 32 or 30 on the upper deck and 24 downstairs.

At a later date car 7 was also rebuilt, but to a different design. It was given three side windows to the lower saloon

and possibly an enclosed upper deck with extended canopies and is stated to have then had a seating capacity of 38/30, a high figure for a two-axle car.

When Mr Douglas was retiring in 1913, a speaker mentioned that he was the first man in South Africa to have built a tram. As the Cape Town system had earlier built some of its own horse trams, this was not strictly correct,

In the upper part of Oxford Street, beyond the city centre, car 14, in rebuilt condition, is outbound for Belgravia about 1912, closely followed by another as yet unrebuilt car. The stop sign is clearly visible on the ornate centre pole. The driver sports a smart uniform, complete with white top to his cap. On the other track, car 4 heads in to the city. (East London Municipal Library, Denfield Africana and Local History Collection)

but perhaps the speaker was referring to electric trams only. It is not clear which tram was involved, but possibly it was no 7, the most substantial rebuild. In any case, Messrs Douglas and Lambe deserved every credit for their work, which they had carried out with very little co-operation from the city fathers.

The livery used in East London was green and cream with gold lining. Cars 10-15 originally had matchboard side panels between the two decks, with cream end panels, but they lost this feature when rebuilt. In early days, no doubt because of the financial problems, the trams were liberally plastered with advertisements, for many different products, to the extent where they became virtually mobile hoardings. The practice was discontinued for some years before 1911 and when it was resumed, it was on a much more restrained basis. The cars carried the system's title EAST LONDON MUNICIPAL TRAMWAYS in English only and on the Preston cars, as built, the third word was spelled MVNICIPAL, to give a classical touch. A colour light route code was operated, with two apertures above the destination box, but details have not survived. Racial segregation was not practised on the trams, but the number of African passengers was very limited, as they then formed only a small portion of the city's population.

All cars survived until the final closure, which took place on 23 October 1935, but none was preserved.

Total number of double-deckers operated:	15

JOHANNESBURG

This extensive system was probably that which, of all overseas tramways, most closely followed British practice. It was one of the very few to renew part of its fleet with modern double-deckers in the 1930s and one of the last using double-deckers to survive, not closing until 1961.

Horse trams were operated in the new city from February 1891 by the Johannesburg City and Suburban Tramway Company. Most of the cars used were single-deckers, but a few, probably five, double-deckers were also acquired. It is thought that they seated 38, with garden seats on the upper deck. Because of hills elsewhere on the system, these were confined to the Belgravia-Fordsburg service. With a period of suspension during the Anglo-Boer war, from 1900 to 1902, the horse cars continued to operate until 1906.

In 1903 the town council decided to acquire the system and establish and work a system of electric tramways, and it appointed Messrs Mordey and Dawbarn of London as contractors for the building of the system. They recommended an initial purchase of 40 double-deck trams, 20 enclosed and 20 open. A further 60 would be required for the full service and the balance should be of whichever type was found to be the most suitable for local conditions. The first tender therefore called for 100 cars and was awarded in 1905 to the Electric Railway and Tramway Carriage Works of Preston. The cars were shipped from Liverpool to Durban in a partly dismantled condition and were then reassembled in Johannesburg. Electric service was inaugurated on 14 February 1906.

One of the open top double-deckers, car 21, in the city centre soon after entering service. (MuseuMAfricA)

An early scene at the city centre terminus in Harrison Street, with car 80 on the left and 47 on the right. The market stalls on the left were later moved to allow construction of the City Hall and the Market Hall on the right was demolished and the area redeveloped as the Library Gardens. (MuseuMAfricA)

Two-axle Trams

Cars 1-20 were open balcony cars, with unvestibuled platforms. They had three side windows in the lower saloon, while the upper deck was open at the sides with six window spaces. Red and white striped canvas blinds afforded some protection from the elements. There were transverse rattan covered seats in the lower saloon and transverse slatted wooden seats upstairs. All cars of this batch were rebuilt between 1923 and 1932 in the workshops of the undertaking. Some received completely new bodies with five side windows on each deck and all were given wooden seats in the lower saloon, to increase seating capacity to 62, though in some cases leather seats were fitted at a later date and seating was then reduced by four. Some received new MetroVick 104 35hp motors but unfortunately none was fitted with air brakes. Car 15 was cut down to single-deck configuration in the winter of 1924/5. Cars 2 and 9 – the first to be rebuilt – were withdrawn in 1933 and five (1, 3, 8, 11 and 13) were transferred to "native" service in 1946. All the others, apart from car 20, were scrapped in the 1950s. That car was initially set aside for preservation at the National Tramway Museum at Crich, but as it had the honour of leading the last tram procession in March 1961, it was decided to retain it in the city. It is now preserved in the James Hall Museum of Transport.

The open top trams took the numbers 21-40. These had five side windows to the lower saloon and a seating capac-

ity of 56, but were otherwise identical to the first batch. Open top cars were very soon found to be unsuited to the city's often cold and wet weather and one was given a top cover in 1907, the remainder being so treated in 1911/12. The first conversion cost only £60 but those carried out in 1911/12 cost either £172 or £174.10s. These cars were rebuilt in the workshops between 1923 and 1931 in the same manner as the first twenty, though two, 27 and 36, were converted to single-deckers at that time. Two, 21 and 28, were scrapped in 1933, being again the first to have been rebuilt. Thirteen were later transferred to "native" service and the last two in "European" service were scrapped in the 1950s.

The third delivery consisted of cars 41-80 and these arrived in Johannesburg in 1906, being identical to the first batch apart from having longitudinal seating in the lower saloon. Car 51 overturned in 1906 and was later rebuilt as a tower wagon. Car 66 was also involved in an accident and when rebuilt took the number 51. A new car numbered 66 was built by the undertaking in its own workshops in 1918. All but three cars were rebuilt between 1923 and 1931, being given new and heavier upper decks with sliding windows, but quite a few retained the three window lower saloons. Many, if not all, were given very comfortable transverse leather upholstered seats on both decks. The three exceptions (55, 64 and 78) became single-deckers in 1924/25. Four trams (46, 56, 63 and 71) were withdrawn before 1936 and cars 45, 47 and 61 became "native" cars

A scene in Eloff Street about 1910, with car 76 outward bound for Twist Street. An early motor car and a contemporary taxi wait outside Chudleigh Brothers store. (MuseuMAfricA)

Car 20 as decorated for the final parade, in the City centre. One of the AEC Regent V buses which replaced the trams, and which had themselves a long life, waits behind. (Author's collection)

An animated scene in Loveday Street on Wednesday 17 January 1945. Airbrake Bogie 195 on the left is still in original condition; it is working service O1 to Bez Valley and is also loading at both ends. 'Springbok' two-axle car 92 for Malvern waits for it to clear the junction. (B.T. Cooke)

in 1946. All others were scrapped in the 1950s except for car 60, which had been earmarked for local preservation, following a recommendation by the Railway Society of Southern Africa. In 1964, however, it was accepted by the Tramway Museum Society in place of car 20 and was shipped to Hull, whence it travelled to Crich. It has since been a stalwart performer on the Society's line, having now run over 11,000 miles there and, its high steps apart, has proved to be extremely popular with visitors. It has also appeared in several film and television productions, variously disguised as a Manchester and a Notts and Derby tram.

Completion of the final batch of two-axle cars (81-100) was slightly delayed and they did not enter service until 1907. These trams had five side windows to the lower saloon, but were otherwise identical to 41-80. Cars 87, 88 and 100 became single-deckers in 1924/25 and all the others were modernised between 1923 and 1932. Cars 90,93,95 and 97 were withdrawn by 1936 and five others (81, 82, 88, 96 and 99) became "native" cars in 1937/38. Car 94 was rebuilt as railgrinder T2 in 1952 and those seven remaining were scrapped between 1953 and 1958.

After buying two lots of bogie cars, the JMT reverted to two-axle cars with 121-135, which were delivered in 1915. They were built by Brush, with electrical equipment by Dick Kerr and had two DK511 50hp motors and K4 controllers. Trucks were Preston standard, identical to the Brill 21E. These were rather more expensive than the earlier trams, costing £1,214 each. In 1930, car 129 was

involved in a collision with a train on a level crossing on Eloff Street Extension and was stored for a time, later re-entering service as a "native" car. About 1933 all the others were given Fischer bow collectors and concentrated on the Mayfair service, where the overhead had been suitably re-aligned. The experiment did not last long and within a few years the cars had regained their trolley poles. Cars 122 and 133 were withdrawn without being modernised but all others were rebuilt between 1931 and 1935, to be finally withdrawn between 1953 and 1960.

During the first world war, JMT experienced a shortage of trams and in 1918 rebuilt a freight car of 1906 as a passenger tram. It was generally similar to the earlier two-axle cars but had enclosed balconies, making it the only totally-enclosed two-axle car in the fleet. It retained the two DK 3A 35hp motors originally fitted, with DB1 controllers. Numbered 136 when converted, it later became 129 when the first car of that number was withdrawn and it was itself withdrawn at some date between 1933 and 1936. As the fleet numbers 137-139 were for many years left blank, it is possible that further conversions were envisaged but not executed.

Collectively the two-axle cars were known as "Springboks", possibly because of the galloping motion produced by the 6ft 6in. wheelbase trucks when running at speed. In 1924 JMT accepted on free trial a set of EMB Pivotal trucks, but no trams were permanently fitted with these as a result. The Spencer Commission's report said that "these cars roll and pitch in a most unpleasant

The smaller of the two experimental cars, car 9, at no.1 depot on 25 January 1945. (B.T. Cooke)

manner". It was unfortunate that the municipality put so much effort into rebuilding the cars without either fitting air brakes or lengthening the trucks. They formed the largest single class of double-decker to be built in Britain for export and one of the largest such classes to be operated outwith the UK, though in later years they were numerically overtaken by the post-war cars in Hong Kong.

All were 26ft 6in. in length by 7ft 3in. wide. Seating capacity was generally 58 (34/24), with the exceptions noted above, and official standing capacity was latterly 18. Before 1934, it would seem that no limit was placed on the number of standing passengers, since the Spencer Commission recommended that a maximum should be fixed. However it should be mentioned that schoolchildren were required to sit three to a seat, thus considerably increasing the capacity of the trams at certain times of the day! All rode on Brill 21E trucks or the Preston equivalent, and had wheels of 33in. diameter. All the original cars and rebuilt 136/129 had two Dick, Kerr 3A 35hp motors and two DB1 controllers. During the rebuilding programme, JMT bought 40 sets of reconditioned DB1 controllers from English Electric and would seem to have fitted these to cars 41-80. As such controllers were by that date out of production, it is likely that EE obtained these from Bolton Corporation, as that operator was then re-equipping its fleet with more modern controllers.

Despite modernisation, it was clear by 1933 that some of the two-axle cars would soon have to be replaced and the city council authorised JMT to buy five experimental cars, to evaluate various designs. In the event, only two cars were bought, of which one, no 9, was a two-axle car. It was built by Metropolitan-Cammell and was 29ft 9in. long by 7ft 3in. wide. Externally it was similar to the trams then being built by that firm for Edinburgh Corporation, but unlike these, car 9 had the very low seating capacity of 48 (30/18), largely as the result of the fitting of a front exit and straight stairs. The official standing capacity of 30 made up for this to a certain extent, but the car was really much too small for the system's needs and the Spencer Commission clearly considered that it had been a waste of money. It was finished to a high standard, with comfortable leather upholstered seats and shaded lamps. Air operated platform doors were fitted. The car rode on an EMB hornless truck of 10ft 3in. wheelbase and had two Metropolitan-Vickers 50hp motors and MV T4B controllers, along with electro-pneumatic control by the same manufacturer. In service this tram proved to have good acceleration and a fair turn of speed. In addition to air, magnetic track and hand brakes, regenerative braking was fitted, but for some reason it proved to be difficult to limit the coasting speed when this feature was in operation, and no 9 was sadly accident-prone. It was fitted with a bow collector when new, but this

74

was soon replaced by the standard trolley pole. The combined cost of this tram and its bogie counterpart (2) was £9,975.

Most of the life of no 9 was spent on the Crown Mines service and after it had run away and demolished a shelter at that terminus in 1950, it was laid up, to be scrapped in 1956.

The "Native" Cars

For most of their existence, the Johannesburg tramways were operated under a policy of racial segregation. In practice this meant that scarcely any service was provided for African passengers. If an African was travelling with a white employer, he was required to sit upstairs on the rear balcony, although a nursemaid accompanying a child could sit in the lower saloon. A service to the area then known as Western Native Township, was begun on 1 October 1919 and to work it, JMT built three new two-axle cars. Two further such cars were added in 1925 and a further three in 1930. All these used trucks and equipment from three freight cars and five sprinkler cars. They were basically similar to the standard two-axle cars as rebuilt, but had deeper rocker and waist panels. Both seating and total capacities were, however, considerably greater, the latter being officially 90, this figure being achieved by the use of longitudinal seating in the lower saloon. In practice this figure was often exceeded and these cars probably hold the world capacity record for two-axle double-deck trams. Internal notices were in English, Afrikaans, Zulu and

A quadri-lingual notice on a bogie car on 'native' service is pointed out by a workman at No. 2 Depot on 18 June 1945. The languages are English, Afrikaans, Zulu and Sesuto. (B.T. Cooke)

Car N9, one of those built for 'native' service from redundant freight cars (in 1930) carries a capacity load on Lower Park Drive near the Zoo on Sunday 28 January 1945. (B.T. Cooke)

N18, here seen complete with driver in white pith helmet, was formerly 88 and was converted for the expansion of services for Africans in 1937/8. It is at Diagonal Street on 1 March 1946, with N31 behind. (B.T. Cooke)

Sesuto. The service lost money and had to be subsidised.

At first these trams were painted silver, the rest of the fleet being then blue, but in 1936 some were repainted olive green and cream. Later the livery reverted to silver with a red and black flash on the dash. They were numbered N1 – N10 until 1947 when the N numbers were discontinued. They then became 227-229, 231-235, 230 and 237 respectively. They were withdrawn in October 1949, when the service to Western Native Township was abandoned and all except 237 were scrapped. It became a wire greasing car during the period when the overhead was being altered to allow the use of sliding shoe collectors and when this process was completed, it was scrapped.

As mentioned above, various cars were transferred from "European" service in 1937/38 and these became N11 – N30. The renumbering sequence is known for cars 22, 23, 29, 35, 37, 38, 82, 88, 96 and 129, which became N20, N21, N17, N25, N26, N27, N13, N18, N15 and N12. The other ten numbers were filled by cars 24, 25, 30, 31, 32, 33, 40, 45, 81 and 99, but it is not known in what order. Car N11 was scrapped in 1946 after a fatal accident on the service to Western Native township and N28 – N30 went three years later. The remaining cars were renumbered in sequence 236 and 239-253 and all had been withdrawn by 1953. After 1946, additional cars were used on these services but retained their original numbers, which were 1, 3, 8, 11, 13, 47 and 61. In the final days of the system, very few such services remained. Some short workings on the J group of services were maintained for African passengers and on these standard Airbrake bogie cars were used. The

small blind below the windscreen carried the designation, in black lettering on a white background.

Bogie Trams

The Johannesburg system had not been operating for very long before it was discovered that the two-axle cars could not cope adequately with certain peak requirements, such as race meetings, and it was decided to obtain some bogie cars to supplement them. To avoid delay, JMT accepted an offer from Dick, Kerr and Company to supply ten cars as an add-on to an order then being completed for London United Tramways (class T, 301-340). The trams were delivered to Johannesburg in the first half of 1907, at a cost, including transport, of £1,369 each, and took the numbers 101-110.

Except for a lack of glazing in the upper deck side window spaces and the full drop windows in the lower saloon these trams were identical to those built for London. Striped canvas blinds were fitted instead of glazing. They introduced the LUT type of staircase with a half landing, sometimes known as a "broken" stair and this design evidently found favour in Johannesburg, since it was repeated on all bogie cars built up to 1931. Dimensions were 34ft 7.5in. by 7ft 3in., height 16ft 5in. and seating capacity was 44/32. Official standing capacity was 20, but this figure was often exceeded. Brill 22E maximum traction bogies were fitted, from which the cars derived their nickname of "ponywheel bogies". Two Dick, Kerr motors of 35hp were, not surprisingly, found to be inadequate and these were later replaced by two Westinghouse 50hp motors. Hand, rheostatic and magnetic track brakes were fitted.

This class was not rebuilt, although the bodywork on some cars was strengthened and some received glazing on the upper deck. All were transferred to "native" service after 1945, retaining their existing numbers. As they became due for overhaul, they were repainted silver. Apart from 108, which was withdrawn after an accident in 1951, they were withdrawn between 1957 and 1960.

The next ten bogie cars, obtained in 1913 from Brush, were numbered 111-120 and were somewhat similar in body design to the cars built by the same manufacturer for Pietermaritzburg, having upper decks open at the sides but with enclosed end balconies. They were heavy trams and, despite the provision of two 50hp motors (probably by Westinghouse) proved to be underpowered for some of the city's steeper gradients. Transverse seating for 50/32 was fitted, this being wooden on the upper deck and rattan in the lower saloon. Standing capacity was again officially 20. The lower saloons were elaborately decorated, the ceilings having green and gold Lincrusta scrollwork on an ivory base. Dimensions were 37ft 6in. by 7ft 4in. The cars rode on Brush equal wheel bogies.

At a later date, probably in the 1920s, the end balconies lost the glazing, but side windows were then fitted to the upper saloon. All were transferred to "native" service in 1941 and renumbered N31-N40 in order. Car N32 overturned in 1946 and was later scrapped, while the others became 254-262, again in sequence, in 1950. All were withdrawn between 1956 and 1960.

A smartly-uniformed driver poses at the controls of Airbrake Bogie 143 at No.1 Depot on 25 January 1945. Details of the LUT-type 'broken' stair can be clearly seen. (B.T. Cooke)

One of the Ponywheel Bogie cars, 102, on 'native' service picks up passengers on the main line outside the Western Native Township on 3 June 1945. Apparently loading at both ends was in force! (B.T. Cooke)

By June 1945 the Brush cars had been converted for use on 'native' services and N31 (ex 111) awaits passengers at the Diagonal Street terminus of these services on 4 June of that year. The dash has been repainted silver. (B.T. Cooke)

The next series of bogie trams was built over a long period, between 1919 and 1931, and with an ultimate total of 65 formed one of the largest classes of double-deck tram to be built outwith the British Isles. All were of the same basic design as 101-110 but rode on equal wheel bogies and were fitted with air brakes. They were therefore known locally as "air bogies". They formed a most reliable class and outlasted many of the streamliners in revenue service.

The first cars were numbered 140-153 and were built by JMT in the tramway workshops at Newtown, using underframes supplied by Brush. The first to be rolled out had its balconies patriotically shrouded in the Union Jack.

One of the first Airbrake Bogies in original condition and livery at City Hall. (National Tramway Museum)

Transverse seats were fitted in both saloons and seating capacity was 48/32, but the official standing load was reduced to 18. Dimensions were 34ft 6in. by 7ft 6in. Four Westinghouse 35hp motors were fitted, along with Westinghouse K35 controllers, and the bogies were Brill 76E equal wheel. Between 1929 and 1933 the upper deck balconies were enclosed and drivers' windscreens were fitted between 1945 and 1947, though an opening was left under the stair landing and the cars were not fully vestibuled. The first to be withdrawn was 149, after an accident in 1957, and two more had gone by 1960, but all the others survived until final closure in 1961. Car 149 was not scrapped but bought by an ex-London Transport driver and repainted in LT colours. It then stood for many years outside his home on the veldt, about 27km from the city. At the time of writing it is still there, still in good condition and it is hoped that it may be preserved permanently.

Brush Equal Wheel Bogie car 116 in original condition in Market Street about 1913. Cars 96 and 124 are on the right. (MuseumMAfricA)

The next batch of cars, 154-169, came out in 1920/21 and were fitted with GE motors and brakes. They were otherwise identical to their predecessors but, with post-war inflation rampant, were slightly more expensive, costing £4,805 each. The balconies were later enclosed as on the first delivery. All lasted until 1958 and three were then sold for scrap, but the balance remained active until final closure. Car 159 was the last to operate in revenue service, in the early afternoon of 18 March 1961. They were followed into traffic by almost identical trams 170-192, built from 1921 to 1924, which however had enclosed balconies from new. These trams also introduced a new livery of grey and blue to the city and were at first known by the public as "Bluebirds". All were given windscreens between 1945 and 1947. Apart from four which were withdrawn after 1958, all formed the mainstay of the service in its final months. One was converted to a bungalow by Regent Metals and exhibited at the Rand Show of 1961, but no sales resulted. Many others were sold for use as garden sheds and the bodies could be found for many years all over Transvaal.

The final batch of air bogies, 136-139 and 193-200, came out in 1930 and 1931. They also received windscreens after the second world war. Metropolitan-Vickers electrical equipment was fitted, with four MV102 50hp motors, along with Brush equal wheel bogies and brakes, the bogies being identical to those supplied to Cape Town in 1924 with cars 101-106 (qv). Seven cars survived at closure and car 200 has been preserved in the James Hall Museum of Transport.

In 1934 JMT took delivery of an experimental bogie car from Metropolitan-Cammell. Numbered 2, it was basically a larger version of car 9 and again of relatively low seating capacity (34/26) due to the provision of front exits and straight stairs. Official standing capacity was, however, 30. Dimensions were 34ft 6in. by 7ft 3in. There were four MV105 35hp motors and MV air and track brakes and the car rode on EMB heavyweight radial arm bogies. Platform doors and a similar interior scheme to that of car 2 were provided. In service this car was more successful than its little sister and it survived until 1959, usually working the Crown Mines service. It was scrapped in 1960.

Airbrake Bogie 147 outward bound for Bez Valley on Kitchener Road, Troyville, seems to be overtaking Uncle Charlie's Bedford breakdown lorry, while a rather weary-looking horse pulls a coster's cart towards the city, (1961). (Pam Eaton)

In 1933, following mounting financial losses and a decline in passenger numbers, the City Council decided to obtain expert advice on both the transport and electricity departments. In 1934 a commission of enquiry was appointed to examine the working of both departments, headed by C.J. Spencer, formerly General Manager of the Metropolitan Electric Tramways in London. The section of the report dealing with the transport department appeared very quickly and made rather depressing reading. From it, it would appear that the trams were generally in shabby external condition, poorly lit internally with 25W bulbs and not particularly clean, either inside or out. The report recommended the general retention and modernisation of the tramway system, the purchase of new high-capacity cars and the fitting of air brakes to the two-axle cars.

Unfortunately the last suggestion was not followed up by

In its final condition, 169 loads an orderly queue of boys in school blazers at Kensington terminus in 1961, while Streamliner 222 waits behind. (Pam Eaton)

A passenger makes a run for car 164 as it swings out of Loveday Street into Commissioner Street on a peak-hour trip to Bez Valley in 1961. The 'robot' (traffic light) post carries a notice about city bus tours which departed from this point. (Pam Eaton)

The larger experimental car, 2, awaits departure from Market Street, probably on the service to Crown Mines, just after eight o'clock on the morning of Wednesday 17 January 1945. An Airbrake Bogie is immediately ahead of it, a Streamliner occupies the middle road, and a two-axle car is turning into Simmonds Street. (B.T. Cooke)

81

Dwarfed by one of the spoil heaps from the gold mines, car 82, one of the Streamliners on M & T swing link trucks, runs along Booysens Road on a short working of the H service to Turffontein Road on 2 March 1945. (B.T. Cooke)

An idea of the high standard of comfort afforded by the Streamliners can be glimpsed from this night shot of 223 in Plein Street, bound for Yeoville, on the evening of 30 August 1939. (B.T. Cooke)

Streamliner 223 (M & T bogies) awaits departure from the siding in Stanhope Street at Malvern terminus in 1961, while a thunderstorm gathers overhead. (Pam Eaton)

A good view of the general outline of the Streamliners is given in this view of an unidentified car (EMB Bogies) outward bound for Malvern in 1961. The track in the foreground is the outward bound track of the Bez Valley route. (Pam Eaton)

A little girl watches the conductor of car 212 swing the trolley at Bez Valley terminus in 1961. (Pam Eaton)

A view of Market Street about 1937 showing two of the Streamliners in their original reversed livery. (MuseuMAfricA)

the Council, but an order for 50 cars was placed with Metropolitan-Cammell in July 1935 and the first entered service almost exactly one year later. These trams cost either £4,641 or £4.657, depending on the type of bogie fitted. When new the "Streamliners" were among the best second generation trams built in Britain and were based fairly closely on the design of car 2, with some modifications suggested by the Leeds Middleton Bogies, the prototype of which had been inspected by a delegation from Johannesburg. They had modern, streamlined all-metal (steel and aluminium) bodies with normal quarter-turn stairs and there were no front exits. This allowed

A period shot of passengers on the upper deck of a streamliner. The wire mesh on the windows suggests that the car is on the Newlands service. At one period, trams on this route were subject to attack by stones and other missiles. (MuseuMAfricA)

these cars to carry 76 seated passengers (44/32), though some sources give the capacity of 78. Official standing capacity was restricted to 16. Dimensions were 37ft 9in. by 7ft 3in. Electrical equipment consisted of four MV109 35hp motors and MV 24-volt electro-pneumatic regenerative control. Half of the class had EMB heavyweight bogies and half had Maley and Taunton swing link trucks. Two further pairs of the former were bought as spares.

There are few views of the smaller of the experimental cars in service. Here car 9 is the middle of three seen from the roof of the City Hall about 1935. (MuseumAfricA)

Fleet numbers were as follows:

EMB bogies: 21, 27, 46, 55, 64, 78,89, 93, 95, 100, 129, 133, 202, 204, 206, 208, 210, 212, 214, 216, 218, 220, 222, 224, 226

M&T bogies: 15, 28, 36, 53, 63, 67, 82, 87, 90, 96, 97, 122, 201, 203, 205, 207, 209, 211, 213, 215, 217, 219, 221, 223, 225.

The streamliners introduced sliding carbon-insert trolley shoes to Johannesburg and after 1945 these were also fitted to the remainder of the fleet. During the changeover period, the overhead had to be greased, hence the conversion of ex-"native" car 237.

Initially the new trams were placed on routes serving the Empire Exhibition in Milner Park but were thereafter distributed throughout the system. Unfortunately there was a wiring fault in the controllers of the EMB cars, which incorporated an EMB air brake interlock to prevent the simultaneous application of power and brakes. Sometimes when the controller handle was moved back, the brakes were released and several runaways occurred, luckily

Not only the cars on the services for African passengers carried capacity loads! It is not clear why this particular car, working on the Crown Mines service, has attracted such a crowd. (MuseuMAfricA)

without fatalities. The fault was corrected, but car 220 later twice ran away again, without serious consequences. Otherwise these trams gave excellent service, especially during the war years, but in the 1950s their bodies began to show signs of corrosion due to electrolytic action. They paid the penalty of being among the pioneers of this form of construction for tramcars. By 1953 it would have been necessary to have spent £600 on each car to keep the fleet on the road and as JMT were not prepared to pay this, the cars were gradually withdrawn as defects became apparent. All were out of service by 1960, but some seem to have returned to traffic in 1961. Before this, in 1958, one appeared on a BBC "Panorama" programme on South Africa and still made a brave sight. Five of the better cars were used in the final procession and all survivors were then sold to Regent Metals and broken up. The only two to escape this fate were 214, which is preserved in the James

Hall Museum, and 82, which was bought by the proprietor of a hotel at Kraalkop, 40 miles from the city. Sadly it has not survived.

The exact livery of the Johannesburg horse cars is not known, but they may have been painted according to route or in a chocolate and cream colour scheme. The first forty electric trams appeared in a light brown and cream livery, but this was soon changed to a deep chocolate with, in the case of bogie cars at least, white or cream upper decks. From 1921 blue and grey were used. The two experimental cars of 1934 were painted cherry red with cream window surrounds. The streamliners retained this livery with the addition of cream upper panels with a red band swept down at each end and a silver roof. These new colours were applied to all cars as they were repainted and the air bogies were also given the streamlined effect, which sat awkwardly on their traditional design. Some of the

1936 cars originally had the red and cream panels between decks reversed and this gave them a very "Edinburgh" appearance. However, this paint scheme did not last for long. The olive green and silver liveries used on the "native" cars have already been mentioned. Advertisements were carried in the early days but were discontinued in 1935 and revived only in 1945. Until about 1957 the standard of maintenance was high and the fleet presented an attractive appearance. Thereafter the trams began to look very run-down and the general effect was not helped by numerous advertisements on the sides and dash panels. Some of the latter incorporated the headlamp in the advertisement, and this practice necessitated the transfer of the fleet numbers to a position above the windscreen.

The Johannesburg fleet was based very closely on the best of contemporary British practice and, because of a process of continual modernisation until about 1950, the trams were able to outlive most British systems, being survived only by Glasgow and Blackpool. Apart from Paris, where different operators were involved, and Hong Kong, where the trams are still in service, it had the largest total number of double-deckers to operate outwith the British Isles and it is good to know that five cars have been preserved, along with a single-deck horse tram.

Summary of the Johannesburg double-deck fleet, as built new or converted:	
Two-axle "Springbok" cars	117
Two-axle "Native" cars	10
Experimental two-axle car	1
Ponywheel bogie cars	10
Brush equal wheel bogie cars	10
Air brake bogie cars	65
Experimental bogie car	1
Streamlined bogie cars	50
Total	264

KIMBERLEY

As with Cape Town and Port Elizabeth, the history of the rolling stock of the two tramway companies which once operated in the diamond city is complicated and such printed sources as there are do not always agree with each other.

Tramway services were first provided in 1887 by the Victoria Tramways Company, which operated horse cars, two at least of which, nos 4 and 10, were double-deckers. The cars were built in New York by John Stephenson. Mules later replaced the horses. The gauge was 3ft 6in.

In 1890 a double-deck battery car was obtained from Mather and Platt Ltd of Manchester, this being the first electric car to run in southern Africa. Its first service was on a demonstration line in Kimberley Park during the Empire Exhibition held in that year and after the exhibition closed, it entered regular service. It was numbered 11, following on from the horse cars, and was a two-axle

double-decker of conventional appearance, with direct quarter-turn stairs and garden seats on the open upper deck. The wheelbase was very short and seating capacity was probably 24/24. The batteries were placed under the floor of the lower saloon. The car worked well enough, but required frequent recharging, the batteries being sufficient for only one round trip of 4.5 miles between Kimberley and Beaconsfield. After a short period of service on that line, no. 11 was placed in store and did not appear again until 1896, when it emerged to operate the newly-opened line to Kenilworth. This line crossed a shallow ford at one point. During a severe thunderstorm, the battery car attempted to cross this ford, now swollen by much rain, and when the water came into contact with the batteries, there was a spectacular short-circuit, fortunately without injury to anyone. The car was towed back to the depot by ten mules and did not run again.

The tramway encountered severe problems during the Anglo-Boer war, when the mules were both requisitioned by the army and, during the siege of the city, eaten as food. The Company therefore decided to convert the system to steam traction and for this purpose bought some steam tram engines second-hand from Bradford. To run with these, they also bought five or six bogie double-deckers from the Electric Railway and Tramway Carriage Works of Preston. These were built for, or along with cars built for the Clontarf and Hill of Howth Tramroad in Ireland. In a history of that line, it is stated that the latter operator had intended to have 14 cars but in the event had taken only 12. While a possible surplus of two cars does not exactly tally with the number bought by Kimberley, it may be that the builder was glad to dispose of two cars at a bargain rate and build others cheaply. The Clontarf cars were 34ft long and, at 7ft 4in. wide, rather wide for contemporary British systems. It might have been difficult to find another buyer. They seated 45/30. Certainly the cars of the two systems appear to have been identical to upper deck level. Both the Clontarf cars and those in Kimberley rode on Peckham reversed maximum traction bogies. Presumably they were delivered without electrical equipment and, if the bogies had already been fitted, would have had to be regauged. For service in Kimberley, the upper decks were roofed and given enclosed end balconies, without windows, but remained open at the sides.

As steam traction did not prove to be entirely satisfactory, the line to Beaconsfield was electrified in 1906 and between that year and 1912, three of the double-deck cars were given motors and electrical equipment. Some single-deck trailers were similarly converted. They appear to have lost the enclosed balconies at this stage, but at some later date they acquired platform vestibules. The date of their withdrawal has not been recorded, but they are said to have remained in service until the 1930s, with one surviving until closure of the system in 1939.

It is unclear if the other Kimberly company, the Kimberley and Alexandersfontein Electric Railway, ever operated double-deckers. One source (Howarth) states that

There are few views of the double-deck cars in service. Car 7 heads into the city past the Kimberley Club premises in Du Toit's Pan Road. (National Tramway Museum)

they obtained bogie double-deckers form Stephenson, but no other source mentions these and no photographs of any such car have come to light.

Total number of double-deckers operated:	4

LOURENÇO MARQUES (MAPUTO)

Although situated in the Portugese colony of Moçambique, this system was to all intents and purposes a British operation.

The concession for an electric tramway was awarded in 1902 by the Portugese government to one F. Breyner, who seems to have been an all-purpose business man and contractor, active in many enterprises in the colony. The concession stated that the cars were to be "of the type used in large cities"; the two nearest large cities which had trams at this time were Cape Town and Durban, so it may have been intended from the start to use double-deckers. Breyner, however, did nothing to take forward the construction of the system.

On 20 January 1903 the Delagoa Bay Development Corporation Ltd was formed in London to provide facilities for this still fairly new city, one of these being the provision of tramways. Most of the capital was British, the Portugese shareholding being limited. (Delagoa Bay was an anglicisation of the Portugese "Baia de Lagoa", referring to the area around Lourenço Marques.) This company acquired Breyner's concession – though it is not clear exactly how or when this was done – and work began on the construction of the tramway system in July 1903. Service began on 18 February 1904. The company appears to have traded as Delagoa Bay Electric Tramways, though the full name of the Corporation appeared on the cars. The track was of metre gauge and, as in metropolitan Portugal at the time, left hand running was observed.

The first trams used were eight built by Milnes (1-8), five of which were available when service began. They had Maguire 21E trucks, two 25hp GE54 motors and BT-H controllers.

After a few days of service, opinion became very

A view of a car on Avenida d'El-Rei Dom Manuel, Lourenço Marques. (Alan W. Brotchie collection)

88

critical of the new cars, which were said to be "very ordinary" and were nicknamed "Banheiras ambulantes" (mobile bathing machines) by one of the local newspapers. It was said that they appeared "old" and looked dull. This gave rise to a rumour that they had been built for Constantinople. While there can be no truth in this, since the tramways in the then-Turkish capital were not to be electrified for another ten years, it is probable that, as they were built at a time when the Milnes factory was in receivership, insufficient care was taken over their construction.

The initial order was supplemented in the autumn of 1904 by four additional cars, built by the Electric Railway and Tramway Carriage Works of Preston, using Milnes drawings. Cars 11 and 12 were reported as being in service on 22 October, but nos. 9 and 10 did not follow until December. They were identical to the first batch and all cars had an overall length of 26ft and width of 6ft 6in. The newer cars had bodies of pitch pine and were reported to be of good appearance, much better than the older cars. It was also reported that "o ciaxhilio do meio movel" (of which an approximate translation would be "the underframe can be moved in the centre") but exactly what was meant by this is not now clear. Possibly there was some kind of radial axle.

These trams had Brill 21E trucks, DK25B motors and DK controllers. All cars had cross-bench seating on the lower deck and longitudinal seating on the upper, capacity being 32/30, assuming that two passengers sat on the front platform. The cars were painted white, although if old postcards can be trusted, the white had a good deal of cream in it.

Article 5 of the original regulations stated that "natives and Asiatics" should travel on the upper deck and in other seats designated by the company for their use. The Asians protested vigorously against their exclusion and took their case to the city council in March 1904. Having discussed the matter, the councillors proposed to amend article 5 to read that they should be allowed to travel on the lower deck if they were dressed decently in a European fashion ("sem que se aprestnem decentmente vestidos a europeia"). This alteration came into effect in 1905. The regulation about dressing could obviously be interpreted in different ways and was therefore something of an escape clause for the Company. It appears that for most of their existence, the trams were in practice restricted almost entirely to European passengers.

The lines seem to have been cheaply and hurriedly built and very soon after service began there were complaints about derailments, dewirements and other accidents. These increased in volume in the second half of 1905 and culminated in a fairly serious accident on 2 December, when a tram approached the Cemetery terminus at high speed and turned over on its side, striking a pole as it did so. Five passengers and the conductor were injured and, according to press reports, the car was totally destroyed ("completamente desfeito"). While the motorman was considered to have been at fault, the press also pointed out the danger posed by the pole concerned and others on the system. Excessive speed seems to have been the most common cause of these accidents, but the overturning of the tram in this particular case may also have prejudiced the use of double-deckers. On the other hand, the Company may have wished to rid itself of the upper decks as a means of avoiding the carriage of African and Asian passengers.

Whatever the reason, the cars did not last long in double-deck form and all had been cut down to single-deck by 1915, though most were probably converted well before this date. From evidence of early but undated postcard views, the work could have been completed by 1910. In their cut-down form, the cars lasted until the closure of the system on 25 November 1936.

PIETERMARITZBURG

The capital city of Natal did not have horse or steam trams, and electric service began on 2 November 1904. The system was operated by the municipality and was of standard gauge. Livery was deep yellow and maroon, with cream relief.

The first cars, numbered 1-6, were built by Brush in 1904. These had reversed maximum traction bogies and Westinghouse equipment. They weighed 11,709kg. Early photographs show the cars with open balconies and Bellamy style top covers over the upper saloon, but these appear to have been replaced by a full length roof at an early date. Reversed stairs were fitted and seating capacity was for 70 passengers. It is not clear why this small system ordered such relatively large, and no doubt expensive, cars.

The second and final batch of cars were two-axle cars on radial trucks with equipment by British Thomson-Houston. These were numbered 7-16 and were also built by Brush. They had full-length upper decks and full-length roofs; the end balconies were enclosed but the upper saloons were open at the sides. Unlike the rather similar cars in East London, the end balconies were glazed. These cars seated only 50 passengers and weighed 8 tons.

Two of the bogie cars, 2 and another car, were cut down to single-deck form in the 1920s, to allow operation by one man. One of these conversions was withdrawn early in the 1930s, but all other cars survived until the final closure in 1936. None were preserved.

> **Total number of double-deckers operated: 16.**

PORT ELIZABETH

Horse trams began operation on 14 May 1881 and the fleet included at least two double-deckers, built by Stephenson. Owing to the topography of the city, trams could operate only along the coastal strip, and the desirable residential area of the hill remained without public transport. The idea of electrification was therefore welcomed when it was put

A view looking north-east up Church Street at the City Hall. A two-axle car emerges from Commercial Street on the left, bogie car 5 is en route to the railway station and on the right another two-axle car leaves for Retief Street. Behind it, another car of the same class completes this busy scene. (Alan W. Brotchie collection)

A scene at what was clearly a remote terminus! Car 13 is one of those built by the Brush company. (MuseuMAfricA)

One of Pietermaritzburg's Brush two-axle cars closed the system on 17 December 1936. Two of the Daimler buses which replaced the trams are on the right. (MuseumAfricA)

A scene in Commercial Road, showing car 16 outward bound on the left while on the right car 6 in its rebuilt condition heads for the City Hall. (National Tramway Museum)

Two of the cars with Bellamy-type top covers shown in the early years of the system, when there was little competition other than that from horse carriages and rickshaws. Car 2 on the right is making for the Retief Street, while the other car is waiting to turn out of Commercial Road. (National Tramway Museum)

The Natal Government Railways was noted for its fine station buildings. Here is that of Pietermaritzburg, with car 15 on a special working. (Alan W. Brotchie collection)

to the municipal Corporation by A. H. Butters in 1894. The first electric tram ran on 16 June 1897. The Port Elizabeth Electric Tramway Company was always very closely associated with the Cape Town undertaking, though unlike the latter it was of standard gauge.

For the opening, ten cars were ordered from Brill, whose order book records all as single-deckers. Photographs of the opening day, however, show at least two double-deckers, having five window saloons and upper decks which were roofed but open at the sides. Canvas blinds could be drawn down to cover the sides and ends in wet weather. These trams would appear to have been identical to the small double-deckers supplied to Cape Town. One source (Gill) states that there were twelve trams in service in 1898, and if all the initial order were single-deckers, there may have been only two double-deckers. Two more must have followed soon afterwards, since there were soon four such trams, numbered 1-4. Two additional similar cars (5,6) arrived at a later date, to be followed by three of the six-window design and by 1911 there were nine double-deckers, 1-9. At least in the early days, these cars sometimes pulled a single-deck two-axle trailer. All cars of this type were still in service in 1926, but two of the earlier cars were cut down to single-deck form in the early 1930s, and only two survived as double-deckers by 1938. These were then numbered 2 and 3, but it is not clear if these were the original cars with these numbers, or whether some renumbering had taken place. One of the conversions was numbered 4 and it may be that the other was car 1, but this is not certain. Car 3 still survived in the 1980s, without its truck and stored in the bus garage.

Eight bogie double-deckers similar to Cape Town's 44-51 were obtained from Brill in three batches. Nos 30-33 were ordered in March 1913 and were a joint order with these cars, to which they were identical. Cars 34/5 followed in 1922 and differed in having reversed stairs. Cars 36/7 were ordered in May 1923 and entered service in April of the following year. They reverted to direct stairs and evidently the management in Port Elizabeth saw no need to follow Cape Town's lead and enclose the upper decks. The only concession to modernity was the use of Brill "Waylo" seats on the upper deck. These were in fact the last double-deckers to be built by Brill and the last to be exported from the USA to another country. All interior fittings were of white ash, and the lower deck ceilings were enamelled white to give a "bright and sanitary" appearance, as the Brill Magazine put it. Seating was 46/36, with seats for five on each balcony.

All Port Elizabeth bogie cars had Brill 22 maximum traction bogies with 33in. driving and 20in. pony wheels. The last four had two trolleys.

Two of the first batch were given more powerful motors around 1923 and in the early 1930s another of the class was "completely reconstructed". No 33 had the honour of closing the system when it was the last car to run in service on 16 December 1948.

As there were ultimately 42 trams in the fleet, double-deckers were in a minority.

Livery was green and cream with the company title carried in full on the rocker panel until the 1940s. In neither Cape Town or Port Elizabeth was racial segregation practised on the trams.

Total number of double-deckers operated in electric service:	
Two-axle	9
Bogie	8
Total	17

This city still had something of the appearance of a frontier post when this view was taken around 1900. One of the original two-axle cars heads towards the City Hall along Main Street, with only horse carts sharing the road. (Author's collection)

Bogie double-decker 35 waits at the terminus at Humewood. (National Tramway Museum)

Bibliography

Tramway Systems of Southern Africa. W. D. Howarth. Johannesburg, 1971

Tram and Trolley in Africa. M. Pabst, Röhr Verlag, Krefeld, 1989

Kimberley Tramways. Richard Sabatini. Kimberley, 1985

Kimberley Tramways. E. Read and A.Spit, in Modern Tramway Review. Ian Allan Ltd, London, 1964

Tracks and Trackless. Peter Coates, Struik and Company, Cape Town, 1976

Cape Trams. Fraser Gill, Cape Town, 1961

Port Elizabeth Tramways. Graham Shields, Port Elizabeth, 1979

Tramways in East London. Brian Patton, Tramway Review nos. 110 and 111, Light Rail Transit Association, London, 1982

Johannesburg Tramways. A. Spit & B. Patton, Light Railway Transport League, London, 1976

Os Eléctricos de Lourenço Marques. Salaomão Vieira, Maputo, 1997

The Dick, Kerr Story. J. H. Price. Tramway & Light Railway Society, Ambergate, Derbyshire, 1993

Dick, Kerr specifications and order cards held in library of the National Tramway Musuem, Crich

Brill order books

Periodicals

The Omnibus Magazine, Vol XIV no. 93, June 1955 (Durban article)

Modern Tramway no.194, February 1954 and other issues

Light Railway and Tramway Journal. January 1901 (Cape Town Brill cars)

Car 2 at North End Terminus, Port Elizabeth. (Frank W. Neave, courtesy MuseumAfrica)

ASIA

CHINA

HONG KONG

Although the tramways of Hong Kong are today synonymous with double-deckers, and the Hongkong Tramways Company has the longest continuous record for operation of such vehicles overseas, the service was actually inaugurated with single-deckers, double-deckers not appearing until some years later. Although the system is still very much in operation, records for the early years are sparse and much of the early part of the fleet history has had to be based on conjecture.

There were proposals for a tramway in 1884, but these did not come to fruition, as it proved to be impossible to raise sufficient capital. The line would have been a steam tramway and the trailer cars would have been double-deckers, laid out to accommodate three classes. Passengers travelling third class would have ridden on the upper deck.

More success attended proposals for an electric tramway and in 1903 Dick, Kerr and Company as contractors began to build a line which was opened for traffic on 30 July 1904. The operating company was originally known as the Electric Traction Company of Hong Kong Ltd, this title being changed in 1910 to Hongkong (sic) Tramways Ltd. Single-deckers were used and the gauge was and is 3ft 6in.

The first double-deckers appeared in 1912. There were ten of these and they rode on Brill 21E trucks of 6ft 6in. wheelbase. They had DK 25B motors and DB1 controllers. The car bodies were built by the Hong Kong and Whampoa Dockyard in Kowloon and were shipped across the harbour on lighters to be finished by the operator. They were open top cars, laid out to carry two classes of passenger. Those paying first class fares travelled in a separate compartment in the lower saloon or – unlike practice elsewhere with a two-class system – on the upper deck. Perhaps because of the local climate, the fresh air of the upper deck was considered an advantage, and this practice was continued as long as a two-class fare structure was in operation. There were separate entrances for passengers travelling third class, these being double width. Although the cars were double ended, only a single staircase was fitted, rising from the inner end of the first class compartment. The cars were fully canopied and vestibuled, but the passenger area of the upper deck extended only to the lower saloon bulkheads. Rails surrounded the upper deck but there were at first no decency boards. Seating capacity was 20/30 and the livery was dark maroon and cream.

In wet weather a trap door could be let down into the

Car 37, the first double-decker, when new. (LRTA collection)

95

well of the stair, to close off the upper deck and prevent water running down into the saloon. Very soon, complaints arose from passengers in first class that, in such weather, their part of the lower saloon became overcrowded and, to allow continued use of the upper deck in rainy weather, light canvas roofs were fitted, with side screens of the same material. A hole was cut in this roof for the trolley standard. Although these roofs marked an improvement, travel in such conditions in wet weather was still not pleasant, as quantities of rain came in through this hole. These trams were numbered 37-46.

A total of 34 cars to the same basic design, numbered 47-80, was added to the fleet between 1918 and 1923, but these had canvas roofs from the start. They also had DK29A 30hp motors. Trucks were of Brill type, but may have been by Brush or to the Preston standard design. The canvas roofs proved vulnerable to the fiercer of local typhoons, and on several occasions were almost completely destroyed when cars were caught on the road in a tropical storm. An unknown number of similar bodies was constructed to begin a rebodying programme for the single-deckers, as the double-deckers seemed better suited to the growing number of passengers. In 1924 one car

One of the cars with canvas roof is seen on Des Voeux Road Central in the 1920s, at a time when the only competition faced by the trams was from rickshaws, one of which waits for custom on the right. The Europeans are all attired in pith helmets. (Author's collection)

was experimentally fitted with a wooden roof, which had a dwarf trolley base. Roll-down canvas blinds protected the sides and ends and, without the hole in the roof, the upper decks were now almost watertight.

In the following year, the first totally-enclosed cars arrived, six being replacement bodies for the remaining single-deckers and six being completely new, these latter cars taking the numbers 81-86. These trams had Peckham P35 trucks of 8ft 6in. wheelbase and the improvement in

riding was so marked that all older trucks were lengthened to 7ft 6in. in 1927. Five similar new cars, 87-91, followed in 1931. During this period, all earlier cars were given fully-enclosed upper decks. The original 26 Brill trucks were replaced by Peckham P22 or P35 trucks.

Six further new cars, 92-97, arrived in 1936, being to the same basic design but with deeper entrance steps and a less sharply angled staircase. These had English Electric 305 33hp motors and were again on P35 trucks. Twelve further

In the mid-1920s, two of the cars fitted with wooden roofs meet in the central district, while one of the new enclosed cars follows car 18 on the right. (Author's collection)

Enclosed car 27 in the central area in the early post-war period. (A.D. Packer collection)

97

Before advertisements had appeared, car 86 heads along Shaukiwan Road in January 1959. (LRTA collection)

cars, 98-109, mounted on Maley and Taunton trucks, entered service between 1938 and 1940, the last being delayed by the outbreak of war in Europe. Car 100 was the first to be fitted with air brakes, which proved to be so successful that the entire fleet had been so equipped by 1941, just before the colony was occupied by Japanese forces.

The Hong Kong tram fleet was run to the ground during the Japanese occupation, only fifteen trams being in operational condition at the time of liberation in August 1945. For the next three years all efforts had to be concentrated on repairing almost all existing cars. The first tram ran in passenger service in October 1945, by which time there was a nominal active fleet of 40 trams. However, by 1948 construction of new trams, to the pre-war design, could be resumed and ten were built in 1948/49. The roofs and underframes for the last seven were supplied by the Taikoo Dockyard and Engineering Company. These trams took the numbers 110-119.

The construction of these cars, to what was by then an outdated design, was something of a stopgap, to cope with the greatly increased number of passengers using the trams in the immediate post-war years. Meanwhile Hongkong Tramways staff were working on a completely new design

and the result of their efforts was seen in 1949, when car 120 appeared in service. It was designed by C. S. Johnstone, who was appointed Assistant Manager in 1949 and General Manager in 1950; he had begun his professional career with Brush of Loughborough. This was the first car in the fleet to be designed for single-ended operation, although it could still run in either direction in an emergency. As a result, non-reversible seats could be fitted in the first class saloon. There were also half-height air-operated platform doors, controlled by the driver, and all handrails were relocated inside the body, to discourage those who tried to hitch a free ride by clinging to the outside of the trams. The new tram seated 68 passengers, an increase of ten over the old design. The trolley base was mounted on rubber, to reduce noise. Dimensions were 29ft 2in. by 6ft 6in. and weight in running order was 12 tons.

Car 120 was very successful and it was decided not only to build thirty new trams but also to rebuild the entire existing fleet to this design. This target was not reached until July 1960, and by then it had been decided to continue the programme with a further twelve cars. Tram 162 was the last to enter service, in May 1964. The last car of pre-war design had run in 1955, those built in 1949 having had a very short life in this condition. Production cars seated only 63 passengers and had slightly shallower end windows in the upper saloon. Most were built by the Taikoo Dockyard and Engineering Company and were then floated across Hong Kong harbour on lighters to Wind Lok wharf, where the tracks then ran close to the edge of the water. The body was then mounted on a temporary truck and taken to the depot for fitting out. However, 25 cars were built by the Company itself and a further ten were constructed by the Hong Kong and Whampoa Docks Company in Kowloon.

The post-war cars ran on either Peckham P22 or P35 or Maley and Taunton trucks, or on trucks of a very similar design built by the Taikoo Dockyard or HKT itself in the workshops. All had a wheelbase of 7ft 6in. From 1956, new cars were fitted with resilient wheels of the SAB pattern and these were later retrofitted to older cars, the extra cost being more than offset by a reduction in maintenance costs.

This standard design proved to be very successful and these trams have since become closely identified with Hong Kong, despite having been replaced by those of a more modern design in recent years. They were strongly constructed,

It is not usual for Hong Kong trams to reverse while in service, and the only intermediate crossover to have a trolley reverser is that at Causeway Bay, here being used by car 129, which will return to Western Market. (D. Beath, LRTA collection)

with teak framing on a welded steel underframe, the outside being covered in aluminium panels. Livery was originally a very dark, unrelieved Brunswick green which made the trams almost invisible at night, although from 1961 this was relieved by the advertisements which were then affixed to the side panels. Car 162 was unpainted when it entered service, but was repainted in normal livery after less than a year in service. In 1969 it was decided to change to a brighter colour scheme. Car 49 was painted yellow with brown window frames, while car 130 was painted jade green with yellow panels and dashes. This green was then adopted for the entire fleet (but not the

yellow panels or dashes) and a lighter shade was used from about 1977. However, shortly afterwards all-over advertising liveries were introduced and these spread to the entire fleet, totally hiding the original livery. Recently, many advertising contracts have not been renewed and cars can once again be seen in fleet livery.

With the introduction of double-deck motor buses by China Motor Bus in 1964, HKT faced serious competition and it was decided to experiment with trailer operation. The rear lifeguard of car 161 was altered to provide space for a towing bar and it entered service with experimental single-deck trailer 1 in August 1964. As this experiment

Trying without much success to shelter from a Hong Kong downpour while waiting to board car 81, at North Point in February 1969. (G.B. Claydon)

was deemed to be successful, twenty further trailers were ordered in two batches from Metal Sections Ltd, while a further single trailer was built by HKT in 1967. To work with these, 21 double-deckers were converted to act as towing cars. In service, the trailers proved to be noisy and rough riding and, as the double-deckers were not really powerful enough for this form of operation, service speeds fell appreciably. Trailer operation ceased in 1982 and, when it did so, HKT built a further double-deck motor car, 163, using parts of trailer 1. Basically this was a standard car, but the toplights in the lower saloon were unglazed.

Until July 1972, double-deck trams required a crew of three, a driver and a conductor for each class. Owing to ever-rising wage costs, it was decided to dispense with one conductor and all cars then had a cash desk and conductor's seat fitted at the rear of the lower saloon. At first, passengers paying first class fares had to move right through this saloon before they could ascend to the upper deck, but a rearward-ascending spiral staircase was soon fitted at the rear of all cars, to allow passenger flow with both classes. However, this turned out to be only an intermediate stage on the way to one-person operation, as was also being practised on buses in the area. On 10 May 1976 the first tram thus equipped entered service and for over a year there was mixed operation, one-person cars being

denoted by a "coin in the slot" symbol and notices. The last two-person car ran on 30 October 1977. The cars were actually converted for "pay as you leave" operation, with a coin box on the front platform beside the driver. This of course marked the end of the two-class fare structure, with a uniform fare of 30c being introduced. To prevent passengers leaving by the rear platform, a turnstile was fitted there, allowing passengers to board only, while lighting on the front platform had to be improved to allow drivers to check what was actually being put into the fare box during the hours of darkness. The system has worked well and certainly helped to contain costs. No other city has ever operated double-deck trams on a "pay as you leave" basis.

During the early 1980s there was some uncertainly over the future of the trams and there was also some thought given to using single-deckers, but once it was apparent that they still had a role to play even after the opening of the Mass Transit Railway, HKT began to consider rejuvenation of the fleet in double-deck form. In February 1986 car 143 emerged from the workshops considerably altered. A new and rather more user-friendly rear staircase was fitted, orange fibreglass seats replaced the wooden ones and the resistances were remounted on the roof at the front of the car. Although at first painted dark green, 143 soon acquired a new livery of orange and grey. It was intended at first to rehabilitate in a similar manner the entire fleet over a period of three years, but after 15 cars had been so treated, it became apparent that it would be difficult to do so over such a short period and in 1987 it was decided instead to scrap cars as they became due for overhaul and to build new bodies and underframes, using trucks and equipment from the scrapped vehicles. The first car to be so treated was car 12, which appeared later in that year. The body was supplied in kit form by Full Arts Ltd and the underframe by W.J. Brown Engineering Ltd, both of Hong Kong. Externally there was at first no difference between the rehabilitated cars and the rebuilt ones, but from car 30 onwards, new cars were fitted with full-height platform doors and, at a later stage, all cars had their lifeguards replaced by deep fenders. With the exception of car 120, which HKT decided to retain in original condition, for inclusion in a possible future museum, the entire fleet had been rebuilt to the new design by 1992. Car 120 was also given a new body, to the original design. Car 12, which had been exported to Vancouver in 1986 to take part in the exhibition of that year, remains there, still in original condition. Plans to remount it on an ex-Bruxelles truck to allow it to operate in San Francisco unfortunately fell through. The Hong Kong museum of history owns car 50, which was transferred to it in 1993.

The first class saloon of one of the post-war cars. The conductor, complete with Bell Punch ticket machine, makes up his waybill. (LRTA collection)

The lower saloon of a car of the same class. Driver and conductor both wear spotless white uniforms. (LRTA collection)

Subsequently the fifteen cars which had simply been modernised were totally rebuilt, this programme being completed by early 1992.

Following these changes, the fleet of 163 trams settled down to a period of uneventful operation. In 1992 car 85 was fitted with chopper control of Chinese manufacture, the equipment later being transferred to car 17, before being removed in 1996. Also in 1992, car 44, which carried all-over advertising livery for Cathay Pacific Airways, was renumbered 165, since the number 44 in Cantonese sounds rather like "death, death" and it was feared that prospective passengers for the air line might be put off by the tram's number. Car 144 was also renumbered 166 for the same

Car 120 was rebodied to the standard post-war style in 1987 and is seen here in Shaukiwan Road in March 1993. (Author)

The contrast of the old and new at Shaukiwan terminus in March 1993. (Author)

reason. In the same year, the traditional foot-operated gongs were replaced by air horns, with a reduction in the number of accidents.

Car 66 was in 1992 fitted with full skirts which reached down almost to road level, in an attempt to reduce noise, although it has to be said that the trams are generally much less noisy than the hordes of buses with which they share the streets. Several other cars were similarly treated but the modification was not generalised on the entire fleet. Likewise a proposal to fit upholstered seats foundered on vandalism after they had been tried in a few trams.

In 1993 car 88 was fitted with a diamond pantograph and ran tests with this within the confines of Whitty Street depot but, although work on the modification to allow pantograph operation has continued, the experiment has, to date, been without result. Several additional trucks were built during the 1990s and in 1996 a new body was constructed for fire drill practice; it stands in Whitty Street depot and carries the number 888. Its construction followed two fires in 1993, in one of which two passengers and the motorman were injured. Following these emergencies, the turnstiles were altered to allow them to free-

In Hong Kong there is (almost) always a car in sight. In fact in this view taken in the central area in March 1993 there are seven, the line of six westbound cars being headed by car 84 bound for Causeway Bay. The car is in its rebuilt condition. (Author)

wheel outwards if necessary. A new double-deck works car was built in 1997. This combines the functions of rail-grinder, overhead line car and sprinkler and, with its half-open upper deck, looks like a less glamorous version of tour car 128.

Since 1995 most bus operators in Hong Kong have introduced only air-conditioned vehicles to their fleets and these new buses have shown up some of the deficiencies in the tram fleet, especially with regard to comfort in the hot and humid weather which often affects the area. In 2000, HKT decided to review the position and commissioned the City University of Hong Kong to undertake research into

such questions as the possibility of using air-conditioned trams. As part of this programme, a new car entered service on 24 October 2000.

This car is numbered 168 and was built by the undertaking in Whitty Street workshops, using components supplied from mainland China by the main bus building contractor for Kowloon Motor Bus. The basic body structure is therefore similar to that of a bus, using aluminium side panels on an aluminium alloy frame, and the tram looks like a rather foreshortened bus. All seating in the lower saloon is transverse, in 2+1 layout, and this marks a distinct improvement on the longitudinal seating of earlier

One of the cars fitted with additional skirting around the wheels was 20, shown here on the stretch of line which still, in March 1993, ran close to the water at Kennedy Town Praya. A land reclamation scheme has since filled in the harbour area on the right and severed the link between the trams and the water. (Author)

Hong Kong works car 200 at the depot in October 2000. (Malcom King)

There are not many older buildings left in Hong Kong, but the Law Courts are a fine example of colonial architecture. Tourist car 28 negotiates the curve from Des Voeux Road Central into Queen's Road at Chater Gardens in March 1993. (Author)

cars. Otherwise the same layout is used. The cashbox at the front is supplemented by an "Octopus" smart card automatic fare collection machine. External livery consists of dark green waist and between decks panels with white window surrounds and a white roof. During the tram's first three days in service in October 2000, no fares were charged. According to TV reports, the cost of a new body is HK$300-400. Two further cars, 169 and 170, entered service in mid-2001. A fourth is currently under construction. It will be fully air-conditioned, with sealed windows. If the new design proves successful, the entire fleet will be rebuilt by 2004, with the exception of cars 120, 28 and 128.

The Special Cars

Although it has always been possible to hire trams, HKT has developed this niche market only in recent years.

In 1977 car 22 was painted silver to commemorate the Queen's Silver Jubilee and was also illuminated for the jubilee procession. For some time afterwards, it was a favourite for private parties and its success in this role may have led the Company to consider the provision of a special tour car for this traffic.

In the autumn of 1985, car 119 was taken into the workshops and completely stripped down before being converted to open balcony condition. It reappeared in February 1986, renumbered 28, with very comfortable interior fittings and painted in a green and white livery, with much polished brasswork. While it does not resemble

any tram which ever operated in Hong Kong – and indeed not many which have operated elsewhere – it proved to be extremely popular both for private hire and for the operation of public "dim sum" tours, in which the fare included the price of a buffet meal. Such was its success that another conversion was soon undertaken, and in April 1987 car 59 was rebuilt to an even greater extent and to a rather strange design. The rear of the upper deck has retained its roof, but the front part is open, giving this tram the appearance of a reversed version of the Frederiksberg double-deckers (qv). The tram is painted red and white, renumbered 128 and named "Victoria". For some time afterwards, car 28 was correspondingly named "Albert". Internally it is finished to an even higher standard of luxury and it was intended to confine its operation to private hire work, but in the event it has seen much service also on tours. Latterly it has been illuminated at night. The public tours were originally very cheap but fares were increased considerably in 1989. Despite this, they remain very popular and HKT is to be congratulated on its use of double-deck trams to develop this market.

Projected Designs

Hongkong Tramways

In 1970 a design was prepared for a semi-streamlined two-axle double-deck car, which bore some resemblance to two

105

Tourist car 128 at the depot. (T. E. Fischer, courtesy Lars F. Richter)

trams built in 1940 by English Electric for Aberdeen Corporation, 140 and 141. Basically this was a modernised version of the standard post-war design with a double-width doorway at the rear and a single-width doorway at the front. The car would have been 30ft 2in. long over fenders and 6ft 6in. wide and it would appear that it would have ridden on an EMB "hornless" truck of 9ft wheelbase. In the plans, it was shown as carrying the number 201. The exact reason for the proposal is not now clear and in the event the tram was not built.

In 1977 HKT drew up plans for a total modernisation of the system, one component of which was the replacement of the entire fleet by 112 new bogie double-deckers, to be followed by a further 14 by 1991 and an additional 23 if a proposed extension to Chai Wan were constructed. In co-operation with the German manufacturer Düwag, a model of the proposed car was constructed. This suggested a long (45ft) but still very narrow bogie car, although with some track respacing the width could have been increased from the proposed 6ft 6in. to 7ft 2in. or 7ft 3in. The car would have been laid out for the existing "pay as you leave" system, but with a double-width front doorway and a double-width doorway at the rear of the offside, for emergency use. The suggested capacity was about 146, although if the body had been widened, this figure could have been increased to about 170. Air conditioning would have been fitted, thus anticipating by quite a few years this now-standard feature on new buses in Hong Kong. Chopper control would also have been fitted. The model was finished in unlined light green. Unfortunately this advanced design had only just been published when a joint team of Hong Kong government staff and consultants recommended

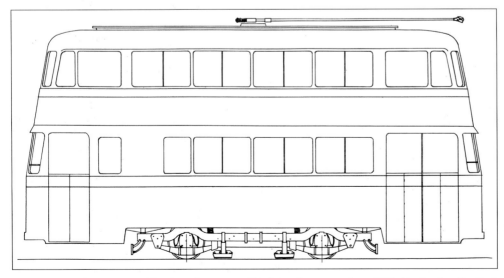

What also might have been. The plans for a streamlined car drawn up about 1970. (Author's collection)

The upper saloon of rebuilt car 143, with new fibreglass seats, presents quite a contrast with the view of a standard car. This illustration dates from March 1986. (Author)

What might have been. The mock-up of the proposed bogie car in the depot yard in 1995, as seen from a passing bus. (Jim D. Schantz)

that the tramway should be converted to "pre-metro" standards with a subway in the central area, and the double-deck project was therefore still-born.

In 1980 Comeng of Victoria (Australia), the builder of the first trams for the light rail system of Tuen Mun, produced a design of a double-decker for Hong Kong, showing a tram with the driving position at the front of the upper deck, reminiscent of the car operated in Chicago in the 1890s (qv). This idea was not pursued.

In the autumn of 1994, HKT began construction of a full-size model of a double-ended, double-deck bogie car, in Whitty Street workshops. This was 37ft 9in long and it was suggested that it would incorporate air conditioning and run on maximum traction bogies. However, the parent company of HKT decided that the proposed tram would be too expensive and the model was scrapped.

TUEN MUN

In 1977-78, a team made up of consultants from Scott, Wilson, Kirkpatrick and Partners, London Transport International and Hong Kong government staff was set up to consider the transport needs of the new town of Tuen Mun in the New Territories. In their draft report, this team recommended that a light rail system would best serve these needs and to work it, they suggested the construction of a fleet of between 60 and 70 very large double-deckers. In overall design, this concept was based on Melbourne's then-new Z class of single-decker, with a length of 54ft 2in. and width of 8ft 6in. Seating capacity would be 103/32, with seat spacing of 3+2 in the upper saloon. Standing capacity, calculated at six passengers per square metre, would have been 112. The cars would have been powered by two 150kW motors carried on monomotor bogies, with chopper control, giving a possible acceleration of 2.24km/second (2) and a top speed of 80km/hr. Unladen weight would have been 21.9 tonnes.

The cars would have been single-ended, with double-width doorways at the front and rear, and two single-width doorways in the middle. As it was proposed at that time to use a flat fare system, a very large space for standing passengers was left between the first two doorways and a smaller space between the second and third, and in these areas there would have been three and two sets of turnstiles respectively. A central forward-ascending and a rear staircase would have been fitted. The car would not have been air conditioned but ample full-depth sliding windows would have assured adequate ventilation. The estimated cost of one tram was estimated at about £200,000, at a time when a new double-deck bus could be bought for about £70,000. The number of trams required was put at 53, with a further 17 if the proposed extension to Yuen Long were constructed.

Initially the parent company of Hongkong Tramways, The Hong Kong and Kowloon Wharf and Godown Company (KWG) expressed interest in operating the system and in turn they engaged further consultants,

Electrowatt Engineering Services Ltd of Zürich. In its report of November 1979, this firm suggested four options of vehicle design, one of which was a double-decker of a length of 59ft 8in. This would again have been single-ended but with four double-width doors. At the same time, the Hong Kong Department of Transport had examined the original proposal and confirmed support for the double-deck principle, but the design first proposed was now modified with four double-width doors.

Various rolling stock builders had meanwhile been approached and Metro-Cammell produced a very attractive design, based on the original concept but showing a car with a single-piece windscreen and front window on the upper deck. Tentative proposals also came from Comeng and, later, from GEC.

Sadly, all these interesting ideas came to naught since first KWG then later the Kowloon-Canton Railway Corporation, who became the actual operators of the new system, firmly rejected the double-deck concept and the only visible reminder of the proposal is the height of the doorway in the depot, which was designed to allow use of such trams. The new Tuen Mun system has certainly been successful, but the use of double-deckers would have allowed more passengers the chance of a seat at peak periods!

Fleet totals

Due to both the lack of records and also to the policy of rebuilding trams, it is very difficult to give an accurate total of the number of double-deck trams which have operated in Hong Kong. The following table is a summary of the position, but it should be borne in mind that in many cases, trams which appear to be new vehicles incorporate many parts of older vehicles.

Open top double-deckers	**10**
Single-deckers rebodied to open top	**18**
Canvas roof double-deckers built new	**34**
Wooden roof cars built new	**6**
Wooden roof cars rebodied from single-deckers	**6**
Enclosed cars built 1931-40	**23**
Enclosed cars built 1948/49	**10**
Post war standard cars	**163**
Cars rebuilt to 1986 design	**158**
Cars rebuilt for special duties	**2**
2000 design	**3**
Total	**433**

Bibliography

Hongkong Tramways. R. L. P. Atkinson and A. K. Williams. Light Railway Transport League, London, 1970

Modern Tramway/Tramways and Urban Transit, various issues, 1970-date

Hong Kong Tramways Handbook. Danny C.Y. Chan. Northcard Transport, Hong Kong, 1997

INDIA

BOMBAY

Tramway operation in Bombay began in 1874, when a USA company, the Bombay Tramways Company, placed in service the first of its horse cars. Only single-deckers were used. The undertaking passed into municipal control in 1905 but a new concession for electric operation was then awarded to the British-owned Bombay Electric Supply and Tramways Company Ltd, whose initials BEST were emblazoned on vehicles and stop signs for many years. The first electric cars ran in 1907 and proved to be very successful. The cars ran on standard gauge tracks.

All the original cars were single-deckers, although several sources mention an order for one 52-seat double-decker placed with Brush in the year of opening. There is no subsequent reference to this car and it seems that it was not built. To handle the increased traffic, which grew from 30 million passengers in 1908 to 40 million six years later, both trailers and coupled sets of motor cars were operated, and in 1912 the Company requested permission to run three-car sets on its busiest services. As many of these ran along narrow streets, the police objected and the idea was not pursued.

On 29 April 1919 the Municipality asked the Company to introduce double-deckers on an experimental basis. This request was agreed to and in September 1920 the first two such cars entered service. One had a lightweight canopy top cover and the other was totally enclosed. Unfortunately it has proved impossible to ascertain whether these were bogie or single-truck cars, though later statistics would suggest that there was one of each. Two more, one of each type, arrived one month later and these were definitely two-axle cars. They had English Electric DK 29A1 30hp motors and Brush controllers, and it is likely that two each were built by English Electric and by Brush.

The experiment appeared to be successful and in the next few years further double-deckers were built. Once again, however, it is impossible to be definite about the number of such cars built in 1921 and 1922. There may have been six or twelve, but they were definitely two-axle cars and they seem to have pulled two-axle single-deck trailers. The number of two-axle double-deckers totalled 15 by 1924, when construction of this type ceased. All were built by the undertaking itself in Kingsway workshops and were numbered 601-615. Details of the equipment have not been recorded. All were out of service by 1936 and were scrapped by 1939. The only known photograph of one of these trams shows a neat, domed-roof design with a front exit, very much a smaller version of the later bogie cars.

Although successful, these trams did not bring the extra capacity needed to cope with the growth of traffic and from 1923 new bogie trams were the rule. These were designed after a careful study of LCC practice and were based closely on that undertaking's E or, more probably, E1 class. In Bombay they were always known as the LCC class. Unlike the LCC trams, however, they had straight stairs and front exits. There is some evidence that the latter were

The only known view of one of the two-axle cars. Car 614 is seen at Flora Fountain in the late 1920s, about to turn into Hornby Road. It is flanked by two LCC class bogie cars, of which 695 is on service 8 for Opera House on the left. (Commercial postcard, courtesy H.E. Jordan)

not used as such but functioned as "purdah" doorways to allow lady passengers to board and alight without coming into contact with male passengers. Other references suggest that all passengers regularly used all doorways, on both the near- and off-side of the trams, although some photographs show the off-side front platform closed off by a chain, as was often done in Britain. By 1929 at least 58 trams of the LCC class were in service, though some statistics give the total as 59. The latter figure would be correct if one of the prototype double-

LCC class bogie car 100 seen at Museum West in 1945. (R.J.S. Wiseman)

deckers was in fact a bogie car. Most were mounted on Brush LCC-type maximum traction bogies and had two DK 29A1 30hp motors. High speed was not a priority in Bombay. Car 656, later 56, is thought to have had English Electric equipment, delivered in 1929 on a trial basis and fitted to this tram at a later date. The cars are thought to have been numbered 651-708 initially and were renumbered 51-108 after 1932. The possible "extra" car may have been 650, but it does not appear in the renumbered series. Some of the class may have had controllers from single-deckers which were then being scrapped, these being of either Brush or BT-H manufacture. Not all cars of this class were exactly alike, as some had flat and some domed roofs. Rexine covered wooden seats were provided for 96 passengers but this was later increased to 110. A contemporary European commentator suggested that the restricted knee-room did not matter much, as "The Indians are a diminutive race"!

From 1933 these trams were improved with air brakes and better seating. Platform vestibules were fitted to most, but as of 1945, 19 still had open platforms and photographic evidence would suggest that, in many cases, the vestibules were removed again after 1946. A further seven cars, 110-116, were built at Kingsway in 1934-35 and all had these improvements from new.

By 1929 the longer distance services running northwards to Dadar and Tank Bunder were feeling the effects of competition from the newly-electrified suburban services of the BB&CI and GIP Railways respectively. The average speed of the trams was only 5.75 mph, with a limitation of the maximum to 12mph; full parallel was seldom attained and was in any case forbidden in congested areas. In a report on the undertaking by James Dalrymple (former General Manager at Glasgow), presented in 1925, it was suggested that speeds should be increased. The maximum was then raised to 18mph, as a result of which average speeds rose to 10mph on almost all routes. The time

seemed ripe for an improved design of tramcar, and in 1929 the Company invited tenders for a tram which would attract passengers. English Electric was successful in obtaining the order and the result was car 751, placed in service in Bombay early in 1932.

This very fine car was, apart from the low horsepower of its motors, fully equal to any of the second generation of British trams, such as LCC 1 or the Glasgow Coronations. In some respects, it showed some affinity with both no. 1 and the Felthams, but unlike these, 751 was designed to have a high seating capacity (50/36) and, as it was not intended that passengers should stand on the front platform, no separate cab was provided for the driver. The commemorative brochure published by the manufacturer mentioned that this platform would be used only by lady passengers.

The body was of composite construction on a steel underframe and all wood used was teak. There was a space between the ceiling of the upper saloon and the aluminium roof, to provide insulation in the hot weather. Overall length was 40ft 5.5in. and width was 7ft 6in. The car's height of 15ft 6in. allowed the generous headroom of 6ft 2in. in both saloons and the unladen weight was 18 tons. Seats in both saloons were covered in red leather, which matched the panelling, while ceilings were lined in red and silver leathercloth with teak mouldings. All handrails were covered in black Doverite and the shaded electric light fittings were chromium plated. Green linoleum covered the saloon floors. The upper half of the windows had shaded "purdah" glass and ventilation was provided by "Ashanco" ventilators in the roof, working through grids in the ceilings. It was normal practice in hot weather for cars in service to run with all windows open on the side away from the sun. Platforms, which had a clear width of 3ft 4in., were enclosed by mechanically operated folding doors and there were straight staircases.

The car ran on English Electric maximum traction

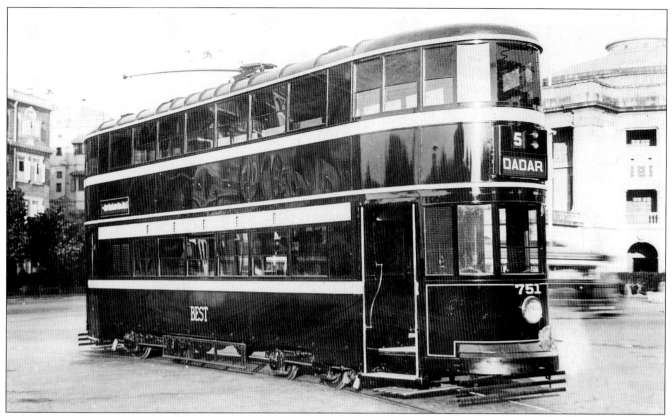

Car 751 when new. (Colin Brown collection)

swing-bolster bogies, with roller bearings. There were two EE DK 105N motors, each of 43hp, and controllers were EE type DB1. Air brakes were fitted and a seat was provided for the driver. There was provision for the later fitting of field shunt equipment, should it be decided to increase maximum speed, but this was not done. The motors were splash proof and the resistances were placed in a cupboard under one of the stairs, both features being intended to cope with the rainfall of the monsoon.

In service 751 proved to be smooth riding and popular

Experimental car 109 with trailer working from Dadar to Museum West is seen on the reserved track on Kingsway on 20 November 1945. Although the war has been over for three months, the car's headlight still carries its war-time blackout masking, while the dash of the trailer has been given diagonal striping. (M. J. O'Connor, Author's collection)

with passengers and crews. It was very soon renumbered 109 and survived until the post-war years, probably until the closure of the system in 1964. The English Electric company, together with A. T. Cooper, Consulting Engineer of BEST, deserved credit for placing in service a tram of such careful design and handsome appearance.

Following the success of 751, it was decided to build more trams incorporating some of its features and, as already recorded, the first to appear were some improved LCC class cars. However, in 1937 a central-entrance design was developed and between then and 1939 23 such cars were built in the Kingsway workshops. Mechanically and electrically they were almost identical to 751/109, but had EE type 305B motors. The controllers were fitted with a device to ensure that the driver paused on each notch when accelerating. Seating capacity was originally for 94 but this was later increased by ten. These

One of the Pullman cars, with trailer in tow, heads inbound to Museum West terminus, sharing the road with two of the BEST's then new Daimler double-deck buses. Note the stop sign, with the pun on the company's title, suspended from the span wire. (Author's collection)

handsome trams, numbered 117 to 139, were known as "Pullmans" and were very similar in layout to many of the central-entrance trams then entering service in Britain, but the stairs rose from the left-hand side of the platform in the direction of travel, whereas on most British trams, they ascended from the right. Sliding doors were fitted. The central-entrance layout had been adopted to speed up boarding and alighting, but for some reason the design did not prove successful in service conditions in Bombay, and in post-war years these cars were rebuilt with end platforms. The stairs, however, remained in the original position. From photographs, it would seem that one or more may have been rebuilt to single-ended configuration, but this cannot be confirmed.

With the outbreak of war, the modernisation programme came to an end. A further 44 sets of motors, controllers and bogies had been ordered in May 1939 for cars to be built at Kingsway, but it is unclear if any of these were actually delivered. Nevertheless, to cope with the growth of traffic, it was found possible to build a further eight cars between 1942 and 1945, to the modernised LCC class design, but

with flat roofs. These must have used either components from scrapped cars, or part of the equipment ordered in 1939. These cars were numbered 140-147. In 1944 there were 96 double-deck trams in the fleet and a further car must have been built soon afterwards.

The system finally passed into Municipal control on 7 August 1947, just one week before the transfer of power from the British Raj. Building of new double-deckers continued apace and there were 123 in stock in 1950, with a further three thought to have been built in the following year. Components from scrapped cars were used in their construction. Bombay was therefore, along with Sheffield and Glasgow, one of the last systems to place in service double-deck trams of traditional British design. There is some confusion about the numbering of these cars; they may have taken the numbers 148-174 and 1 and 2, but some views suggest that they may have been 148-170 and 1-6. These cars differed from earlier examples by having angled end panels, rather than the rounded ends of the pre-war design.

In 1945 the Pullman double-deckers and car 109 were

used on services 1,2 and 9, these being variations on the route that ran from the central area northwards to Dadar and King's Circle, which incorporated a fair amount of reserved track. The LCC class worked on services 6, 7, 8 and 19, the first three of these running along Girgaum Road and the last along Sandhurst Road. The cars built during the war were confined to 6 and 7. Bombay also had a service numbered 0, which ran from Museum East terminus southwards to Sassoon Dock and the LCC class also operated on this. One of the perennial problems of the Bombay system was the operation of an efficient service in the very narrow streets of what was, in the days of the Raj, often called the "native town", the area north of the Fort district, between Crawford Market and Pydhonie. Although it might have been assumed that double-deckers, requiring less road space for a given number of passengers, might have been used to advantage on services in this area, they were not then so used. After municipalisation in 1947 double-deckers, mainly those of post-war build, did appear on services 13 and 16 which traversed part of the area concerned, using in part one-way working in some narrow streets.

In 1945 35 double-deckers were shedded at Colaba, in the depot adjacent to the Company's head office, while the remainder were based at Kingsway, which was both a running shed and workshops. The trams were painted light crimson with cream relief and gold lining, the Pullman cars having a slightly streamlined effect. During the Second World War, some trams were painted grey-green and white, without lining, a colour scheme which did nothing to

enhance their image. In this period also, when a modified black-out was enforced in India, black and white diagonal stripes were painted on the dashes of many trams. This practice was discontinued as soon as the war had ended. In the period after 1945, double-deckers had the cream band below the upper deck windows swept down over the ends, giving the cars the appearance of a bogie version of the then-standard Edinburgh two-axle cars. In all trams there were designated seats for women passengers and for smokers and the conditions of their use were rigorously enforced by other passengers. However, commentators noted that the smell of tobacco tended to pervade the entire car, despite the designated seats.

The fare structure was for many years based on a maximum fare of one anna, which was equivalent to about 1d in British terms, and the company had to fight hard for higher fares when extensions were made. The fare structure then became complicated by half-anna and 2 anna fares. Added to this there was an extensive range of transfer facilities. Tickets were designed to prevent, as far as possible, abuse of these and had to be checked and punched accordingly. Given the numbers carried and bearing later BEST bus practice in mind, it would seem certain that two conductors were carried on double-deckers. First class fares were tried only briefly until 1908 and after these were given up, the Bombay tram became very definitely a conveyance used only by the poorer sections of the community and thus had the same proletarian associations as their counterparts in Britain. The commentators mentioned above noted in 1947 that "Europeans, higher grade Eurasians (ie Anglo-Indians)

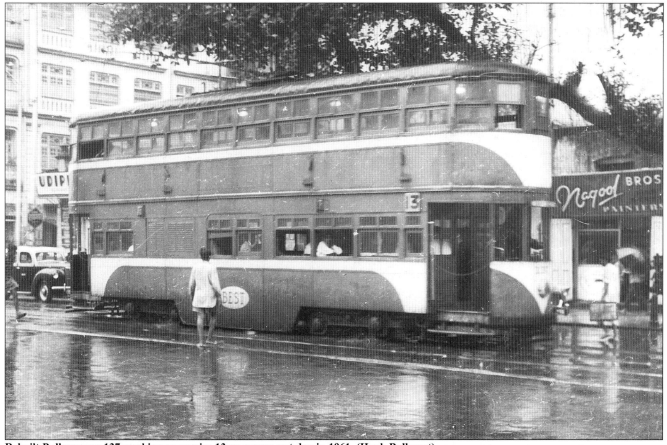

Rebuilt Pullman car 137 working on service 13 on a very wet day in 1961. (Hugh Ballment)

113

One of the war-time cars, 145, with a flat roof, seen here at Flora Fountain on 27 September 1944, with a central-entrance Pullman car behind. (M. J. O'Connor, National Tramway Museum collection)

Post-war car 170 on service 16 in 1961. A rebuilt Pullman car follows. By this date the Ambassador car, based closely on the Morris Oxford, has begun to appear on the streets, although a Morris Minor follows the Pullman tram and a Ford Prefect is passing 170. (Hugh Ballment)

LCC class car 97 working inbound at Victoria Terminus in 1945. (R. J. S. Wiseman)

which were mainly double-deck. Out of a total fleet of 426 motor cars at the time of municipalisation, only 97 were double-deckers and, while additional such trams were subsequently built, 25 additional single-deckers were purchased from New York in the post-war years. Nonetheless Bombay was the last major city to operate traditional British-style double-deck trams, these continuing to run for eighteen months after Glasgow had closed. Since then the city has become famous as one of the world's major operators of double-deck buses.

Fleet total	
601-615, 1920-24, Original two-axle design	15
651-708, 1921-29, LCC class (1)	58
(later renumbered 51-108)	
751/109, 1932, Experimental car	1
110-116, 1934-35, Modified LCC class	7
117-139, 1937-39, Pullman central-entrance	
class	23
140-147, 1942-45, Wartime LCC class	8
148-174, 1947-51, Post-war class (2)	29
1, 2	
Total	**141**

Notes
1 There may have been a bogie car numbered 650
2 These cars may have been numbered 148-170 and 1-6
Total number of double-deckers operated: 141 or 142

and the wealthier Indian sections of the population seldom, if ever, use the trams".

Another unusual feature was the operation of trailers with double-deckers. Between 1942 and 1944, 30 diminutive single-deck two-axle trailers were built at Kingsway for use with the Pullman cars. These seated 32 passengers and rode on Brill 21E trucks from scrapped cars. Their riding qualities no doubt left much to be desired as they pitched along the reserved track of Vincent Road in the wake of the bigger cars, but they did help to handle the record war-time traffic.

It fell to the lot of LCC class car 103 to close the system on 3rd March 1964 when, crowded inside and festooned with passengers clinging to the outside, it left Bori Bunder for Dadar fifteen minutes late at 22.00. There was no closing ceremony but large crowds turned out to watch the car pass and the then General Manager, Shri B. Ghate acted as conductor and issued the last tickets. No trams were preserved but 45 sets of maximum traction bogies and controllers were sold to Calcutta, where they may well be still in service.

The use of double-deckers in Bombay was an interesting adaptation of British tramway practice to Asian conditions and the translation seems to have been largely successful. But it should be noted that the BEST tramways were basically a single-deck system. In 1945 there were in all 15 services, seven of which did not see any double-deckers and single-deck cars often operated as extras on services

Bibliography

The Tramways of Bombay. R.J.S. Wiseman BA. Tramway Review nos. 157-161, LRTA, 1994/5

The B.E.S.T Story. S.N. Pendsay. Bombay Electric Supply and Transport Undertaking, Bombay, 1972

BEST – A Review. S.M. Bedi. BEST, Bombay, 1981

The Bombay Tramways. R.W. Dean and M.J. O'Connor. Unpublished paper, written in 1947, in the library of the National Tramway Museum, Crich

86-seater Tramcar for Bombay. The English Electric Company Ltd, 1931

A History of The Bombay Electric Supply and Transport Company Ltd. P.D. Mahaluxmivala. Bombay 1936

JAPAN

OSAKA

This system had the only double-deck electric trams to operate in Japan. They were first used on the 3.12 mile long route linking the port to the city centre, which opened on 13 September 1903 and was the first municipal tram system in the country. The track was of standard gauge.

There were three double-deckers, variously recorded as

Electric car of Harbor Osaka. 　　車電の港築 (勝名阪大)

A view of car 3, showing the trolley projecting from the canopy. (Commercial postcard, Allen Morrison collection)

3, 5 and 9 and 5,9 and 10. The bodies were built in Japan by the Kisha company and they rode on two-axle Herband trucks, supplied from Germany. The cars were of fairly British appearance and were of course laid out for left hand running. They had seven-bay enclosed lower saloons and transverse seating on the upper deck, which was reached by reverse stairs. A light canopy covered the central portion of this deck. Possibly to give adequate clearance for traffic to the port, the overhead on this line was strung at a very high level above the roadway and the trolley poles on these trams were not in the usual position, but were fixed to the base of the canopy, just above the staircase and stuck out behind in a most unusual manner. When the track was later doubled, double overhead as used in Cincinnati was installed, but it is not clear if the double-deckers were rebuilt for this form of current collection. They were all withdrawn in 1911. No particular reason for the adoption of double-deckers has come to light.

In 1953 the city council decided to celebrate half a century of tramway operation and a replica double-decker was constructed on the 79EX truck and the underframe of a car of the 1920s. As this replica was intended for operation on the city streets, under overhead which had by then been relocated to normal height, it had to be built to a reduced height and a wire cage was placed around the bow collector. The longitudinal seats in the lower saloon are very low and there is again a light canopy roof over part of the upper deck. When the tramway system closed in 1959, this replica was stored, along with other museum cars, in the paint shop of the metro. The collection has since been transferred to Morinomiya depot.

Parts of double-decker 3 are preserved in a museum at the Takarazuka amusement park on the Hankyu Railway, an interurban line which runs from Osaka to northern suburbs.

Bibliography

Modern Tramway no.424, April 1973
Sayoanara Streetcars. R. Forty. Interurbans Special 70, Interurban Press, Glendale, California, 1978

MALAYSIA

JOHORE

In the 1890s, the Sultan of Johore in Malaya constructed a steam tramway using engines and bogie double-deck trailers built by the Falcon Engine and Car Company, predecessors of the Brush Company. The cars had central entrances and provided accommodation for three classes, first and second being in the lower saloons. Nothing is known of the later history of this line.

Bibliography

Bus Journeys through Malaya in the 1950s. F. W. York. DTS Publishing, Croydon, 2001.

AUSTRALASIA

AUSTRALIA

ADELAIDE

The capital of South Australia was in horse tram days served by no fewer than seven companies, most of which used British-style double-deckers. Many had a light canopy roof fitted to the upper deck. One such car, 18, has been preserved by the National Trust of South Australia. It belonged to the Adelaide and Suburban Tramway Company and started life in 1877 as a single-decker, built by Stephenson in New York. The upper deck was added at a later date.

In 1889 a Julien battery car was tried. The vehicle used was adapted from a standard double-deck horse tram built by Duncan and Fraser. The batteries were placed under the seats and the car was driven by a portable controller. With its equipment the car proved to be too heavy for the track, and the wheels tended to jam on curves. The experiment was no more successful than that in Sydney.

BALLARAT

Double-deck horse trams were operated in Ballarat by the Ballarat Tramway company from 1887 until electrification was completed in 1913. These were built by Duncan and Fraser of Adelaide and were of conventional British design. Two cars survived as garden sheds and one of these, which turned out to be car 1, was rescued for preservation in 1985. After a complete rebuilding, involving many hundreds of hours of work by members of the Ballarat Tramway Preservation Society, the tram re-entered service in 1992. It now runs on the truck of former Melbourne cable car 88, with the brake gear from 461.

BRISBANE

Horse tram services began on 10 August 1885, operated by the Metropolitan Tramway and Investment Company Ltd. Both double- and single-deck cars were used, the former being of typically British appearance. They were, however, supplied by Brill and Stephenson from the USA.

The system was sold in 1895 to the Brisbane Tramways Company, and electric operation commenced in July 1897. No further double-deckers were used.

LEONORA

One of the world's most obscure tramways was that which served this gold-mining town, located about 180 miles north of Kalgoorlie. In the late 19th century, when it was at the heart of a thriving industry, a line was built to link the town centre with the suburb of Gwalia, a distance of about 2.5 miles. To work this line, two small saddle-tank steam locomotives were bought, and these hauled at least two double-deck trailers. These were two-axle vehicles, with an enclosed saloon and an upper deck fitted with a canopy roof, but open at the sides. This had knifeboard seating. The line was electrified in 1908 and the steam locomotives and trams disappeared.

MELBOURNE

The Victorian capital was widely known for its large cable tram network, but horse cars did play a small part in its transport system in the 19th century, and in fact the first tram line to be opened used such cars. This ran from Fairfield station to Thornbury and service began in 1884 with double-deck cars which, from contemporary sketches, would appear to have been single-ended. A line from Cheltenham station to Sandringham via Beaumaris also used double-deckers, of a more conventional double-ended design. This line ran from 1887 and expired after a lingering death in 1914. Other horse car lines and the cable lines used only single-deckers and the Victorians have since shown little enthusiasm for double-deckers whether as trams, buses or, most recently, electric trains.

SYDNEY

The capital city of New South Wales is one of the few cities to have operated successively three quite distinct tramway systems, two of which used double-deckers.

The first of these was a horse car line along Pitt Street from Circular Quay to Redfern, opened on 23 December 1861. This line was owned, and at first worked by, the New South Wales Government Railways. The first two horse cars were imported from Britain, where they had been built by Starbuck and Prentis in Birkenhead. They were identical to the cars used by G.F. Train on his line there, having knifeboard seating on the upper deck, an iron ladder for access to that, and nine side windows in the lower saloon. At first they carried the names "Old England" and "New Australia", but later were more prosaically numbered 1 and 2. Seating capacity was 18/18, and twelve standing passengers could be carried. Length was 24ft and British records give an unladen weight of 2.4 tons, but Australian records

A side view of car 82 as a double-decker at Randwick workshops. It is coupled to single-deck motor car 93. (V. Solomons collection)

give the weight as 5.8 tons. Due to the gradient of Pitt Street, four horses were assigned to each tram. The trams were already in poor condition when unloaded, and it seems that they did not survive for long. Two further similar cars were built in the railway workshops at Redfern, car 3 appearing in May 1864, and a second car 2 one year later. Owing to opposition from local businesses, the line closed on New Year's Eve 1866, and the two remaining trams were rebuilt as single-deck railway carriages, in which form they lasted until about 1895.

However, the idea of a tramway did not die, and in 1879 Sydney's second system began operation with a line from Central Railway to Hunter Street via Elizabeth Street. This line was to be operated by steam tram engines, but as the date fixed for opening drew near, it was clear that these would not arrive in time, and to allow the service to begin as planned, two double-deck horse cars were built by the local firm of Hudson Brothers. These were again numbered 1 and 2 and were used to open the service on 16 September 1879 and for eleven days thereafter. They were based on the 1861 cars but had rather primitive staircases to the upper deck in place of the iron ladders. The cars became redundant when steam service began, and it is stated that one was displayed at the Melbourne International Exhibition of 1880. If this was so, it would seem strange that New South Wales chose to be represented by an example of what was, by then, outdated technology.

In 1938 single-deck electric car 94 was rebuilt as one of the 1861 cars, but was not then further preserved.

To work with the steam tram engines, the NSWGR introduced a variety of double-deck bogie trailer cars. While these were of high capacity, they seem to have been poorly constructed, and none lasted very long. All were classified A. Class A consisted of six cars, numbered 3 to 8, built by Gilbert Bush and Company for Brill in 1879. Originally these had open compartments in the lower deck, but these were fitted with sliding doors during refits in 1882/83, when the light canvas roofs were replaced by wooden ones. Length was 35ft and total capacity was 30/60. Early weakness in the upper deck pillars caused these cars to be cut down to single-deck form between 1886 and 1889.

Classes A1 and A2 were virtually identical, but could be distinguished by their elliptical roofs, and totalled 7 and 22 cars respectively. They were built by Hudson Brothers. Numbers were 1, 2, 42-46 (A1) and 21, 22, 24-41, 107 (A2). Again all were cut down by 1892.

The three cars of class A3 (48-50) entered service in 1882/83 as three-axle cars but were very soon remounted on bogies. Classes A4 (51-80) and A5 (81-94) were built as two-axle cars but proved to be unstable and were all rebuilt as bogie vehicles by 1884, the last seven being so altered prior to delivery. Cars 95-98 formed class A6 and were built as bogie cars. On all these classes, seating was reduced to 20/40. By 1886 signs of decay were appearing with dropped end platforms, and all were officially withdrawn between 1888 and 1894, though some continued to exist on the duplicate list for some time thereafter. Many were scrapped, but some were converted to single-deckers.

There were also two classes of self-contained double-deck steam trams, which were intended to be used in place of locomotive-hauled trains in off-peak periods. The first was supplied by Kitson of Leeds in 1881 and was a single-ended car, totally enclosed below and with a light roof over the upper deck. The front bogie carried the power unit, which had a vertical boiler and two inside cylinders. Seating, for 28/24, was longitudinal on both decks. The car, classified D and numbered at first 46 and later 50, was used on the service from Bridge Street to Redfern; at the former terminus and at the depot, turntables were installed for its use, while at Redfern it turned on a triangle. It required frequent repairs and was withdrawn by 1885, the engine portion being then used to power a traverser in the workshops, while the body, shorn of its upper deck, became a railway carriage.

While the Kitson car was still fairly new, the NSWGR ordered some further units to be built by Baldwin, to the design of their own rolling stock engineer. These cars, classified D1 and numbered 70-75 (power units) and 100-106 (bodies) entered service in 1883/4. They differed from the Kitson car in having compartments to the lower deck and two staircases, and were also somewhat longer, at 38ft. Seating capacity was 40/40. These cars were powered by pairs of compound engines, each with four cylinders. It is not clear why there was a surplus body, but perhaps this was intended to cover repairs. Once again these self-contained cars, known as "Jumbos", proved to be unsuited to Sydney's hills, and in 1887 the class was cut down to single-deck form and transferred en bloc to Newcastle. They were little more successful there and all were scrapped by 1896.

However, thoughts were already beginning to turn to electrification and, to assess whether this could be done without the expense and complication of overhead wires, trials were made in 1888 of a battery car provided by the Australian Electric Tramway Company. This double-deck car, of very British appearance, may have been built by Brown, Marshall of Birmingham, and used the Julien battery system. It was a two-axle car with end platforms and garden seats on the upper deck. It was tried on the line from Botany to Bridge Street in June 1888 but proved to be unsuccessful in heavy traffic and may then have been moved to the line at Sans Souci, before disappearing into obscurity.

Electrification on the overhead wire system duly went ahead and in the early years of the twentieth century the Sydney system enjoyed great popularity. One of the penalties of this was overcrowding, which was especially severe on the line to Dulwich Hill and about which questions were asked in the State Parliament. In 1906 it was decided to try using double-deckers to overcome this problem, and two class C two-axle trams, 33 and 82, were accordingly rebuilt in Randwick workshops. The platforms were extended and enclosed upper saloons with short end balconies were added. The upper saloon seated 28 passengers on 2x2 seating inside and four seats on the balconies.

Lower deck seating remained at 26. Very steep reversed stairs were fitted and there were front exits under the stairs. To avoid clearance problems, the cars were not fitted with trolley poles and had therefore to run permanently coupled to single-deck cars 92 and 93 – even so, the overhead wires had to be raised in certain places. The cars rode on Peckham Metropolitan two-axle trucks, and as single-deckers had two 36hp motors. Although there is no specific reference to the motors used in their double-deck form, or indeed as to whether or not they retained their motors, it may be assumed that they did. There were many C class trailers in existence when these trams were converted, and these could have been used if non-motored cars had been envisaged. Nor would non-motored cars have coped with the gradients between Enmore and Central Railway inbound, and from Circular Quay outbound, especially when crowded with passengers enjoying a novelty ride.

Both sets entered service on 25 March 1907, being timetabled to work 13 trips between Enmore and Circular Quay. Naturally enough, most passengers made for the upper decks and there were reports of passengers standing upstairs and even on the end balconies. Matters improved after such practices were forbidden, and the sets were not used on Saturday evenings and Sundays, when there was likely to be heavy pleasure riding. However, delays were still experienced on George Street in peak hours, and from May the sets operated only to and from Central Railway during the evening peak. Upper deck passengers also complained about the pitching motion of the cars. In October it was decided to discontinue the experiment, and the sets last ran in traffic on 17 January 1908. The cars were then reconverted to their original design.

While they were running, an enterprising film maker used one of the double-deckers as a mobile platform from which to make a film of George Street. The result is excellent but unfortunately he did not think to include any shots of the cars themselves.

Although a large fleet of double-deck motorbuses, and even a few trolleybuses, was later operated in Sydney, no other double-deck electric trams were used, although at one point drawings were prepared for the fitting of upper decks to trams of class N. The problem of peak hour traffic was instead solved by the use in multiple of bogie toast rack cars of much higher capacity than the two-axle double-deckers. There is a photograph of a car of class J carrying a good load of passengers on its roof en route to Watson's Bay in 1908 – but this is simply an overloaded single-decker!

VICTOR HARBOR

The world's newest double-deck horse trams operate this line.

Victor Harbor is a pleasant holiday resort situated about 60miles south of Adelaide, and just off shore lies Granite Island, connected to the town by a timber trestle bridge.

From 1894 to 1955 a horse tram line ran over this and along the shore of the island for a total distance of about 1.25 miles. The line was built by the South Australian Railways and used their gauge of 5ft 3in. Double-deck cars were used. When the trestle was resurfaced in 1955-56, tramway operation over it ceased, though it continued on the island in the latter year. Total closure followed in May 1956.

In 1986, as part of the state's sesquincentennial celebrations, the line was rebuilt, using railway-type track, and four new double-deckers were built in a local marine workshop. These resemble the original cars, with knifeboard seating on the upper deck and longitudinal seating inside. They are of welded steel construction, clad with plywood and timber, and must be the heaviest horse cars ever built. They are fitted with roller bearings and, as the line is totally flat, and high speed is not required, they do not pose much of a problem for the hefty Clydesdales which pull them. There are five of these, and one is used per car. The driver also acts as conductor and guide, and for much of the journey the horses get on with the job with minimal supervision – a unique form of automatic operation!

Service began on 14 June 1986 and has continued ever since. Trams run from 10.00 to 16.00 in winter and for longer in summer, and a visit to the line can be highly recommended. Victor Harbor can be reached by an infrequent coach service from Adelaide, though at certain times steam-hauled excursion trains are run.

TASMANIA

HOBART

It is a curious fact of tramway history that this relatively small city, with a population in 1890 of under 30,000, situated in one of the smaller, though important self-governing colonies of what was then the British Empire, should have been one of the first cities in that empire to construct a complete electric tramway system, and also one of the first anywhere to have used double-deck cars with that form of traction. Prior to the arrival of the trams, the inhabitants of Hobart relied on horse buses, some of which were double-deckers, and horse cabs for local transport.

Despite having obtained an Act of Parliament in 1884, the Hobart Tramway Company had been unable to raise sufficient capital to allow it to build the horse or steam tramway authorised in that Act. In 1889 a local businessman and member of the board of HTC, Mr J. Wemyss Syme, announced that he was negotiating with an English syndicate to build a cable tramway and, to raise further capital for his project, he and another director went to London in 1890. Through the good offices of the Agent General for Tasmania, they met both British financiers and representatives of Siemens Brothers, who were then looking for a suitable system to advertise their products in the

Eight of the original Hobart cars at the depot entrance in MacQuarie Street, probably around the opening date. (MTT archives)

southern hemisphere. The upshot was that in 1892 the company was taken over by the Hobart Electric Tramway Company Ltd, registered in London, and this new company then concluded an agreement with Siemens to finance, build and equip, and for six months to operate, a system of electric lines in Hobart. The system duly opened without any ceremony on 21 September 1893. It was a very brave pioneering effort, since at that time only the system in Vevey (qv) had any experience of operating double-deck electric trams, and then only on one line and with a different form of current collection. The gauge was 3ft 6in. and the original track was lightly laid, the 40lb running rails being second hand from the main line railways. Mr A. C. Parker came from England as Siemens' representative to oversee the construction of the tramways and stayed to become General Manager in 1893.

To operate the system, a fleet of 20 short canopy double-deckers was imported from Britain, numbered 1-20. According to contemporary reports, the first tram arrived complete, apart from the roof, while the remainder arrived in ckd (completely knocked down) condition, to be assembled locally. This must have been quite a daunting task for local workmen with no previous experience of assembling a double-deck tram from a kit of parts, and some of the later body defects might have been the result of this inexperience.

These were the first conventional electric trams to be built in Britain for export. They were built by the Lancaster Railway Carriage and Wagon Company Ltd, and it is thought that this firm also supplied the trucks, since these do not resemble any trucks made by Siemens. Since no similar cars were in service when the cars were designed, the builders took their inspiration from four cars which they had delivered to the Blackpool conduit tramway in 1885, of which car 4 still exists. The Hobart trams, however, more closely resembled the slightly larger Blackpool trams 5 and 6. The bodies were constructed of teak and ash, with mahogany window frames, and seating was 24/24. It seems that considerable standing loads were carried on special occasions, when the cars sometimes carried over 100 passengers. Length was approximately 30ft, and unladen weight was about 10.5 tons. Single-width entrances on the platforms could be closed off by metal gates. The cars were powered by two Siemens 12.5hp motors, which operated in series only and were controlled by switches and resistances, rather than by the later type of controller. Contrary to later practice, the handle for these was worked by the driver's right hand and the hand brake by his left. Maximum speed was officially 12mph but this was sometimes exceeded. Current was collected by two rectangular bows mounted on the supports for the roof. In early days these bows consisted of iron piping revolving in a steel shaft, the diameter being 5in. Later the piping was abolished and the collector was simply a steel rod of 6.22in. diameter sliding along the overhead. No lubrication was provided, though drivers

Car 4 (1) in Main Road, New Town about 1893. As yet the crew do not have any uniform. (MTT archives)

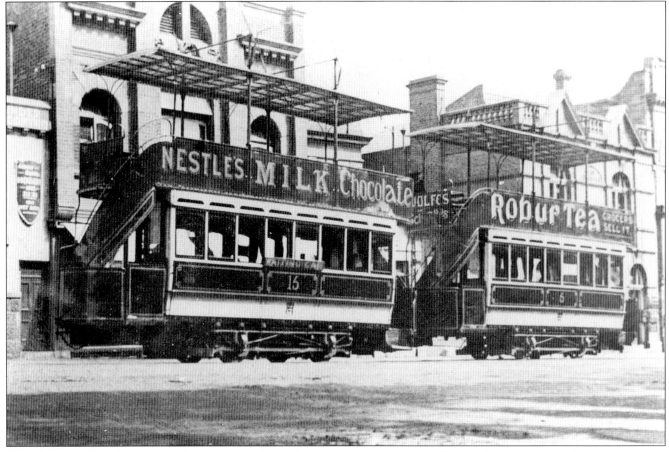

Cars 15 and 6 of the original fleet in the city centre in their later days. The former carries a 'Waiting Car' board below the saloon windows, indicating that it was in reserve and was not, for the time being, in service. (Martin Jenkins collection)

were supposed to grease the bows at every terminus. Short of climbing onto the roof, it is not clear how they would have done this, and perhaps they did not always remember to do so, since it was remarked that these bows were noisy in operation. A square electric headlamp was mounted on the canopy and internal lighting was provided by two lamps in the lower saloon.

Despite being pioneers, these trams worked reasonably well, and the speed with which the entire system was commissioned reflected great credit on all concerned. The only significant problems were caused by the inferior track, which led to frequent derailments, and by the motors, which had a distressing tendency to burn out in the early months of operation. Perhaps it was just as well that the cars were fairly light! However, a contemporary diarist, the wife of one of the conductors, recorded that the cars ran "easily". She also mentioned the use of the trams for pleasure riding "by all classes" and that women, including herself, enjoyed travelling on the upper deck, presumably a novelty for them. (In later years, the upper deck was normally a male preserve.) The habit of pleasure riding continued in Hobart after it had become passé elsewhere, and a later commentator mentioned that, when visitors from the country were being entertained, it was customary to take them for a ride on a double-decker, as late as the 1930s.

The class remained intact until 1905 – although car 18 had been cut down to single-deck form in 1902 – and the last to be withdrawn was car 3 in March 1922. The average

life span for these trams was just over 21 years, by no means a bad record for such original vehicles. Despite their good performance, they did not bring any further business in Australia for Siemens or for their builders.

By 1903 the HET Company had decided that additional rolling stock of an improved design was necessary and in that year built car 22 in their own workshops. In dimensions it was almost identical to the original fleet, but rode on a Peckham truck and had only seven side windows to the lower saloon. It was mentioned that this car had "an improved means of access"; this referred to the wider platform and normal width entrance, compared to the cramped platforms and single-width entrance of the older cars. This new feature would, Mr Parker claimed, "avoid jostling". There was also a round headlight mounted on the canopy and the twin bow collectors were of a different design. This tram did not enter service until October 1904, owing to delivery problems with the truck, and it was probably scrapped in 1922. The General Manager said that this tram cost only £300 to build. Given that a "cheap" tram for a British operator would have cost about £600 at the time, this is an incredibly low figure, and it may be that the tram incorporated parts which were already in stock.

Earlier in 1904 a second prototype appeared. This was a bogie car, still of short canopy design. The body was built by Hurst, Nelson of Motherwell, Scotland, who may earlier have tendered to supply single-deckers to HET. It was to a slightly dated design. The four-window saloon was of typically British design for the period, with glass

Car 17 (1) Elizabeth Street, Hobart, c.1912. (Alan W. Brotchie collection)

Second generation car 8 (II). (H. J. King photo, Queen Victoria Museum)

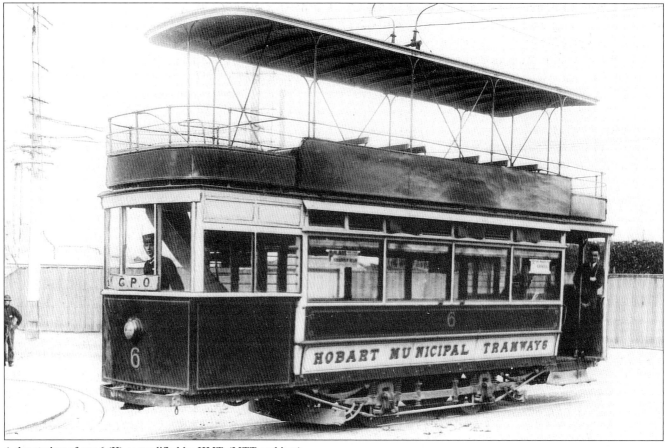

A depot view of car 6 (II) as modified by HMT. (MTT archives)

ventilators above the windows. The upper deck was roofed but open at the sides and ends. The car rode on Brill 22 maximum traction trucks, ordered in October 1903. As the order did not specify 22E trucks, the frames for these may have been cast, rather than forged. Total capacity, at 58 plus standees, was considerably greater than that of the earlier double-deckers and the public appreciated its smooth riding qualities, but the car cost over three times as much as 22 (£1,100), and evidently the additional expense of a bogie design was considered to outweigh the advantages, since no further such double-deckers were purchased. This car was the first in the fleet to carry a green and cream livery. This car was out of service by 1918, as it was found that the body had been badly affected by rot, and was scrapped in 1920, the bogies being used under a new single-decker, 42. However, the layout of the body had clearly been found to be satisfactory and five similar two-axle cars, 27, 12, 8, 2 and 6, were built by HET between 1905 and 1910.

In 1912 two further cars appeared, 10 and 28, and on these full length canopies and platform vestibules were fitted. Reversed stairs replaced the former quarter turn design. These cars were not identical, since 10 is believed to have had a Brill 21E truck of 7ft 6in. wheelbase, while 28 originally had a Conaty truck as used in Birmingham. The five earlier cars had by 1916 been given extended upper decks and enclosed platforms, with flat fronts in the style of 28. With these two trams, new construction by HET ceased and the system passed into Municipal control on 3 July 1913.

One of the first matters to engage the attention of the new owners was that of the overhead, and as early as 1 August 1913 the Council approved the installation of copper running wire as a means of improving the performance of the tramways. This wire arrived on 30 January 1914. At the same time the early bow collectors on the double-deckers were replaced by an adapted version of the standard Siemens bow. This form of current collection had not previously been used on double-deckers, and the frame had to be reduced in height to avoid clearance problems. A shoe manufactured from aluminium alloy and copper was used for the sliding contact (single-deckers had the standard bow). These bows had one or two grooves which were packed with lubricant, and this method of current collection proved to be a great improvement over that originally used. From 1928 Fischer plates were used in the bows, but while these proved successful on double-deckers, they were unsuitable for single-deckers. Hobart was in fact a pioneer of this form of bow collector on double-deckers, as its use had not at that date begun on those British systems such as Glasgow which later standardised on Fischer bows. Although they were then uncommon on double-deckers, the bow collectors worked well in Hobart, and in the decade from 1918, only six accidents to the overhead were attributed to the trams.

As the municipality had retained the services of the General Manager, A.C. Parker, there was no change in vehicle policy, and what was now Hobart Municipal Tramways went on to build 34 more double-deckers to what had become a standard type, though in Hobart the concept of a standard tram was relative, since scarcely any two cars were exactly alike! This was a two-axle design, with a four window lower saloon and an open upper deck given some protection from Hobart's often bitter winters by a roof which did not extend the entire length of the car. Overall length was 30ft 6in., and weight was approximately 11 tons. Seating (wooden) was generally for 58 passengers, being longitudinal in the lower saloon and transverse upstairs, though several trams had seats for 62 passengers. The trams carried as many standees as could squeeze aboard, and it was not uncommon for passengers to stand on the upper deck balconies and saloon. Construction began with car 11 in 1914, and a total of nine cars were built in that year and the next, these being required to cater for extensions which the Council had built. In January 1916 Mr Parker reported that the old cars were "very shaky" and, despite wartime conditions, obtained approval for six more new trams. This programme continued through 1917, when car 41 appeared. There was then a gap until 1921, when five more were built, and this programme continued until 1925. Three of the later cars, 56-58, were actually built by the local firm of J. Hurburgh. While there were variations between batches, the main outward difference was that most of the cars built before 1917 had flat dashes, while later examples had round fronts. Hobart's double-deckers did not have conventional lifeguard trays, but some protection was afforded to anyone who fell in front of a tram by a rudimentary barrier, fitted to the original cars

and repeated on later examples. Including trams built under HET auspices and later modified, there were 40 standard double-deckers.

With the exceptions noted below, most cars rode on Brill 21E trucks, almost all having a 7ft wheelbase, though cars 7, 10 and 29 had rather longer trucks with 8ft wheelbase. Exceptions were Brill Radiax trucks fitted to 29 and 30 around 1925 and the Peckham P21 truck of 8ft wheelbase placed under the former at a later date. Car 7 also had a Peckham P21 truck in 1935. Cars 7, 11, 17 and 19 had trucks made by Clarke, Chapman and Company of Glasgow, believed to have been engaged as sub-contractors to the UEC Company. Due to wartime pressures on shipping space, these trucks did not arrive in Hobart until four years after they had been ordered, and in the meantime the cars concerned ran on trucks from older cars. In 1933 most of the earlier cars had two GE58 30hp motors, but car 18 had GE60 motors of 28hp, while those built later had 35hp motors, either GE249 or DK30B1. Numerous changes were made after that date. As the system operated on 550V, motors were downrated from the normal horsepower. Most cars had GE controllers, but fourteen had EE DB1 controllers. It should be noted that HMT had a long history of remotoring and retrucking its trams and, owing to lack of official records, the complete story may never be known. Cars built from 1917 had air brakes and these were retrofitted to some earlier cars.

Given the short wheelbase used, it is not surprising that the double-deckers are remembered for their pitching

One of the last double-deckers in service, car 44 waits at Sandy Bay terminus in December 1948. (Ken Flood, also Martin Jenkins collection)

Car 10, then one of the newest cars in the fleet, had a moment of glory on Saturday 11 October 1913 when it carried the official party to open an extension of the Sandy Bay line from what is now Nutgrove Avenue to the corner of Beach Road and Sandy Bay Road. (Tasmanian Government archives)

The traffic light and the pillar box on the left give the intersection of Elizabeth and Liverpool Streets a distinctly British appearance in this view taken about 1934. Car 59 on the former is outbound to Lenah Valley. (Ian Cooper collection)

Car 22 (l) and 30, the latter bound for Glenorchy, wait at the GPO terminus c 1934. (J.D. and G.C. Nowell)

motion, especially when used on the hilly Lenah Valley branch.

While the last of the standard double-deckers was under construction, the first car of a new design appeared on the streets, when car 62 entered service on the Cascades line in May 1925, to be followed shortly afterwards by 63 and 64. These cars had rear entrances, single-width front exits and straight stairs located within the body rather than on the platforms. The offside front exits could be closed off by canvas blinds. The roofs extended the full length of the car and the ends, but not the sides of the upper decks, were enclosed. On car 62 the ends of the upper deck were set back by 1ft from the ends of the body, possibly as a safety measure; this car had curved sides as on the standard trams. The following two had straight sides and full-length upper decks. Seating capacity was 62. Peckham P21 trucks of 8ft 6in. wheelbase were fitted, allowing a lower floor level than on previous cars, and there were two DK105 50hp motors and GE K68 controllers. Length was again 30ft 6in. and weight was 11.5 tons. It seems that these cars proved to be rather too fast for Hobart conditions, since resistors were later fitted on their roofs to keep line speeds within suitable limits.

These trams represented the nearest approach in Hobart to a totally enclosed double-decker. As in the UK, the engineers in Hobart were always very cautious about the operation of enclosed double-deckers on narrow gauge track, especially as some routes had steep gradients, while at other places trams were exposed to the full force of gales blowing in from the ocean. As late as December 1921, HMT engineers were still expressing concern on this point,

but in 1924 a university professor recommended that enclosed trams could operate with complete safety, and the new cars were ordered in the same month.

One of the new routes opened under Municipal control was that to Proctors Road, opened by the Mayor on 21 October 1922, using new double-deck car 20. In fact this line, like that to Cascades, was not really viable and perhaps this had been anticipated, since discussions had already begun with the Union, ATEA, about one-man operation, but these were not successfully concluded until 1924. ("One man" is correct in this context since Hobart at no time employed women drivers, and women conductors only from 1942 until 1960.) The first cars built for this type of operation were single-deckers, but from July 1928 eleven double-deckers were rebuilt to allow the driver to collect fares. The first two to be so treated, 51 and 52, had in fact been built as one-man single-deckers for use on Proctors Road, but upper decks for them had been constructed at the same time and placed in store. In 1928 these were fitted to the cars. These top decks were of a slightly different design, since the roof extended for the full length of the upper deck, which was still completely open at the sides, and they had higher side panels around the balconies. Five other cars were standard double-deckers which were rebuilt. A single-width doorway was cut in the front platform, the rear doorway was closed off and the staircase was displaced to the offside and turned around. Above the driving position an opening was cut in the roof to allow the driver to pull over the bow collector at a terminus without leaving the tram. These conversions were carried out in 1930 and 1932. In 1930 and 1931, the three

Car 52 running in its double-deck form in MacQuarie Street on the Cascades line c.1934. (J.D. and G. C. Nowell)

trams with enclosed ends were also converted, but in this case the only alteration was the removal of the rear entrance and the transposition of the stair to the other side of the body. Finally, standard tram 56, which had been damaged in an accident, was converted both to the semi-enclosed design though with shorter glazed sections to the upper deck – and for one-man operation in 1930. All these trams had folding doors fitted to the platform, but, while one-man single-deckers had full safety interlocking, as on US Birney cars, the double-deckers lacked this refinement.

Until Hong Kong converted its fleet in the 1970s, Hobart was probably the only system to work a fleet of double-deck trams in this way. As there were far more one-man double-deckers than were required for the routes to

Car 1, as converted for one man operation is on a short working to Lambert Avenue on the Sandy Bay line. It is seen at the city terminus in MacQuarie Street, with the Town Hall in the right background. (Ken Flood)

Cascades and Proctors Road, they were also used on the main lines and this practice was a source of complaint by the tramwaymen's union until all such cars were withdrawn in 1947. Externally there was nothing to indicate whether a car had a crew of one or two and, while regular passengers no doubt learned to distinguish the two types of double-decker, the position with single-deckers was much more confusing. Normal fares with tear-off paper tickets applied, and photographs suggest considerable delay at central area loading points. It was always

Car 63 in original condition. (P. W. Duckett collection)

the aim of the Municipality to run the transport system as a self-supporting enterprise, and no doubt the one-man double-deckers helped in this respect.

In 1931 it was decided that all new trams should be single-deckers, suitable for operation with one or two crew members. However, the double-deck fleet remained intact until 1938, when car 27, which had by then become 27A, was withdrawn. Many others were officially replaced by new single-deckers but continued to exist on the duplicate list with "A" added to their numbers. During the war the trams coped well with crowds of forces personnel and munition workers, and the double-deckers played a full part in this effort. They seemed to have many more years of life ahead, but in fact, with the ending of the war, their end was imminent.

The condition of the track on the Sandy Bay line had given cause for concern in the 1930s, and approval for reconstruction and doubling of the single-track sections had been given in April 1939. For obvious reasons nothing could be done in the next few years, and by 1946 both track and road surface were in poor condition. On 15 February of that year, car 63 derailed and overturned on that route and was so badly damaged that it had to be scrapped. Car 1 followed suit on 20 November, on the same route but with less serious consequences. There was however a considerable outcry in the media about the operation of "unsafe" double-deckers, and this was reinforced on 30 July 1948 when 49 overturned at almost the same spot as the latter accident. This time there were some injuries to passengers and the conductor, fortunately none of a serious nature. Just two months later work began on conversion of all double-deckers to single-deck form, and this was completed in May of the following year, 31 trams being so treated. As there were then 69 trams in the fleet, this represented a loss of capacity of about 22% and there was overcrowding on all services for some years, until the building of new cars and the closure of some routes alleviated the

problem. It was clearly a panic reaction, as double-deckers had operated with an excellent safety record for 55 years, but in view of public anxiety and the prolonged delivery time for new rails – some had been on order since February 1945 – there was perhaps no other course of action open to HMT.

The conversion was not, however, the end of the story. When the last tram ran in 1960, car 141 was preserved by members of the Tasmanian Transport Museum Society and, over the years, members considered the possibility of preserving a double-decker. It seemed an unlikely proposition, but in 1974 the body of car 46, in its cut-down state, was offered for sale in a newspaper advertisement and this was duly acquired by the TTMS. Over the next nineteen years much painstaking work restored the tram to its original condition. The lower deck, which still had its original seats, was completely renovated, while a new upper deck was constructed, using original seats and staircases from other tram bodies. The roof, side panels and bow collector were new. The tram also has some electrical equipment but as of 2001, it still lacks a truck. In 1993 members were rewarded for all their hard work by seeing a double-deck tram once again traversing Elizabeth Street, albeit on a low-loader, when 46, beautifully repainted and polished, was paraded before an admiring public. Apart from 46, four other double-deck bodies are still extant, those of cars 7, 17, 20 and 28. The last of these is beyond repair, but car 7 is in reasonable condition and car 20 is being restored for eventual preservation in Sydney. The idea of preservation has now been widened to incorporate active plans for a heritage line.

No 141 was for a number of years stored in the Hobart railway roundhouse before finally going to the newly established Tasmanian Transport museum. Although on display there for many years it has never been made operational because the tramway side of that museum concentrates only on static exhibits.

Car 62 as rebuilt for driver only operation in service c1934 on the Cascades line. The location is MacQuarie Street at Franklin Square. (J.D. and G.C. Nowell)

Partly obscured by a very decorative lamp standard, car 63 as rebuilt, uplifts passengers in the city centre in 1947. (Roger Greenwood collection)

In the mid-1990s, Hobart City Councillor Alderman Darlene Haigh became interested in the possibility of returning some old Hobart tramcars to operational condition for use in a tourist tramway. Several alternative routes were considered, including one to North Hobart following the old Moonah and Glenorchy line. However the route now favoured is one which will run across the Hobart waterfront area to link Salamanca Place with Hunter Street, a distance of about one mile. This would take the form of a single 3ft 6in. gauge line with a centrally located passing loop extending one city block.

One of the challenges facing the City Council and other supporters of the plan was the acquisition of old tramcar bodies suitable for restoration and of finding equipment to allow these to be made operational again. At this stage the Council has in its possession No 39 (single-decker built in 1917), No 17 (double-decker put into service in 1919), No 7 (double-decker built in 1917), and No 118 (bogie single-decker built in 1941). Of these, the body of No 39 has been completely restored, and the body of No 17 is almost complete. It was to be unveiled at a ceremony in Hobart in December 2001 and will carry the livery of 1915. The Council has also obtained some ex-Lisbon GE59 motors which are to be refurbished for use in newly constructed Brill 21E trucks.

The schedule for completion of major infrastructure is dependent on the availability of finance, and several options are currently being explored. Whilst there is no firm schedule for the tramway to commence, it is generally hoped that it will be operational by 2004 to coincide with Hobart's bi-centennial and should ensure the success of this imaginative scheme. The Hobart tramway system had many features that set it apart from other Australian tramways, and when the heritage line is in operation, the chance to ride once again on the top deck of a Hobart tram is likely to be popular with enthusiasts, residents and visitors to the Island State alike and should ensure its success.

It is thought that the original HET cars were probably varnished rather than painted, since there are references to a dark brown colour scheme. Later they may have been maroon, with yellow dashes. After car 23 arrived, this livery was replaced by a green and cream colour scheme. Owing to difficulties in obtaining paint during the First World War, a car was repainted grey and white in July 1918, and this paint scheme was applied to the entire fleet after the war. In 1933 the livery was changed to larch green and off-white, this latter being replaced by cream in 1934. In early days the trams were liberally plastered with advertisements, but this practice was discontinued when the municipality assumed control. It was revived in a more restrained form later, being then limited to the side panels of the upper decks and the dashes. The company, and later the city, monogram, were placed in the centre of the lower panels with the fleet number. Trams were decorated to celebrate special occasions and one of the original cars was thus treated for the relief of Mafeking in the

Anglo-Boer war, while a standard double-decker commemorated the Coronation of King George VI in 1937. Illuminated trams do not seem to have been used.

The double-deckers served Hobart well for 56 years and, until their last years, had a good safety record. They are still remembered with affection, and it is good to know that, thanks to the efforts of the TTMS members, these memories can (quite literally) be kept green by car 46. In the future they will be strengthened by the even more exciting plan now being developed for Hobart.

Summary of Hobart double-deckers:	
Original trams	**1-20**
Prototype cars for fleet renewal	**22, 23**
Standard cars built by HET	**12, 8, 2, 6, 27, 10*, 28**
Standard cars built by or for HMT	**11, 29, 30*, 17-19, 21*, 36, 15*, 37, 38, 7*, 9, 41*, 1*, 3*, 43-45*, 13*, 46-48*, 49*, 59*, 20*, 22*, 60*, 61*, 57*, 5*, 56*, 58* (* air brakes)**
Cars with enclosed balconies	**62-64**
One-man, ex single-deckers	**51, 52**

Total number of double-deckers operated 67 (one bogie, 66 two-axle)
Standard cars rebuilt for one-man operation 1, 5, 13, 41, 43, 56

Bibliography

The Tramways of Australia. S. Brimson. Dreamweaver Books, Sydney, 1983

The Tramway Museum, St. Kilda. C.A. Andrews et al. Australian Electric Transport Museum (SA) Inc. Adelaide, 1982

Destination Subiaco. Ed J. Richardson. Traction Publications, Melbourne, 1957 (W. Australia)

New South Wales Tramcar Handbook, parts 1 & 2. K. McCarthy and N. Chin. Southern Pacific Electric Railway, Sydney, 1976

The South Western Lines of the Sydney Tramway System. D. R. Keenan. Transit Press, Sydney, 1992 Trolley Wire, February 1993 (Ballarat)

100 Years of Melbourne Trams. Metropolitan Transit Authority, Melbourne, nd

Destination G.P.O. Ed J. Richardson. Traction Publications, Canberra, 1971 (Hobart)

Hobart Tramways. Ian G. Cooper. Transit Australia Publishing, Sydney, 1993

Hurst Nelson Tramcars. J.H. Price. Nemo Productions, 1977

Videos

Trams, Tracks and Trolleys – The Story of Tasmania's Electric Tramway Systems. Winning Post Productions, 1993

The Wonderful Tramways of Mr Parker and Mr Jinks. Roger Greenwood. Efftech Pty Ltd, 2000

NEW ZEALAND

Despite the very strong links between this country and Britain, the double-decker, whether bus or tram, has seen only very limited use in New Zealand.

AUCKLAND

Horse trams first appeared in Auckland in 1884 but only single-deckers were used. In 1899 the undertaking, which had been in financial difficulties, was acquired by the British Electric Traction Company, who registered in London the Auckland Electric Tramways Company Ltd and began electrification of the system. The lines were built to standard gauge and the first electric tram ran in 1902. Control passed to the City Council in 1919.

Among the cars ordered for the start of electric service were six double-deckers, which were numbered 17-20 and 38/9. These trams, which formed class C, were open top vehicles built by Brush and ran on that firm's type D equal wheel bogies each of 4ft wheelbase and having wheels 30in. in diameter. There were two Brush 1200 40hp motors and Brush H4 controllers. The cars were fitted with Spencer pattern track brakes and, in view of what was to

happen, it is interesting to read that there were two slipper brakes to each bogie and that a pressure of 4,000lb could be applied to each if necessary. They had full-length canopies, reversed stairs and the flush, match-boarded sides allowed the considerable overall width of 7ft 2in. Seating capacity was 46/34 but no standing passengers were allowed. Two conductors were carried, one for each deck. Livery at first was red and cream, but it was found that this did not wear well, possibly because of the amount of dust on the streets, and it was changed at an early date to orange with blue lining. Before 1911 this was again changed to green and cream.

On Christmas Eve 1903, car 39 was involved in a very destructive accident when it ran backwards out of control on the Kingsland route and collided with the following single-decker, three people being killed and over fifty injured. At the inquest, the jury found that the accident was due to the failure of the ratchet (hand) brake and the motorman's panic which had prevented him using the "other" (slipper) brake. The particularly sad timing of this accident may have been responsible for the disfavour with which double-deck vehicles were later held in New Zealand, but there was nothing to suggest that the accident was in any way due to this form of construction.

Weight was 13.5 tons and perhaps the class was found to be underpowered, since all cars were given four motors between 1909 and 1911. When this change was made, car

Double-decker 19 carries a capacity load on the Ponsonby service, while a Brush-built single-decker bound for Kingsland follows behind. (Graham Stewart collection)

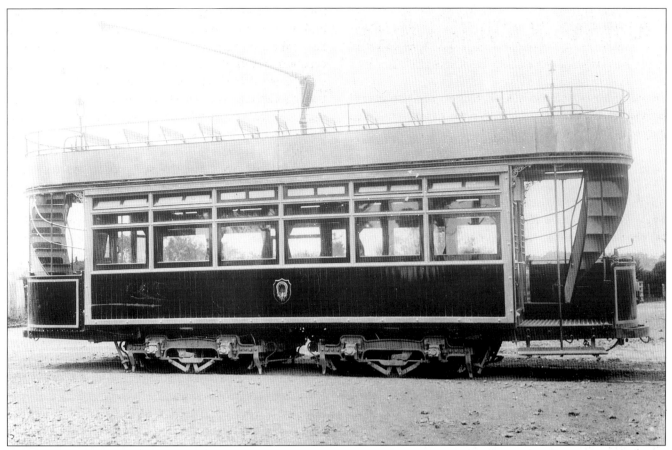

A builder's view of one of the double-deckers. (Graham Stewart collection)

17 briefly had B-TH B6 controllers, but in 1911 it received GE K6 controllers, which were also fitted to the rest of the class. Air brakes and drivers' windscreens were fitted at the same time and the canopies were rebuilt. From the same year, ten standing passengers were allowed in the saloon. In November 1918 car 17 was decorated to celebrate the end of the First World War. Each side was covered by a representation of the Dominion flag, illuminated at night, and the destination blind read "PEACE".

The cars were not otherwise altered until they were cut down to single-deck form in 1923. They were finally withdrawn in 1948, except for 38 which had served as a rail grinder and lasted almost as long as the trams themselves, being withdrawn in 1955. The body of car 17 has been saved for restoration at the Museum of Transport and Technology, Auckland.

The total number of trams operated in Auckland was 269 and it can be seen that the double-deckers formed a very small percentage of the fleet.

CHRISTCHURCH

This city had the longest tradition of operating double-deckers in New Zealand. Part of that tradition was the operation of trailers behind successively steam, horse and electric cars, a practice which continued until the 1950s. No other city had comparable experience of running double-deck trailers behind single-deck electric trams. The city used standard gauge.

The history of the pre-electric era is fairly complex. On 9 March 1880 the Canterbury Tramway Company began a service between Cathedral Square and the railway station, using steam tram engines and open-top double-deck trailers. Further routes were soon opened, and it was not uncommon to see the engines pulling up to six fully loaded trailers. There were originally nine of these, 1-9, built by Stephenson of New York. They were followed by seven similar cars, 10-16, built by the local firm of W. Moor and Sons in 1880/81, car 10 being the first tram to be built in the country for street tramway service. Three single-deckers appeared in 1882 and in the following year another local firm built the last double-decker to be bought by the CTC, car 21. Horse traction was used on the city lines from 1882, with the same cars.

In March 1886 the City Council opened a line which was almost immediately leased, first to a Mr O'Malley then to the CTC, and from 7 December 1888 to the New Brighton Tramway Company. To work it, two double-deckers were built by another local firm, Booth and Mac Donald, and were numbered 1 and 2.

A third operator, the New Brighton Tramway Company, began service on 15 February 1887. The first two cars were single-deckers, but from 1887 to 1894 eight double-deckers were bought, cars 3, 4, 6 and 8 being built by W. Moor, while 5, 7, 9 and 10 were built by Boon and Stevens, later Boon and Company, yet another local firm. The trams were similar to those of the CTC, but introduced to Christchurch the practice of having alternate windows in the lower saloon having wooden panels, instead of full glazing. The NB Company sometimes worked its horse cars in multiple, with four horses pulling two trams.

Yet another operator appeared on the Christchurch scene on 1 September 1893, when the City and Suburban Tramway Company ran its first car. It ultimately had ten double-deckers of conventional design, of which two were built by Moor. However, it also introduced a completely new and in fact unique design of open double-decker. The trams built to this design had open lower decks, with knifeboard seating, a straight staircase arranged across the car and knifeboard seating on the upper deck, and were known locally as "cage" trailers. There were four such cars, probably built by local firms. No accurate record of the fleet numbering has survived. The CST also practised multiple unit operation.

In 1893 the Canterbury Company went into liquidation and its assets were taken over by The Christchurch Tramway Company Ltd. It added to its fleet another twelve "cage" trailers, some built in its own workshops, some by Boon and Stevens. These were probably numbered 22-24, 33-35, 38, 39, 41, 42, 44 and 45. There were also four new conventional double-deckers, probably numbered 31, 32, 36 and 37. In addition, the CTC's single-deckers 17-19 were rebuilt as double-deckers.

All Christchurch steam-horse cars had knifeboard seating on the upper deck and, apart from the "cage" cars, all had quarter-turn stairs and seven or eight side windows in the lower saloon, though, as stated, on some cars these were not all glazed.

In 1905 and 1906 all these companies were merged into the Christchurch Tramways Board and all trailer cars were taken over. There was in fact an awkward exchange between the Board and the Council, when it emerged that the latter had not been informed that its two trams had been taken over. The Board first assured the Council that one car had been scrapped, when it proved impossible to sell it for £3, and that the second was lying derelict in a yard in New Brighton. Matters became even more difficult when it was discovered that car 2, far from being derelict, had been completely rebuilt. The Council was offered the value of car 1 when it was taken over plus £10 for car 2, and ultimately settled for these amounts.

The CTB had been set up in 1903 and had been proceeding with electrification, the first electric tram running in June 1905. Quite remarkably, 55 of the double-deck trailers taken over from the private companies were rebuilt to work behind electric trams. In the case of 53 cars, this involved the fitting of platform gates, electric wiring, lighting and buzzers and new axles with steel wheels and tyres. These cars were then numbered 52-124 in the CTB fleet. The enclosed saloon cars took the numbers 52-70 and 84-100. All except cars 84-86 were 25ft 6in. long and 7ft wide and seated 46 passengers, though cars 84-86 were slightly shorter and seated only 42. All weighed 3.25 tons. Exact details of the renumbering have not survived but it is thought that 55-70 were ex-Canterbury Company cars and 85-92 and 94 ex-New Brighton Company cars, while 95-100 were definitely ex-City and Suburban Company.

Cars 71-83 were "cage" trailers rebuilt with new quarter-turn stairs and having seats for 48 passengers. Their dimensions were 25ft by 6ft 6in. Trailers 101-104 did not appear until 1907 and were also "cage" cars which retained their straight stairs for electric operation. The first two had curved dashes, the second flat fronts. These were definitely ex-C&SC cars. Dimensions and capacity were as for the previous batch. Cars 71,75 and 77-79 had the lower decks enclosed in 1923, reducing seating capacity to 46, while 103 was cut down to enclosed single-deck form in 1946 to become a staff bicycle trailer.

The CTB staff in 1905 designed a large bogie trailer which was then rebuilt from two of the other cars by Boon and Company. This unusual tram, now numbered 51, had a central doorway for lower deck passengers and end platforms with quarter-turn stairs for upper deck passengers. It rode on two bogies and was 43ft long, with seating for 92 passengers, though it was credited with being able to carry up to 200. Seating was longitudinal in the lower saloon and knifeboard upstairs. It had been envisaged that all former saloon double-deck trailers would be so treated, but in the event 51 remained the only one of its kind. It was variously nicknamed "Jumbo" and "Rotomahana", the latter being the name of a well-loved and very pretty ship of the inter-island steamer express. This tram was finally scrapped in the late 1930s.

The trailers continued in use for pleasure traffic and on race days until the 1950s, though after 1940 they were not used after dark during winter months. Car 100 was trailer to the last electric car to leave New Brighton in October 1952, when its upper deck provided a suitable bandstand for the kilted stalwarts of the Caledonian Pipe Band. The last was withdrawn in 1954, the year of the closure of the system, when car 72 was in the last set to run to Papanui on 11 September.

However, that was not the end of the road for the trailers, since enclosed car 91 and "cage" car 74 have been preserved at the Ferrymead museum near the city, where they see service with the equally long-lived Kitson steam tram engine 7. The bodies of two others, 64 and 84, await restoration at Ferrymead. The former is one of the original Stephenson cars of the Canterbury Company.

The use of such a large number of double-deck trailers over such a long period was unique to Christchurch. No other operator anywhere managed to coax such long service out of ex-horse trams, and their longevity says much for the soundness of their original construction and of the rebuilding for electric operation. That had no doubt been cheaper than ordering new cars which would be used only at certain times of the year and it was also useful that no alteration of gauge was involved. As Christchurch is a fairly flat city, the use of trailers did not present problems which might have been the case elsewhere. As in North America, the use of double-deckers here was closely connected with heavy pleasure traffic to the beach and to race meetings, rather than with urban service.

It should be noted that the above is a summary account of a very complicated history and readers who wish to know more are referred to the books listed in the bibliography.

However, apart from its trailers, the CTB did operate some conventional double-deck electric trams. Three of its original fleet were double-deckers, numbered 24-26, and it was one of these which was driven by the wife of the chairman of the Board to inaugurate electric service in June 1905. These cars were built by Stephenson in the USA and were bogie vehicles with enclosed, eight window saloons and open upper decks. Rattan seats were

A three-car train returning to Cathedral Square from Addington racecourse in December 1949. Electric single-decker 157 has trailer 65, with enclosed saloon, and 'cage' trailer 101 in tow. Given the loads being carried, it is not surprising that the cyclist seems to be overtaking the convoy of trams! (Graham Stewart)

fitted in the saloon, where passengers also enjoyed the luxury of electric heaters. The cars were not originally vestibuled but the platforms were enclosed after the first winter of operation. Front exits were provided, though the platforms seem to have been rather narrower than usual elsewhere, and there were reversed stairs. Providence type lifeguard trays were originally fitted but these were later replaced by those of conventional British design. In 1907 large steel hoops were fitted to the upper decks, to protect passengers in the event of a dewirement.

The double-deckers ran on Peckham 14D5 maximum

traction bogies and had air brakes. There were two GE67 40hp motors and it is thought that GE K10 controllers were fitted. Seating capacity was 46/32. Length was 33ft 6in. and width 7ft 6in. and unladen weight was almost 15 tons. The double-deckers usually operated on service 3 to Summer, a line with heavy pleasure traffic, and on this service pulled one or two double-deck trailers. However, it was found that they were slow to load and unload and there were also problems of visibility for motormen. They were cut down to single-deck form in 1918 and became trailers in 1920/21, being finally withdrawn in 1952. However, the

Double-decker 26 in Cathedral Square when new. (Graham Stewart collection)

body of car 26 has been preserved and is currently undergoing restoration to original condition by the Transport Historical Society. It had been planned originally to order six double-deckers and the numbers 27-29 were left blank for some years, but in the event no more were built and these numbers were taken by new single-deck cars.

Livery of the CTB trams was Paris green and cream until about 1930, after which it was white and green until the mid-1940s. The final colour scheme of the trams was green and stone.

WELLINGTON

This city had begun tramway service with steam trams in 1878 but these were not totally successful and were later replaced by horse cars; a few double-deckers were used latterly. It is thought that most of these were built by Brill. The exact number of double-deckers is unknown, but two were numbered 15 and 17. They were two-horse cars with knifeboard seats on the upper deck. When the city purchased the lines from the Wellington Tramway Company in 1900, councillors celebrated by touring the system in one of these cars. The gauge of the horse tramways was 3ft 6in.

After the laying of new tracks to a gauge of 4ft, electric service began on 30 June 1904. Macartney, McElroy were contractors for the work.

Among the first cars delivered were twelve double-deckers, 1-12, which, with scarcely any alteration, would have looked at home on any British system. These were two-axle open top cars with reversed stairs, built by the British Electric Car Company at Trafford Park and fitted with two GE54 25hp motors and GE B18 controllers. They rode on Brill 21E trucks of 6ft wheelbase. Length was 27ft 6in, width was 7ft and seating capacity was originally 55, though the distribution between the two decks has not been recorded. The system's title – WELLINGTON CORPORATION TRAMWAYS – was emblazoned on the rocker panel in true British municipal style, and the only feature which marked these trams as different to those on home systems was the provision of full-drop opening windows in the lower saloon.

A further three similar cars were built by Dick, Kerr in 1905, numbered 34-36. The only visible difference from the first batch was the fitting of four ventilators above the lower saloon windows. One of the double-deckers was used to convey the Mayor and members of the City Council to view the extension into the heart of the city in 1905, and later to welcome the US fleet to New Zealand. All these cars seem to have received three-piece windscreens at a fairly early date in their careers, probably by 1909, but full vestibules were not fitted. Following the passing of the Tramways Act by the Dominion Parliament in 1913 – New Zealand was one of the few countries to regulate the details of tramcar design by Act of Parliament – the off-centre trolley masts were re-located to the centre line of the upper deck, with the loss of one seat.

Cars 2-12, 34 and 36 were withdrawn in 1931, but car 1 survived until 1940 and was then repaired to take part in the centennial exhibition of that year, being broken up

Car 6 attracts a crowd of very curious spectators as it makes the first trial run in 1904 (Graham Stewart collection)

shortly afterwards. Car 35 was used as an illuminated advertising tram – during the war years it functioned during daylight hours only – and so lasted until 1950. In 1985 car 7 appeared on the 45c stamp of a set commemorating vintage transport.

Shortly after the second batch of double-deckers was delivered, the first single-deck "palace" tram entered service. This design, which was to become typical of Wellington, was an enclosed toastrack, clearly based on Sydney's trams, with sliding doors to the compartments. The design proved to be so successful that it was decided to try it in double-deck form and six trams were ordered from the local

Car 36 of 1905 would have looked at home on any British system. It is bound for what was then called the 'Government Station', Wellington at that date having two railway termini. (Graham Stewart collection)

firm of Rousse and Hurrell, later Rousse and Black. The cars of this unique design entered service in 1906, numbered 47-52. There were five compartments to the lower deck, each closed off by sliding doors, and facing pairs of full-width seats, there being originally no centre aisle. Two GE57 motors, each of 40hp, were fitted, with GE B18 controllers. The trams rode on Brill 22E maximum traction bogies. Overall length was 36ft and width 7ft. Reversed stairs rose from the end platforms, which were separated from the driving position by a partition. This allowed the operation of a system of passenger flow for upper deck passengers, these being asked to board at the rear and alight at the front. Smoking was allowed on the open upper deck, but only to the rear of the trolley mast. Seating capacity was originally 93. Windscreens were fitted from new but, like the two-axle cars, these trams were not fully vestibuled.

These trams were nicknamed "Big Bens", being credited with carrying almost 200 passengers when used on services to rugby matches, although their normal employment seems to have been on workmen's specials. The Tramway Act of 1913 required all trams to be fitted with a centre aisle

and the cars were rebuilt accordingly, having a central entrance and two saloons in the lower deck. The end platforms were still used for the upper deck only. At a later stage consideration was given to enclosing the upper deck and drawings were prepared showing the cars with an enclosed upper saloon and end balconies. Windows were spaced to match those of the lower deck and the slightly domed roof extended over much but not all of the balconies. This modification was not actually carried out.

All cars remained in service until 1954, when 48-52 were scrapped. Car 47 was retained as a maintenance car for use

Palace car 51 in original condition is also bound for the Government Station. (Graham Stewart collection)

Car 48 in rebuilt condition at Riddiford Street in 1949. The conductor swings the trolley as the car reverses after a peak hour trip to Island Bay, the destination of the following single-decker. Car 48 will return to Newtown depot. (Pam Eaton)

in the Hataitai tram tunnel and thus lasted until 1962, almost to the end of tramway operation in Wellington, to be then preserved in the Museum of Transport and Technology in Auckland. Despite the success of this design, no further trams were built to it, either in New Zealand or elsewhere.

Wellington's trams were painted red and cream with, in the early days, very elaborate gold lining on the waist panel.

OTHER OPERATORS

New Zealand's first tramway, and one of the first to operate anywhere, was a single line at Nelson, which began service on 7 May 1862, running two miles between the town and the harbour. A single tram was built by Keary and Company of Sydney, but was unlike those then in use in that city, being of a decidedly boxy appearance. It seated 40 passengers and access to the knifeboard seats on the upper deck was by steps and footholds cut into the bulkhead, rather than by a stair. The car was known as the "city bus" and that title was painted on its rocker panel. A second, rather more roomy car was built in the 1870s. The first car was withdrawn about 1881 and was replaced by car 3. This vehicle was built by the local firm of Gorried and Son and looked rather more like a conventional tram-car. It is depicted on the 24c stamp of the series mentioned above. Service continued until 30 May 1901, when the line was taken over by the local council and closed.

Double-deck cars ran in Dunedin behind both horses and steam engines. The Dunedin City and Suburban Tramway Company began service in July 1879 and the first double-deckers were built by Stephenson and Scandia of Norway. The two cars built by the latter firm had been ordered by the New Zealand Railways for serv-

ice in the Hutt Valley as contemporary horse trams. In December 1880 the depot was destroyed by fire and all records and almost all trams perished in the blaze, only two trailers surviving. Replacement trams were quickly ordered, of which two were double-deckers from Brill. Three similar cars later came from Stephenson.

The system was sold to the municipality in February 1901, the take-over date being fixed for 21 March. However, on 14 February another fire destroyed the depot and 16 of the 32 trams then owned. Electric municipal service used only single-deckers.

A single double-deck horse tram was built in 1887 for Invercargill. Although initial reports praised the smoothness and silence of upper deck travel, the car proved less popular when winds were blowing in from the Antarctic and no more were built.

Total number of double-deck trams operated on electric systems:	
Auckland	6
Wellington	21
Christchurch (motor)	3
Total motor	30
Christchurch (trailer)	54
Grand total	84

This is a very small percentage of the total number of electric trams operated.

Bibliography:
The End of the Penny Section. Graham Stewart. A. H. and A. W. Reed, Wellington and London. Revised and enlarged edition, Grantham House Publishing, Wellington, 1993
When Trams were Trumps in New Zealand. Graham Stewart. Grantham House Publishing, Wellington, 1985
Always a Tram in Sight. Graham Stewart. Grantham House Publishing, Wellington, 1996
Fares Please! Graham Stewart. Grantham House Publishing, Wellington, 1997
Tramway and Railway World, 14.9.05 (Christchurch), 7.11.07 (Wellington), 1903 (Auckland)
Modern Tramway, no.286, October 1961, no.333, September 1965, no.376, April 1969, no.403, July 1971

NORTH AMERICA

CANADA

TORONTO

Only two double-deckers are known to have operated in Canada. On 1 July 1893 the Toronto Railway Company took over operation of the line opened in the previous year by the Toronto and Mimico Railway and Light Company between Sunnyside and Mimico Creek, a line which depended on summer pleasure traffic for much of its revenue. A photograph taken in 1893 shows one of two double-deckers, 10 and 11, used on this line and probably built by the TRC for it. It appears to be a two-axle, open top cross-bench car, with six seating bays downstairs and a knifeboard seat on the upper deck. Seating capacity would have been approximately 35/30, depending on the actual layout. The stairs were arranged for left hand operation, although traffic in Ontario drove on the right. The name of the builder is not known, although there is a strong resemblance to the cars of the Douglas Southern cars in the Isle of Man. The cars, which operated in summer only, were later cut down to single-deck configuration and were scrapped about 1904. Two large cross-bench single-deckers were placed in service on this line in 1896 and it is said that these had been originally conceived as double-deckers, similar to but much larger than 10 and 11.

USA SYSTEMS

The double-deck concept was not unusual in street railway history in North America. The first ever tram or streetcar, built in 1832 for the New York and Haarlem Railroad, had seats on the roof as well as a space for luggage, and in the later part of the 19th century, several street railway companies in New York, Pittsburgh, Boston and a few other cities operated horse-drawn double-deckers. Car builders such as John Stephenson also built many examples of the type for export.

The first recorded order for a double-deck car to run in electric service was received by Brill in February 1888 for delivery in May of that year. This was for an eight-wheel car for the City Electric Railway in Little Rock, Arkansas. No further details have come to light and it may be that the car was not built.

WASHINGTON DC

The first line which is definitely known to have used double-deckers in conjunction with electric traction was the Eckington and Soldiers' Home Railroad, a line in the north-eastern suburbs of Washington city. It was one of the first electric lines to be opened after the pioneer line in Richmond, and began service in the autumn of 1888. It used originally the overhead system throughout but from 1890 it was obliged by the US Congress to use some other form of current collection in the central area and, pending the development of an alternative system, it opened an extension with horse cars.

To run with its new single-deck electric cars, this company bought seven double-deck trailers, numbered 8-14, from J.G. Brill in December 1888. These were placed in service in the following year and operated in times of heavy traffic; apart from the Home in the title, this line also served the Catholic University. These cars were two-axle double-deckers with quarter-turn stairs, short canopies over the platforms and a canvas awning over the upper deck. They were 26ft long by 7ft 10in. wide and weighed just over 3 tons unladen. They were painted in a red livery and appear to have been laid out as for left hand running, probably to allow the platform of the trailer to be adjacent to that of the motor car. The lower saloon seated 28 passengers on transverse seats and was convertible for summer use, when the waist panels could be removed. There was a knifeboard seat on the upper deck but its capacity is not recorded – it would probably have been about 24 passengers. In 1898 the line amalgamated with others to form the City and Suburban Railway of the District of Columbia, and on 3 December of that year suffered a disastrous depot fire. It is thought that all the double-deck trailers perished in that fire and certainly they did not run again after that date.

The design of these trailers set a pattern for most later double-deck electric cars built by Brill.

WEST BAY, MICHIGAN

At almost the same time as these cars were entering service, Brill received an order for two double-deckers for the City Street Railway in this town. It is not certain that these were electric cars and nothing further is known about them.

Trailer car 13 of the Eckington and Soldiers' Home line with single-deck motor car 5, seen c.1891 in North Capital Street, north of Florida Avenue . (Handy Studios, Washington DC National Capital Trolley Museum collection)

PITTSBURGH (1)

Another almost contemporary order came from the Pittsburgh Traction Company, which was building the first of the city's three cable lines. The line's engineer, A.D. Whitton, believed in using bogie enclosed trailer cars which were 28ft long and at least one of these, or possibly two were double-deckers built by Brill. An illustration published in the Street Railway Journal in October 1904 shows a single-ended car with eight side windows and an enclosed front end. The upper deck is open with a knifeboard seat and the car is lettered Schenley and Highland Parks. It may be assumed that it was bought to cope with heavy pleasure traffic to these and the cultural centre in the Oakland area of the city. The actual date of construction of this car is not known. The line closed as a cable operation on 23 August 1896 and the car was presumably scrapped.

PITTSBURGH (2)

The steel city first saw an electric double-decker in 1890 when the Federal Street and Pleasant Valley Passenger Railway Company built what was claimed to be the largest electric streetcar of the time, being 36ft long. This was a bogie double-decker – the first of its kind to run anywhere – which could seat 40 passengers on the open upper deck and 52 in the saloon. As it was fitted with only four 15hp motors, its performance on Pittsburgh's hills when fully loaded could hardly have been very lively. It carried the number 76 and may have been named COLUMBIA. The top deck passengers were accommodated on two longitudinal benches fore and aft of the trolley mast and it is not clear how passengers actually reached these seats, as no stair is visible in photographs. It was claimed that 160 passengers were carried by this car on one occasion. Although it was reported that the car ran successfully in 1890, particularly on long runs and excursions, the upper deck was removed after that year and the whole experiment may have been little more than a gimmick.

OAKLAND

The first real attempt to use double-deck cars in electric service was made in Oakland in 1893. One of the companies operating in that city, the Highland Park and Fruit Vale Railway Company, had in 1891 bought from Brill or (more probably) Pullman, eight double-deck horse cars to the design patented by its president, E.C. Sessions. In this design, upper deck passengers sat on a bench formed by the clerestory of the lower saloon, their feet resting on eaves which projected slightly beyond the sides of the car. Access was by two quarter turn stairs ascending from the middle of the rear dash, to serve each side of the upper deck. The conductor stood on the platform between the stairs and the reduced platform space must have led to delays at stops. When the line was electrified in 1893, these cars were each given a pair of Thomson-Houston 15hp motors and mounted on Taylor trucks. They were 23ft 4in. long and could seat 52 passengers. The cars were single ended and fitted with front windscreens, though the driver's platform was open at the sides. Upper deck passengers also enjoyed the shelter of a windscreen and a roof, though there was no protection at the side. The cars seem to have been successful and continued in service until the company was taken over by Oakland Transit in 1898.

SIOUX CITY

In 1893 five double-deck cable car trailers were placed in service by the Sioux City Cable Railway Company. These cars, of very British appearance, apparently laid out for left hand running, were built by James A. Trimble of New York. They were single truck cars, with quarter-turn stairs and a completely open upper deck. The upper deck had a knifeboard seat for thirty passengers, while twenty could be accommodated in the lower saloon. It is not now clear why this company in a relatively small city chose to use double-deckers, but it had laid out an amusement park at the outer end of its line, and it may be that the double-deckers were bought in the anticipation of heavy traffic to and from this park.

This company had a distinctly chequered history and operation ceased on 15 May 1894 after a spectacular accident in the power house. The fate of the double-deck cars is not recorded.

Pullman-Sessions Demonstrators

Sessions clearly saw that, if his design were to appeal to managers of busy city lines, he would have to produce something rather larger than the little Oakland cars and to do so, he teamed up with C.L. Pullman, brother of George Pullman, in Chicago. In 1891 three double-deck electric cars were built there for demonstration purposes. One was a bogie version of the Oakland cars and the other two were centre entrance bogie cars, known in the USA as "center vestibule cars". For their time, these were impressive vehicles, the first being 33ft 8in. long by 7ft 4in. wide, with an overall height of 14ft 9.5in. There were in fact two entrances on each side, between which an outward-facing double width staircase ascended to a half landing, from which a single width stair served each part of the upper deck. This deck was not therefore continuous in the modern sense but was really four separate quarter decks. An electric seat counter indicated to those on the platform which seats were vacant, though how effective and how child-proof this was has not been recorded. The driving positions were housed in enclosed compartments at each end of the upper deck and the motorman was able to adjust the trolley by a system of pulleys, mirrors and ropes, without having to leave his cab. Two trolleys were fitted and it appears to have been normal practice to use the leading trolley in service, rather than the rear one as in British practice. The upper deck was covered, but in summer was open at the sides, while portable panels and sashes allowed it to be completely enclosed in winter. Seating capacity seems to have been 40/40, each part of the upper deck seating ten. Estimated total capacity was 160, though it is not clear

where all the standees would have been accommodated. Braking was by a "new friction system, exceedingly simple and so delicate that it could be operated by a child". Presumably this meant some kind of improved hand brake. As the unladen weight was over 12 tons, there must have been some strong children around in Chicago at that time! The price was $3,500 or about £730 at the current rate of exchange, considerably more than for a British car.

Comparison with other contemporary double-deck designs, such as that supplied to Hobart in 1893, shows just how advanced the concept was. Sadly, its later fate was not in keeping with its deserts. In the autumn of 1891 it was demonstrated to the West End Street Railway in Boston, and was used on the busy service between downtown Boston and Harvard Square in Cambridge for a period of 40 days. That operator had expressed an intention to order four Pullman-Sessions double-deckers. The public seem to have liked it, though perhaps some of the interest was from its novelty value. It variously carried between 159 and 290 passengers on each trip (though not all at the same time), but management did not like its great height or the twisting spiral stairs. It seems to have run in Boston in open condition, which, if correct, would appear to be rather strange, given the cold weather which can be experienced at that time of the year in the city. It was returned to the builder in December. No explanation is given as to fare collection in urban operation, but it would seem to be almost certain that two conductors would have been employed. The order for four cars was not confirmed and the next double-deck vehicle to operate in Boston was a Safeway bus used for an equally brief period in the summer of 1926. The tram was later sold to the Louisville Terminal Railway Company, a corporation whose ambitions exceeded their capital. Electrification of a network of lines was planned, to a gauge of 5ft, but in the event only three miles had been constructed when foreclosure occurred in 1896. In the intervening period the double-decker was towed in service by a Patton single-deck gas (diesel)-electric car.

The end platform car was after some time sold to the Tiffin, Fostoria and Eastern Electric Railway in Ohio and ran there successfully until at least 1903.

The second centre entrance car was slightly shorter than the car which ran in Boston (30ft 4in.). It failed to attract any buyer and in 1893 it was put on display at the World Columbian Exposition at Chicago. The car had sprung seats and was fitted with both oil and electric lamps. It shared its stand in the Transportation Building with four other Pullman built cars, two of which were double-deckers.

In 1889 William Patton had been granted three US patents for electrical transmission of the output of a gasoline (oil) engine and he had subsequently teamed up with Pullman to put his ideas into practice. The first railcar was completed in 1890 and he then turned his attention to street railways. A three-axle end platform Patton gas motor car, 25ft 8in. in length, with an open upper deck and open platforms and stairs was shown. This rode on a "special" three-

The lines of COLUMBIA can be appreciated in this view of the car at Celeron Park, with a load of passengers in their Sunday best. The motorman stands by his cabin on the right and the other driving position can be clearly seen. (Fenton History Center, Jamestown)

Another view at Celeron, taken about 1900. The car can scarcely be seen for the passengers and the members of the Silver Current Band (from Franklin, Pa.) posing in front of it, but this view typifies the use made of electric cars for pleasure riding in the USA. If the musicians were also travelling as passengers, COLUMBIA was carrying a load in excess of 86 on this day! (Fenton History Center, Jamestown)

axle truck, but the name of the builder has not been recorded. Internally the wooden slat seats were covered with carpet.

There was also a bogie trailer, 34ft 6in. long, open on top but with enclosed ends and central entrance and staircases. This car also had sprung seats and combination oil/electric lamps. This was probably the cable car trailer which was recorded as having been built in 1892 for the City Railway of Chicago.

The Pullman cars were painted royal blue with gold lining and fitted out in mahogany. It is recorded that other Pullman double-deck cars ran during the Exposition on the Calumet Electric Street Railway, which served the model township of Pullman, but details of these have not survived.

One of the first visitors to the Exposition was A.N. Broadhead, President of the Jamestown (NY) Street Railway. Two years previously he had electrified and expanded the horse car system in that city. Mr Broadhead was so taken by the centre-entrance double-deck motor car that he immediately bought it and had it shipped back to Jamestown, along with two small steamboats and a quantity of equipment for his amusement park. A Ferris wheel from the 1895 state exposition in Atlanta, Georgia, was added in 1896. Presumably the builders were so glad to effect a sale that they did not mind the car being removed almost as soon as the Exposition had opened its gates to the public! The car reached its new home on 30 May 1893 and was placed in service exactly a month later, running a charter for a special party to Lakewood. It then entered service as an extra fare car on that line. In 1895 it was transferred to run to the new Celeron Park. Like Lakewood, this park was located at the south end of Chautauqua Lake and attracted much pleasure traffic in summer; the steamboats had been bought for use on the lake in conjunction with the car lines. The car did not carry any number but was named COLUMBIA.

COLUMBIA created quite a sensation in western New York and became very popular. As operated in Jamestown, one part of the lower deck was designated a smoking compartment and the other a ladies' saloon. Both saloons were now upholstered in rich plush. However, most passengers made for the upper deck and often let other cars go by to wait for COLUMBIA. The track on the line was not particularly smooth and upper deck passengers were often treated to something of a gentle "ocean wave" effect as it sped along. For many years, this car was worked by one particular conductor, a man of large girth and size, who nonetheless managed to make his way around quite easily. Probably because of its weight, COLUMBIA did not run onto the jetty at Celeron to connect with the lake steamers as other cars did, and turned on a loop at the edge of the park.

The car had a long life and was popular and much photographed; it could well be claimed that this was North America's most successful double-decker. It was withdrawn from service about the time of the US entry to the First World War, probably in 1917 or 1918 and was then stored in the rear of the depot in Washington Street. It was still there in 1923, but had clearly not run for some time. In 1926 the depot was sold and the car was scrapped.

The fate of the Patton car has not been recorded. Pullman withdrew from the partnership soon afterwards and, without substantial financial backing he was unable to continue with his designs. The cable trailer likewise disappeared into obscurity.

SAN DIEGO

For the inauguration of electric service on 22 September 1892 the San Diego Electric Railway used two Brill two-axle double-deckers, numbered 1 and (presumably) 2. These had a California style seating layout on the lower deck and knifeboard seating on the upper deck. As available space on the platforms was taken up with seats and the staircases, the controllers were mounted on outriggers from the dashes. These would appear to have been Brill's illustrated catalogue number 632, and had seating for 22 passengers on top, 14 on the open-end seats and 12 in the saloon on the lower deck. They were small cars, of dimensions 25ft 9in. long by 6ft 7in. wide and unladen weight was 4 tons 4cwt. Brill advertisements stated that these cars could also be supplied with a covered upper deck, but there is no evidence that any operators took advantage of this design.

Some years later, in October 1893, a bogie version of this design was placed in service by the operators of the line which linked the Hotel del Coronado to a ferry to San Diego. This line had previously had bogie double-deck trailers, built by the Saint Louis Car Company, to work with the steam locomotives which the electric cars replaced. These trailers closely resembled many which were operated on steam lines in Britain and some were cut down to single-deck form to work behind the electric cars. The electric car was numbered 41. It is not known how long any of the San Diego cars lasted in service.

SARATOGA

In 1892 the Union Electric Railway Company of Saratoga ordered four central entrance double-deck cars identical to COLUMBIA for service on the line from Saratoga Springs to Saratoga Lake. Three were still in use at the turn of the century, by which time the owners were the Saratoga Traction Company, but when the city lines were amalgamated with the radial system in the Hudson Valley, the cars were scrapped.

SANDUSKY

A similar car was ordered in February 1893 for the Sandusky, Milan and Norwalk Electric Railway, another rural line. Operation began in Norwalk in the autumn of that year, and in 1895 the line linked up at Sandusky with the Peoples' Electric Railway. This operator also had

Car 41 at the Tent City on Coronado Beach, across the bay from San Diego. The line was extended to this point in 1901 and the photograph dates from this period. (Colin Brown collection)

double-deckers, used on the line from the Soldiers' Home to Oakland Cemetery, but these were rather smaller Brill two axle cars with open canopies and platforms, a canvas roof over the upper deck and quarter turn stairs. These cars had been delivered in 1893 or 1894. It is not known exactly how many cars there were of this design, but one was numbered 16 and they carried the Brill catalogue number 629. They were 26ft long by 7ft 4in. wide and seated 22/22. They would appear to have formed the model for cars which Brill later supplied to systems in Cape Colony. In 1901 the two lines were combined into the Sandusky, Norwalk and Southern Railway, which very soon afterwards became part of the large Lake Shore Electric Railway system. It is not known how long any of the double-deckers lasted in service.

TOLEDO

In February 1892 the Robinson Lines of Toledo ordered four Brill double-deckers for delivery in April of the same year. These were of a different design, being roofed but open on both decks. The single quarter-turn stair curved down to the edge of the platform. The lower deck had seven cross bench seats, which were stated to be reversible, a rather strange facility as the cars themselves were single ended. Upper deck seating was on the knifeboard pattern and total seating capacity was 24/35. It was also said that these cars could seat about sixty passengers "in orderly fashion". They were 35ft long by 7ft wide and weighed only 4 tons unladen. The manufac-

turer claimed that this was less than the weight of an "ordinary 16ft closed car". Height was 15ft 3in. and the cars rode on Brill type 13 trucks. They were used on a circular route in the central area of the city but did not prove satisfactory, and were withdrawn in 1896 when the Robinson Lines were absorbed into the Community Traction Company.

ELMIRA NY

In 1893 this town's West Side RR placed in service three double-deck cars. There is some uncertainty about these two-axle vehicles, since some sources give them as trailers built to be pulled by single-deck electric cars, and it is not clear whether 1893 was their original date of build or date of conversion to motor cars. In any event, the trolley was mounted on a kind of framework over the stair and, as there was no room on the platform for a controller, this was mounted on an outrigger over the dash. They were double ended trams, with open upper decks. The name of the builder has not been recorded.

BRIGANTINE

In the spring of the same year, Brill supplied two very large bogie California-style double-deckers to the Brigantine Transit Company, which had just built a line six miles long running north from Atlantic City, in an attempt to develop this rather bleak stretch of the New Jersey coast. Unusually, this line operated only for the three and a half

144

months of the summer season. The cars, numbered (?) 1 and 2 were single ended and top covered, though the upper deck was open at the sides. Windscreens were fitted on each deck. Total seating capacity must have been around 100 passengers. The cars rode on maximum traction bogies. The line was actually operated under lease from the Philadelphia and Brigantine Railroad and, when the latter was washed out in a winter storm in 1903 and subsequently abandoned, the tram line followed suit in the next year. The double-deckers were presumably scrapped.

MILWAUKEE

In 1893 the American Street Railway Association held its annual conference in Milwaukee and the car selected to convey delegates around the city was a Brill double-decker, numbered 251 and lettered "Milwaukee Street Railway". This was in fact one of three demonstrators which the firm was exhibiting. It was a fairly small car, measuring 25ft by 7ft 6in., with six side windows to the lower saloon, and would seem to have been based closely on the firm's double-deck horse cars. Seating was provided for 44 passengers. It rode on a type 21 truck and had two General Electric 25hp motors. Seating was longitudinal on both decks and the upper deck was protected by a light roof. An advertised feature was the shelter afforded to the otherwise open platforms by the short canopy and quarter turn stair, which rose directly from the entrance step. Transverse seating on both decks was also advertised as an option.

Despite the publicity, no sale was made in Milwaukee and the fate of the car is not known.

ALTOONA

For the opening of Lakemount Park in 1894 by the Altoona and Logan Valley Electric Railway in Pennsylvania, the operator purchased six double-deck trailer cars of similar design to 251 but with three side windows and California-style seating in the lower deck. The platforms were rather longer and the dashes extended well beyond the stairs. Two at least were built by Brill and one of these was numbered 22. They were all destroyed in a depot fire in 1898.

TERRE HAUTE

The only double-decker to be built in 1894 was a two axle motor car (70) for the Terre Haute Street Railway. It was an end platform car with knifeboard seating on the upper deck, which was roofed but open at the sides. It was credited with being able to carry 175 passengers and a surviving photograph shows it festooned with people, but it is not clear if this represented normal service conditions. The car was built by Pullman. Its career as a double-decker was brief and it was soon cut down to single-deck form.

NEWBURGH

In 1895 the Newburgh and Orange Lake Electric Railway bought from Brill one double-deck trailer similar to those supplied to Altoona, but with four side windows to the saloon and having quarter turn stairs placed against the dashes. The builder's extended canopies covered the platforms and there was a light awning roof over the upper

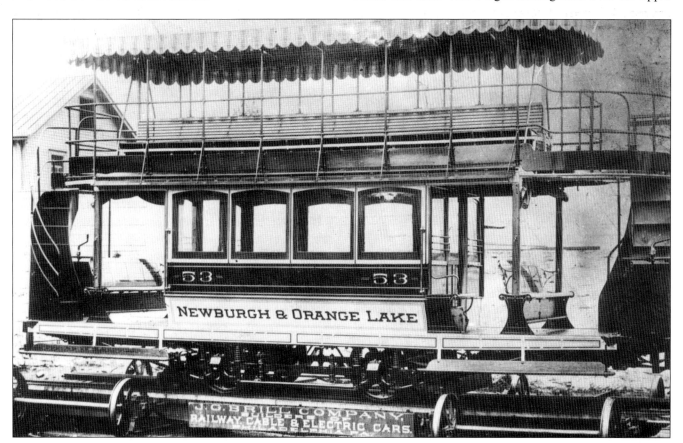

Trailer car 53 of the Newburgh and Orange Lake line. (Alan W. Brotchie collection)

145

deck seating area. Seating capacity would have been about 34/24. It was numbered 53. This line ran between Newburgh on the Hudson River, where connection was made with the steamers of the Hudson River Day Line, and Walden in the Wakill valley, serving en route the resort of Orange Lake. To allow it to be used on other lines which had low bridges, the car was cut down to single-deck in 1899.

BRILL BOGIE CAR

The Brill catalogue also offered a double-deck bogie motor car, type 631. It was a large car, 35ft long by 7ft 6in. wide and the lower saloon had ten side windows. Height over the canopy was 15ft. There were short canopies over the platforms and the upper deck had a light canopy roof, but was completely open at the sides and ends. It could seat up to 72 passengers and unladen weight in running order was 5tons 9cwt. The car rode on Eureka maximum traction bogies. This would seem to have been the design of two cars which were ordered in July 1891 for the Grant Park Electric Railway of Chicago. No further details of this operation have come to light.

HARTFORD

An order for one double-deck car, to be numbered 6, may have been placed with Brill in March 1896, but there are no further details and no record of the car in service.

CHICAGO

In 1896 the Chicago General Railway Company ordered a Pullman-Sessions centre entrance car, 50, for use on its main line in the southern part of the city. Probably because of the disruption caused by the Pullman strike of 1894, the order was sub-contracted to a local builder, Wells and French. While closely resembling earlier cars of this type, this car was of even more advanced design, since it made use of all-metal construction, the framing and panelling being of steel plate. Despite this, it was about 30% lighter than the wooden cars, although the exact weight is given vaguely by one source as "around ten or eleven tons", while another quotes the incredibly low figure of "about 8.92 tons". Whichever figure is correct, this was clearly a light car for its size and capacity. The lower saloons were completely enclosed, while the upper deck was convertible, being open sided in summer and fully enclosed in winter. Seating capacity was 36 inside and 44 upstairs and estimated total capacity was 200. In recognition of the local climate, doors were fitted at the entrance to the saloons, to lessen draughts in winter. Two equal wheel bogies were fitted and there was a Westinghouse 40hp motor on each axle, this provision being over-generous for the level lines of Chicago. There was a driving cab at each end of the upper deck.

Sadly, this fine car had a short career. It had been in service for only one year when the city built an underpass with insufficient headroom for a double-decker on its route. It then spent a year on a branch line taking sightseers to view the works on the Lake Michigan Drainage Canal (the direction of flow of the Chicago River was being reversed in the interests of public health). It was then placed in store and finally scrapped on the unification of all the city lines in 1908. No other double-decker ran in the city and it can be said that this car did not have a chance to prove itself. However, double-deck buses were later operated by the Chicago Coach Company and a fleet of similar buses, from cities as diverse as London and Vienna, is still used on sightseeing work.

SYRACUSE

In 1898 another manufacturer entered the double-deck market when Jackson and Sharp of Wilmington, Delaware, built four very large cars for the Syracuse, Lakeside and Baldwinsville Railway. These cars had 15 cross-bench seats on the lower deck and knifeboard seats on top; the lower deck probably seated 60 and it was said that "on a pinch" 100 could be seated upstairs. The upper deck was reached by stairs which were basically straight, with only a slight turn at the bottom, and this feature necessitated the fitting of very extended platforms. This may have caused top-heaviness and there are records of some accidents, though none was of a serious nature. Nevertheless, the double-deckers were stated by the manager of the line to be "eminently satisfactory" and a second batch of identical cars was purchased. It is not known how many were included in this second delivery. The lake mentioned in the company's title was Onodonga Lake and the large cars were nicknamed "whales" by tourists. In general the "whales" seem to have functioned well enough while the line was a fairly short one doing most of its business during the summer months, but extension to Oswego, making it into a true, year-round radial of 40 miles, sealed their fate and they were cut down to single-deck around 1908. In this form they survived until about 1930.

TAMPA

A two-axle double-deck car with enclosed lower saloon, end platforms and stairs and an upper deck roofed but open at the sides ran in Tampa in the 1890s. It was a Pullman-Sessions car and was operated by the Tampa Suburban Rail Road, carrying the number 2. The line had only three cars in total. It is said that, when Pullman secured this order, Brill immediately counter-attacked and obtained an order for a second double-decker, but there is no record of any order for such a car from Brill.

However, this was not the only double-decker to run in the city. The central area was served by the Tampa Street Railway, which was owned by a businessman named Chapin. His wife, Emilia, was one of the leading lights of Tampa society in the '90s and for her use a double-deck private car was bought. The upper deck was used partly as a bandstand and partly as an observation platform. The car had its own motorman, Frank Folson, and when not engaged in carrying Mrs Chapin on her social round, he would take the car into town to collect shopping or pick up visitors at the railroad station. When the Chapins left the district about the turn of the century, this unusual car was scrapped. It appears to have been the only double-deck private car to be used outwith the British Isles.

HORNELL, NY

It is thought that a double-decker may have run in this town, but no details now survive.

MINNEAPOLIS

In 1898 the Twin Cities Rapid Transit Company began construction of cars of its own design, mounted on trucks supplied by outside manufacturers. These large cars were specially designed to withstand the rigours of the local climate and proved successful in service. In 1904 it was decided to construct one of these cars as a double-decker, to handle the crowds on lines which ran to beauty spots on the local lakes, on which the company also operated steamers, and on three "sightseer" services which operated during the summer months.

Accordingly in 1904 car 1092 of class E-4 was either built as a double-decker or built in such a way that conversion to this form would be an easy matter. Accounting records indicate that the upper deck was actually added in July 1905. The car was mounted on a composite wood and steel underframe and weighed 23tons 4cwt as against 18tons 9cwt for a conventional E-4. It was 45ft long. As the

overall height was 4ft 8in. above that of a standard car, the overhead line had to be raised in some places to allow the car to operate. This then caused problems of dewirements with standard cars. Some nervous passengers were also concerned about their proximity to the overhead line when riding on the upper deck.

As first built (or converted) the car was an open topper with twelve four-seat cross benches on the upper deck. Access to these was by gangways built on the arch roof at the side of the car, with a straight stair of eight steps ascending from the front platform through the front bulkhead. The seats were raised about 15in above the gangways, rather in the fashion of a British lowbridge double-deck bus. Handrails and side screens were fixed to upright posts of gas pipe, 1in. in diameter, which were bolted into special fittings built into the roof at the sides. Very soon a canvas roof was fitted, with waterproof curtains which could be pulled down at the sides in the event of rain. The trolley was then moved from its place on the roof over the rear platform to a base on the new roof. Like all cars in the Twin Cities, this car was single ended. It could seat 99 passengers and standing capacity was given as 65. The car apparently operated with success on charters in 1905, but there is no evidence that it ever ran in regular service, nor did the planned removal of the upper deck in winter take place.

Undeterred by the inconclusive nature of this experiment, the company in May 1906 built a second double-decker, 1145, as part of the order for class G-6. This car had a steel underframe and was a real giant. It had a permanently enclosed upper deck, with a flat roof and windscreens front and rear; there were no windows in the sides of the upper deck, but these spaces could be enclosed by blinds which rolled down in channels in the window

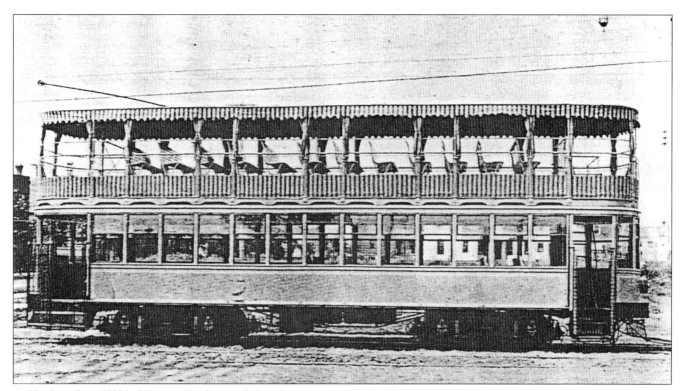

A side view of car 1092 in Minneapolis after the fitting of a top cover. (William J. Olson collection, courtesy of Aaron Isaacs)

pillars. It seems that these were not totally effective, since passengers tended to seek the shelter of the lower deck if a shower came on. As the lower deck could be entered only from the rear platform, this could not be done until the car stopped and the mass transfer of passengers from the upper deck then led to delays. The upper deck extended aft only as far as the rear bulkhead and the trolley was mounted on the roof over the rear platform, which was fitted with large gates of the standard type. There were thirteen cross-bench seats for five passengers each, these being reached by a sunken gangway on the left side of the car. Assuming that the lower deck could again seat 51, this would have given a total seating capacity of 116, making car 1145 one of the largest double-deckers ever to operate anywhere. The stair ascended from the front platform and there was space for luggage at the front of the upper deck. Total weight was 27 tons and to cope with this, the car was given four 75hp GE 73 motors.

There were plans to build more double-deckers and the next fifty G-6 cars were given the heavier underframes which would allow them to carry the additional weight. In the event only 1146 had any such work done, but records indicate that this was not completed and the others all emerged as single-deckers. It was found, not surprisingly, that 1145 was hard on the track and again there was a problem with the overhead. It was also too high to fit inside the workshops at 31st Street and presumably maintenance had to be undertaken in the open. This did not endear it to the maintenance staff, and would in any case have been impossible in a Minneapolis winter.

Car 1145 ran for three months in the summers of 1906 and 1907 on the newly opened 18 miles long Minneapolis-Excelsior line, when a two-hourly service of double-deckers was advertised. Since the running time in each direction was 45 minutes, this would suggest that only one such car was in service. The high average speed (24mph) should be noted. It seems that it did not run in 1908 and the upper decks were removed from it and 1092 in 1909, though 1145 at least continued in service until 1940.

PITTSBURGH

Around 1910, traction companies in North America began to study the possibility of using cars with a low, or lower entrance, both to speed up boarding and alighting and also to reduce platform accidents with their associated claims. Among the first operators to put such cars into service was Pittsburgh Railways, which introduced a batch of centre entrance trailers in 1910. These proved to be so successful that thoughts turned to running motor cars of similar design and, there being no suitable motor on the market, the General Superintendent of PR, P.N. Jones, himself designed a 30hp motor which could be used with wheels of 24in. diameter. In 1912 the first car fitted with this motor took to the rails. Attention was then given to the idea of building a double-deck trailer on the same principles.

In August 1912, car 6000 appeared, built from three summer cars – 1503, 1562 and 1689 – two of these being connected by steel drop frames, with a centre well 13ft long between the two bodies. The floor of this well was only 17in. above rail level and thus required only a single entrance step. The floors of the end sections were 30in. above rail level and thus required only one further step into the lower saloon, and the overall height, at 14ft 3in., was not much greater than that of a single-deck car. Seating was longitudinal in one part of the lower saloon and on a conventional knifeboard on the upper deck. In the other half of the lower saloon, transverse seating was tried and total seating capacity was 52/60. With a full complement of seated passengers, total estimated weight was 18 tons 15cwt. In practice, the car could and often did carry almost 100 standees. The light weight was in part due to the lack of any lining to the ceiling of the lower deck or the roof, the floor of the upper deck being laid directly on the cross-members.

The car was single ended and there were two off-centre doorways 7ft apart, each being 3ft wide. Hand-operated doors were at first fitted, since the normal pneumatic equipment would not fit into the available space, but later it was found possible to modify this equipment to allow manually-controlled pneumatic operation. The doors then made a 90 degree sliding turn when opening, similar to the original design on the Docklands Light Railway cars. The conductor stood at the fare box facing the rear door and passengers going to the upper deck filed past him and used the stair on the offside of the car. Those leaving the upper deck used the nearside stair and the forward door was used for exit by all passengers. A small landing was fitted at the foot of the each stair, provided with a guard rail to turn passengers in towards the interior of the car and prevent doorway accidents. The entire design was well arranged and the only drawback was the narrow stair width of 18in., this being due to the narrowness of the car bodies used.

Car 6000 went on trial on 4 August 1912 and entered service just three days later. It proved successful and its design was patented by Jones. As a trailer, it was used first on a service linking the city centre to a ferry wharf serving Brunot's Island, where race meetings were held. Later it was used during the evening peak on various services and at week-ends it also ran to either Forbes Field, when ball games were being held there, or to Highland or Schenely parks.

The car entered service as a convertible and had little side panelling on either deck, but later in the same year it was enclosed and motorised, still as a single ended car. Four Westinghouse 328 motors, of 30hp each, were fitted. No separate driving position was provided, the control rods being simply led up behind the curved seats at the front of the lower saloon.

Impressed by the success of 6000, the PR management then ordered five double-deckers from the St Louis Car Company, these being delivered by rail early in 1913. They were numbered 6001 to 6005. In many respects they were

The rather skeletal outline and the low height of Pittsburgh 6000 are well illustrated in this view of it in service as a trailer behind a handsome single-deck interurban car. (Bradley Clark collection)

One of Pittsburgh's purpose-built double-deckers working on service 73 on 29th. August 1923. It is in the dark red livery used before the Pittsburgh Railways changed to a colour scheme of traction orange, and has paused to allow work to continue on the overhead line from the Autocar tower wagon. A motor cycle combination stands by with a spare ladder. The view was taken in Oakland and the building on the right was then the Hotel Schenley. It is now the William Pitt Student Union of the University of Pittsburgh. To the right the Steel City Automobile Company offers a parking lot – competition for the streetcars has arrived! (Miller Library Collection, Pennsylvania Trolley Museum)

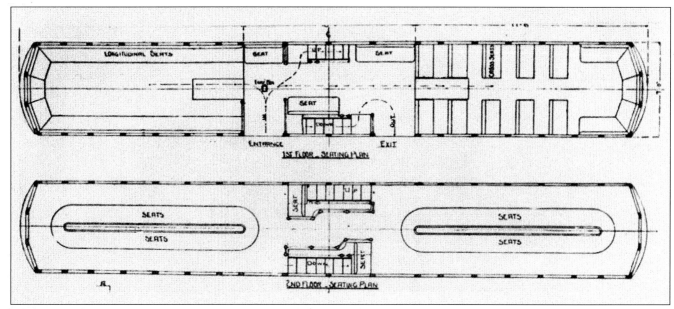

The interior layout of the Pittsburgh 6001. (Pennsylvania Trolley Museum)

similar to 6000 and used identical motors, but they were built of steel, and were initially double ended. Folding seats were fitted in the centre well, to be used on whichever was the offside. Seating capacity was 56/54. There were still no driving cabs, the driver standing at the front end and operating the master controller and brakes by a system of rods which passed up through the partitions separating the seats. Removable handles were provided for these rods. The small master controllers were actually located under the end seats. To achieve the very low overall height, the trolley base was recessed by 4in. into the roof. Despite the low height, headroom in both saloons was 6ft, increasing slightly in the centre well. Unladen weight was 17 tons 3cwt or 352lb per seat.

When the new cars arrived, car 6000 was transferred to work with them out of Bunker Hill (Highland) car house, normally on service 78 South Highland, but occasionally on services 70 and 71. In 1915 the 78 and 73 were combined as 73 Highland and the cars ran regularly on that. These services all had good end-to-end loadings and thus maximum use was made of the high seating capacity, while the dwell time at intermediate stops mattered less. At first they were used in all-day service, but later were relegated to peak hour workings only, sometimes being used on school specials. It is thought that they were seldom operated as double ended cars and may have been converted to single ended configuration at some date. All were withdrawn in 1924 and were broken up in 1925 (6000) and 1927. They had been moderately successful but would have been unable to cope with the faster schedules then being introduced, and it was of course impossible to run them as one-man cars.

NEW YORK

The use of a double-deck tram in New York also arose from the earlier introduction of a design of tram with a low step height. In March 1912 the New York Railways Company, which operated in Manhattan, placed in service the first "stepless" car, designed by the line's general manager, Frank Hedley, and rolling stock engineer, J. Doyle. This was a single-decker with a central entrance only 10in. above rail level. Manhattan in 1912 was expanding in the vertical rather than the horizontal plane – a skyscraper of 55 storeys had just been built – and road space was at a premium, militating against both multiple unit and trailer operation. As the new "stepless" design had proved to be successful, Hedley and Doyle decided to try it on a double-decker; it was hoped that the ease of boarding and alighting would avoid the prolonged dwell times at stops which had bedevilled earlier double-deckers, especially if combined with staircases which were easier to use than the spiral version of the Pullman-Sessions cars. Accordingly car 6000 was ordered from Brill and, after a trial run with dignitaries, it entered service on 14 August 1912, just five months after the prototype single-decker and two days after its namesake, Pittsburgh 6000. Early passengers commented on the total absence of any kind of swaying motion and said that the upper deck was as steady as the lower deck, even on curves. At first it normally worked on the Seventh Avenue line linking 59th Street with South Ferry, but it soon migrated to the Broadway line and spent most of its life there.

As this car was intended for use on conduit lines only, there was no need to fit a trolley and it had the incredibly low overall height of 12ft 10in., allowing it to pass freely under the elevated railway structures of Manhattan. It was probably the lowest top covered double-deck tram ever to operate anywhere. The knifeboard layout of the upper deck, as patented by Sessions, was adopted to give adequate headroom in the lower saloon, despite the low overall height. Length over cab ends was 44ft 10in. and width was 8ft 3in. The car had a steel frame and steel panelling and had an unladen weight of 20 tons 4cwt.

As on the single-deckers, (which carried approximately half the total number of passengers), there was a single central doorway of 3ft 10in. clear width, having power-operated sliding doors interlocked with the controller. The step height, however, had to be increased to 11in. above rail level and the ends of the ramped saloon floors were 7in. higher. The conductor had a fixed, raised position in the vestibule, which was spacious enough to absorb the number of passengers boarding at most stops. The Brill Magazine optimistically stated that the complete success of the single-deckers assured the success of this double-decker, apparently disregarding the difficulty of channelling twice the number of passengers through the same width of doorway in the same time. A "Car Full" sign could be displayed, allowing the car to run past stops when necessary and it was claimed that, with the doors closed and a total absence of any external projections, there was no danger of would-be passengers trying to climb on board.

Internally all the low floor cars were finished to a very high standard, with enamelled stanchions and handrails and shaded electric lamps in glass bowls. Seating had been quoted as 44/44, but official records give 38/41. Standing was allowed on the upper deck, where passengers stood alongside the windows, which were fitted with handrails, and the corresponding figures for standees are either a total of 83 or 42/46. The low centre of gravity and the weight of the frame probably meant that the practice of standing on the upper deck was not as dangerous as may be thought. Seating was covered in sprung rattan and the lower deck had longitudinal seats, except for one pair of transverse seats located towards the end of each saloon. These seats were thus fitted to provide clearance for the pony wheels, but they had the unfortunate effect of reducing gangway width at this point to 18in. at floor level. Unlike the Pittsburgh cars, the stairs, which had a total height of only 5ft 2in, were fitted at the outer ends of the lower saloons, against the bulkheads and rising from between a pair of curved end seats. A short central flight of steps branched into two narrower flights which gave access to each side of the upper deck. Thus every passenger had to pass through one or other of the lower saloons and the constant movement must have been very uncomfortable for those seated there, despite the width of the central aisles. It had been hoped that positioning the stairs at the ends of the saloons would encourage passengers to clear the platforms but, as on the single-deckers, it was found that passengers were reluctant to "pass right down the car" and the congestion remained.

The driver benefited from a cab which was more roomy than on the single-deckers, the length having been increased from 30in. to 4ft. The cabs had five windows and were outside the bulkheads, rather as in the London Felthams, and, like the single-deckers, car 6000 was fitted with safety fenders around the bogies and anti-climbers at the ends, to reduce the risk of telescoping in an accident. In the interests of pedestrian safety, this car was also fitted with two extension fenders, connected to the bogies and the lifeguard trays under the cabs. These fenders were

interlocked with the master controller and the motorman could, by releasing the deadman's handle or taking his finger off the button in it, instantly shut off current, apply the brakes and drop the lifeguard tray. However, as these projected 1ft 2in. beyond the car ends, they proved in service to be vulnerable to glancing contact with other road vehicles and they looked rather odd. The rather fearsome frontal appearance combined with the heavy weight earned for the car the nickname of the "Broadway Battleship".

Mechanically car 6000 was identical to the single-deckers, having Brill maximum traction 62E bogies and a deadman's control system. The car was powered by two Westinghouse 310G3 60hp motors, with the manufacturer's electro-pneumatic control. Air brakes were fitted and an automatic selector varied braking power according to passenger load. It was hoped that this facility would reduce braking time and so allow 6000 to maintain a high average speed. How successful it was has not been recorded.

With New York's summer humidity in mind, the car was designed as a convertible and numerous opening windows were fitted in the lower saloons. Nevertheless, with a capacity load on board, the atmosphere on a hot day must have been unpleasant, especially as smoking was allowed on the upper deck. It would have been even worse when the car was enclosed for winter service but a forced air ventilation system provided some relief. This was the Cooke system, in which an exhaust fan was used to create a vacuum in the interior of the car; fresh air would then enter over the heaters in the lower saloon and would rise as it warmed, to be expelled from the upper deck. It was claimed that this system could provide a minimum of 350 cubic feet of fresh air per passenger per hour. Its operation was regulated by variation in the fan motor field according to passenger load, but there is no record of how successful it was in practice. There was also a "magnaphone" to allow the conductor to announce stops in advance to upper deck passengers by three "announcing horns" in the upper saloon. This device was located on his desk and it was stated that it was "similar to an ordinary telephone transmitter". It was hoped that these announcements would encourage them to start making their way downstairs in plenty of time for their stop and so reduce delays.

However, despite the "magnaphone" and the careful design of the stairs, the single central doorway became a bottleneck in service and the car gained a reputation for delays at stops. Given a maximum passenger load of 176 passengers, this was hardly surprising, since only two passengers could board or alight together, and at busy stops there could be a dwell time of over a minute. The shields were later removed from the bogies, leading to rumours that the motors were prone to overheating. Again, given the loads carried, this would not be surprising. However, car 6000 survived in traffic until either 1922 or 1925 (sources differ), by which time most of the fleet had been converted for one-person operation and, as it was impossible to adapt

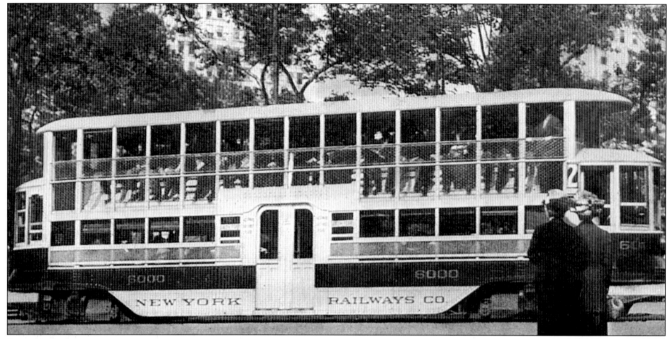

A side view of New York 6000 in its summer guise, also taken about 1913. (Colin Brown collection)

the "stepless" cars for this, most of them went after a very short life.

This design was a praiseworthy attempt to re-think the concept of the double-decker from first principles and it certainly had many good features. Only one doorway could be fitted if the conductor was to be able to supervise boarding and alighting passengers, but this was clearly a weak point in the design. The positioning of the bogies at the far end of the car, necessitated by the low floor design, subjected the middle of the frame to stresses, which were magnified by the increased weight compared to the single-deckers, and in turn this weakness made it necessary to locate the stairs towards the ends, rather than in the central position adopted in earlier and later double-deckers of this layout. Nonetheless the basic concept was sound and reappeared in modified form in cars built in 1923 for Valparaiso (qv) and later in many cars built in Britain in the 1930s and 1940s. As such it can still be seen today on the "Balloon" cars in Blackpool.

COLUMBUS

In the following year, the Columbus Railway, Power and Light Company obtained a very similar car, also from Brill. It was ordered because the weight per passenger in such a car was lower than in either a motor/motor or motor/trailer set and it would thus be cheaper to operate. The actual figures were given as 16.48 cents/mile, 15.23 cents/mile and only 11.12 cents/mile. As the main street of the city, High Street, was traversed by no fewer than ten of the sixteen services operated, it was also expected that the use of a double-deck tram, occupying less road space per passenger, would lessen congestion. Another advantage claimed was the greater facility for those who wished to smoke.

The tram was numbered 1000. It also ran on 62E bogies,

but the diameter of the driving wheels, 33in., was greater than the 29in. of car 6000. It was also slightly longer than that car, at 45ft 6in., and, in light of experience in New York, the doorway opening was increased to 4ft 2in. Both these alterations were made to ease passenger flow within the car and the greater length allowed a more spacious layout at the foot of the staircases. The width of the gangway at the point where the transverse seats were located was also increased by 1.5in. However, the driving cabs had to be shortened by 10in., although the semi-circular ends which were fitted did allow some more internal space. Brill quoted a seating capacity of 85, but the operator claimed only 83. There was room for 88 standees. The height of the body, 12ft 5in., was slightly lower than that of the Manhattan car, but as it was fitted with a trolley, the overall height of car 1000 was 13ft 2in. This was still a very low height for a double-decker. Two General Electric 201a motors, each of 55hp, were fitted, along with K36 controllers (which were interlocked with the doors) and air brakes. Car 1000 cost $6,500 (about £1,280 at contemporary rates of exchange), and it was expected to have a top speed of 25mph, and to be able to maintain a scheduled speed of 8.5mph with seven stops per mile.

The single conductor had a post on the platform by the unused centre door, with a folding seat, change desk, footrest and farebox. The floor of this platform was 11in. above rail level and it could accommodate ten passengers. Electric heaters were provided, and forced draught ventilation was maintained by fans driven by a motor placed under the cab roof at one end. Car 1000 could be modified for summer use, by removal of the side panels of the upper deck, but as the windows in the lower saloon remained in place, it was not a true convertible. Internal finish was in cherry wood, metal parts being painted to match. Stanchions were enamelled in white. There were no straps for standees but handrails were fitted over the longitudinal seats in the lower saloon and along the windows of the upper deck.

In service car 1000 was a failure. Clearance problems prevented it from operating on certain lines and on the High Street line, its great capacity was used only for a few blocks in the city centre, where the delays it caused at stops slowed down other services. After four or five years of irregular use, it was withdrawn in 1917 or 1918 and scrapped.

WASHINGTON DC

In 1913 the Washington Railway and Electric Company placed in service a very handsome double-decker, also numbered 1000. This car was built by the Southern Car Company of High Point, N. Carolina (a Brill subsidiary) and was equipped for both conduit and trolley operation. The reason behind the building of a double-decker was to reduce traffic congestion and it was to be tried on a variety of services; there may also have been an idea of using it on sightseeing duties.

The car was somewhat higher than the cars dealt with above, at 15ft 2in., though this was still lower than many contemporary British cars. The doorway was 4ft 8in. wide, but the doors were manually operated and this feature no doubt increased the conductor's work. Headroom in the lower saloon was a generous 6ft. The bogies were in the conventional position, but the central entrance still allowed

a fairly low step height. The car was very strongly constructed and had a sheathing of steel plates, with lattice steel end columns to support its weight. The driving cabs were enclosed within the body and the car had a pleasantly rounded external appearance.

Unfortunately although this car closely resembled those in Pittsburgh, the awkward position of the stairs of New York 6000 was copied, although in this case there was no structural reason for so doing. Actual seating capacity was 100, arranged 50/50, no figure being given for standees. In each lower saloon, there were three pairs of transverse seats and the longitudinal seats were placed by the stairs, to ease internal passenger flow. Upstairs there were both longitudinal and curved end seats. There were no driving cabs and the motorman simply stood between the curved seats at the end of the saloon.

The car rode on Baldwin equal wheel bogies, with wheels of only 61cm diameter, and had four GE 32hp motors.

Once again the double-decker proved to be unsuccessful in city traffic and car 1000 was cut down to single-deck form after only three years. As car 895, it survived until 1938.

Summary

In the majority of cases, the use of double-deckers in North America was closely associated with pleasure traffic, either

Columbus 1000 poses in front of the state capitol of Ohio. (Colin Brown collection)

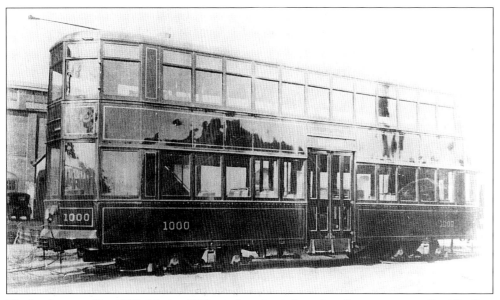

The handsome outline of Washington 1000 seen in a depot view when the car was new. (Leet Brother, Washington DC – National Capital Trolley Museum collection)

However, the experience gained with double-deckers in the early 1890s no doubt helped Brill to win some contracts, such as that for cars for Cape Town, a few years later.

Preserved Cars

No original double-decker has been preserved in the USA. However, from 1955 several double-deckers were imported from Britain or Ireland for preservation. The first to cross the Atlantic was Blackpool Standard 144, which went to the Seashore Museum in Kennebunkport, Maine in that year. It was repainted into its original red and white livery and was for some time used on the shuttle service linking the entrance with the workshops in the museum grounds. However, it has not run for some years.

Subsequently the same museum obtained three other British double-deckers. The first was Liverpool's official last tram, two-axle "Baby Grand" streamliner 293 of 1939. It was followed by ex-London Transport Feltham 2085 (via Leeds), and lastly by Glasgow Coronation 1274. None of these cars has ever run at Seashore.

After the closure of the Hill of Howth line in Ireland in 1959, car 2 was obtained for preservation by the Orange Empire Trolley Museum of Perris, California. After some initial concern over the name of its destination, the car was stored in a shed in Dublin docks until 1960, and then shipped to Los Angeles via Glasgow. It has since been regauged to standard gauge and partially overhauled and runs from time to time in passenger service.

In 1964 the Glenwood Trolley Park in Oregon acquired another Blackpool Standard, 148. It saw little if any service there, but in 1987 was transferred to operate on the Williamette Shore Line, running out of Portland. As the line is not electrified, power is provided by a small diesel generator coupled to the tram. It has run successfully there ever since and has proved most popular, although by 1999 it was beginning to show signs of body wear, probably because it has been operating on railway type track, rather than standard tramway grooved rail.

The same museum also acquired the illuminated "Blackpool Belle" tram, which could carry passengers on its upper deck and should thus be classed as a double-decker. It did not run in Oregon and has since been scrapped.

In 1967 the Trolleyville museum at Olmstead Falls, Ohio, obtained yet another Blackpool Standard, 147. Unfortunately the operators had not taken the height of the car into account and it was unable to operate, being stored in the open for two years. Thereafter it was placed under

to natural beauty spots or to amusement parks, which were themselves often owned by the operating company. Leaving aside the cars built in 1912-13, at least ten of the operators in the USA and the only one to run double-deck cars in Canada, used these solely for pleasure traffic and it was in this field that they had their greatest, albeit limited, success. While this was quite different to practice in other countries which used similar cars, it must be remembered that in the early years such traffic must have posed problems of peak loadings for street railway management, possibly even greater than those of city working, and it was as a solution to those problems that the double-decker was viewed. It also had novelty value and for this reason encouraged pleasure riding in its own right.

In city service, the double-decker proved to be almost totally unsuccessful. Only the little Oakland cars of the early days almost managed to avoid this trend, but even they lasted for only five years. The car built for Chicago in 1896 was of very advanced concept and nothing like it was seen in the UK until an experimental car built for Liverpool in 1914. It seems not to have had a fair trial from either the operator or the civic authorities and, had this not been the case, the later history of vehicle design in North America might have been different.

The cars built for city service in the years before the First World War were again of advanced conception and, especially in their provision of low height entrances, anticipated practice of recent years. But, by the time they entered service, designs such as the Peter Witt cars in Cleveland were appearing and by their advanced layout and ease of fare collection providing advantages which the double-decker could not hope to match. The cars in Pittsburgh came closest to success, but by the 1920s, the tide had turned in favour of one-person operation and their requirement for a crew of two sealed their fate. Elsewhere the attempt to funnel a peak load of well over 100 passengers through a single doorway of, at best, a clear width of 4ft 8in., would seem to have been doomed from the start.

<table>
<tr><td colspan="4">Summary of double-deckers built for electric operation in USA and Canada</td></tr>
</table>

Trailer	Bogie	2-axle	3-axle
Washington	1	7	
Pittsburgh	1+6		
West Bay		2*	
Oakland		8	
Boston/Louisville	1		
Jamestown	1		
Pullman dems.			1 (G)
Pullman township	?		
Grant Park E Ry	2*		
Hartford		1*	
Saratoga	4		
Chicago	1		
Sandusky/Norwalk	1	1*	
Toledo		4	
Tiffin	1		
Elmira	3		
Brigantine	1		
San Diego	1	2	
Terre Haute		1	
Newburgh		1	
Altoona & LV		6	
Syracuse	4+?		
Tampa	2 (1 private)		
Hornell		1*	
Milwaukee	1 (Dem.)		
Twin Cities	2		
Manhattan	1		
Columbus	1		
Toronto		2	
Totals	35*+?	36*	1
Grand total		72*+?	

* Figure cannot be verified
(G) Gas-electric motor car
Double-deck cable car trailers were also operated in Sioux City (5). Chicago (1) and Pittsburgh (1)

Dimensions of some US double-deckers

System	Car no	Length	Width	Height
Pittsburgh	76	36'		
Oakland		24'		
Jamestown		33'8"	7'4"	14'9½"
Chicago	50	35'8"	7'11½"	13'6"
Toledo		35'	7'	
Milwaukee	251	25'	7'6"	
Twin Cities	1092	45'	8'8"	16'4"
Twin Cities	1145		9'2"	16'8"
Pittsburgh	6000	48'	7'7"	14'3"
Pittsburgh	6001	47'2"	7'10"	13'8"
New York	6000	44'10"	8'3"	12'10"
Columbus	1000	45'6"	8'3"	13'2½"
Washington	1000	42'9½"	8'6"	15'2½"

cover, but, apart from a repaint of the upper deck, no work was carried out on it and 147 slumbered quietly in the depot for over thirty years, a home for the local racoons. In 1999 an approach was made to the museum to discuss the possibility of returning the car to Blackpool, to form part of the heritage fleet, and it was agreed that it should be exchanged for open "boat" single-decker 606. Much money was raised from sponsors and in October 2000 147 was shipped from Baltimore to Liverpool, the upper and lower decks being separated, and the former braced, for the voyage. It returned to its native town in torrential rain on 23 October and was re-assembled before being towed into the depot. By September 2001 the workshop staff in Blackpool had almost completed the rebuilding and it was formally handed over to Blackpool Transport at a ceremony on 27 September, many of those who had sponsored it being present. It is hoped that 147 will re-enter service at Easter 2002.

In 1976 the city of Detroit built a 900mm/2ft 11.5in gauge tramway on Washington Boulevard – one of the few streets in the city centre which had not carried a tram line – to link the main hotels with the Cobo Hall convention centre. The length was just under one mile and the project was intended to help with the revitalisation of the city centre which had become somewhat run down. The choice of the unusual gauge was dictated by the availability of trams from Lisbon which were acquired in ready to run condition. The line opened on 20 September 1976 and is worked by the city's transport department. In 1980 the city obtained a five-year lease on ex-Burton and Ashby double-decker 14, whose body had been preserved by a local group. This car was one of a class built by Brush in 1906 and originally ran on a 3ft 6in. gauge truck. The car was shipped to the USA in May 1980 and was then hurriedly made ready to run in time for the Republican Party convention which was held in the city in July of that year, when the line was also extended by about 400yd. The work of restoration was carried out in Topton, Pa., and included mounting the car on an ex-Lisbon truck and the fitting of air brakes. As there was no time to undertake research into detailed matters of painting and lettering, the tram entered service in an approximation of the Burton and Ashby red and cream livery. Shipping and restoration costs were met by Michigan Bell Telephones and the car carried advertisements for their services. When the original lease expired, the local group in England accepted a cash offer for the car from the AmenTech Corporation and it has remained in Detroit ever since. It has proved popular and has seen service even in snowy weather, though only a few hardy souls have been prepared to brave the open upper deck in a Detroit winter! However, it has been little used in recent years.

Bibliography

The Cable Car in America. George W. Hilton. Howell North Books, Berkeley, CA, 1971

Trolley Car Treasury. Frank Rowsome. McGraw-Hill Book Company, New York, NY, 1956

The Time of the Trolley. William D. Middleton. Golden West Books, San Marino, CA, 1987

The Hedley-Doyle Stepless Streetcar. Henry Elsner. N.J. International, Hicksville, NY, 1997

Pittsburgh Double-Deck Cars. M. McGraw and C. Benjamin. Pennsylvania Railway Museum Association Inc, 1962

Double-Deck Electric Tramcar for Chicago, USA. Article in The Engineer, 8.7.96

Double-Deck Electric Railway Cars in the United States of America. William H. Watts II. Modern Tramway 1943 and (slightly condensed) Bulletin 57 of the Central Electric Railfans' Association, November 1944.

100 Years of Capital Traction. LeRoy O. King Jnr. Dallas, 1972

Trolleys of Jamestown and Chautauqua Lake – a New Look. Helen G.Ebersloe, Chautauqua Region Press, Westfield NY, 1998 (Published for Fenton Historical Society, Jamestown).

The Highlights of Blackpool's Trams, Steve Palmer. Tramroad House, Blackpool, 2001.

Periodicals

Street Railway Journal, various issues

Electric Railway Journal, various issues

Modern Tramway, various issues

Journal of the Fylde Transport Society, 2000 and 2001.

MEXICO

GUADALAJARA

This city bought two double-deckers in 1908, the year the system opened. They were built by McGuire Cummings and numbered 50 and 51. They were rather longer than the cars used in the capital, having nine side windows to the saloons, and the upper deck was roofed but open at the ends and sides. It is not known how long they lasted in this form.

MEXICO CITY

The Mexico Electric Tramways Ltd was registered in London on 13 April 1898. This company was also part of the Butters group and shared a London office and other facilities with Cape Electric Tramways and the Chilian Electric Tramways and Light Company Ltd. The aim of the new company was to purchase and electrify the tramways of Mexico's capital and locally it used the name of Ferrocarriles del Distrita Federal. H.A. Butters and Alfred Parrish were members of the board of directors. Charles Parrish, although not directly involved, had mining interests in Mexico in addition to those in Chile. It was intended to put the Chief Engineer from Cape Town, William B. Rommel, in charge of electrification.

If Rommel actually did go to Mexico, he could not have stayed long enough to achieve anything very much, since early in 1898 he was moved on to become engineer in Lisbon. His successor at Cape Town, Albert E. Worswick, had proved to be a disastrous appointment there and had performed so badly, particularly over the matter of current leakage, that after a year it had become imperative to replace him there. He was accordingly moved to the Mexican post in place of Rommel as soon as the new company was formed, with apparently scant regard for the feelings of the Mexicans in the matter. However, he seems to have done rather better in America than he did at the Cape, although the MET dividend had fallen to zero by 1902.

Worswick had had experience of Brill bogie double-deckers at Cape Town and that no doubt explains the purchase in 1900 of six similar cars for Mexico City, numbered 58-63. They were very similar to the cars built for southern Africa, having eight window saloons and a light roof over the upper deck. This however had enclosed ends and doors in the bulkheads to give access to the stairs, although a photograph suggests that car 59 had open ends. The stairs rose directly to the bulkheads and the platforms were completely open. One commentator brightly mentioned that this arrangement "saved complications with the stairs"! The platforms were in fact unusually spacious, with a length of 6ft. Transverse seating was fitted on both decks, with rattan seats in the saloon and wooden seats upstairs, the probable seating capacity being 36/32. Brill 27G maximum traction bogies were fitted and dimensions were 34ft 6in. x 8ft 2.5in. The cars looked as though they had been built for left hand running, although Mexico drove on the right, but had openings on either side of each platform and this no doubt allowed them to adapt to local conditions.

In the event, their life as double-deckers was brief. The system was acquired by a Canadian company in 1905 and the cars were cut down to single-deck configuration.

Total number of double-deckers operated (all bogie):	8

Bibliography:

Latin America by Streetcar. Allen Morrison. Bonde Press, New York, 1996

Tramway and Railway World, 13 March 1902

Tracks and Trackless. P.R. Coates. C. Struik, Cape Town, 1976

E. Garcke, Manual of Electricity Undertakings, various numbers 1898-1902.

CENTRAL & SOUTH AMERICA

ARGENTINA

BUENOS AIRES

The capital of Argentina had at one time a very extensive tramway network, operated initially by several companies, of whom the British Anglo-Argentine tramways Company was the largest. Despite this British connection, the use of double-deckers was very limited. The first horse trams ran in 1870 and some of these were double-deckers built in England by Starbuck. There were also a few twin stair cars as used in Chile and some other companies used double-deck cars, but most of the city's horse trams were single-deckers.

La Capital

This British company was the second in the city to electrify its system, service beginning in December 1897. In January of that year it had ordered two double-deck cars from Brill, one with a 22ft body and one of 17ft, for delivery in April of that year. These were apparently followed in March of the same year by an order for 41 18ft cars. In 1899 a further 12 cars of the same type were ordered, to be followed by a further 15 in 1900. It may be assumed that the 22ft car was mounted on bogies, while all the others were two-axle cars. They were all of that firm's standard design but arranged for left hand running. The latter formed the largest single order for double-deckers to be placed with this manufacturer.

The cars were shipped from the USA in ckd (completely knocked down) condition and assembled in Argentina. The two-axle cars were of short canopy design with a light roof over the upper deck. Seating capacity was 24/24, with transverse seats on both decks and the cars were designed with the climatic conditions of the city in mind, being noted for their light and roomy appearance. As the headroom in the centre of the lower saloon was 7ft 4in., this is not surprising! There were full drop windows in the lower saloon and these could be covered with wooden jalousies, of cherry with maple

BUENOS-AIRES Paseo de Julio

A view of an almost-deserted Paseo de Julio about 1900 with one of the two-axle cars of La Capital in the foreground. (National Tramway Museum)

slats. Another feature which was commented on was that of very high stair rails, designed to minimise on-board accidents.

Dimensions of the two-axle cars were 29ft 6in. x 6ft 8in. and they rode on Brill 21E trucks of 6ft 6in. wheelbase, with wheels of a diameter of 33in. There were two GC1000 motors.

The bogie car was basically similar, but had eight side windows in the lower saloon. The upper deck seated 32 and it is likely that the capacity of the lower saloon was for this number also. It is not known if, or for how long the company actually ran this car.

It appears that, in the early days and despite the high stair rails, the double-deckers of La Capital were somewhat accident-prone. The cover of the weekly satirical magazine Caras y Caretas of 8 April 1899 is illustrated with a drawing of a winged skeleton holding a quite passable representation of one of the two-axle cars, with the following verse underneath:

Quiso la muerte un dia
Que non quedase aqui bicho viviente
Y como outro recurso no tenis
Nods mando este tranvia
Con el que esta matando a tanta gente.

An appropriate translation might be:
When Death resolved one day
Not to leave anyone living here
And as she had no other tool to hand,
She sent us this tramcar
With which she kills so many people.

Buenos Aires and Belgrano

This was the third largest tramway company to serve the city and the first to inaugurate electric operation, in 1897. In 1907 it had 90 cars and in 1908 it was taken over by the Anglo-Argentine. In 1898 it bought some 50 cars from Jackson and Sharp of Wilmington, Delaware, including at least twenty-one double-deckers. These took the even numbers from 20 to 40. They were short canopy cars without the upper deck landing of the Brill cars, and of course were also designed for left-hand running. The upper deck seated 32 passengers and the lower saloon probably accommodated a similar number, in both cases on transverse seats. There was a light roof over the upper deck, which was open at the sides and ends, and some protection from the weather was afforded by canvas blinds which could be rolled down to enclose the upper deck completely. These cars were very similar to those supplied by the same manufacturer to Guadalajara, Mexico (qv). Little is known of their subsequent fate but some may later have been sold to Pelotsa, Brasil (qv).

Corporacion de Transportes de la Ciudad de Buenos Aires

In June 1938 this company was created by Law No 12,311 to acquire, co-ordinate and operate all the passenger transport systems in the city, with the exception of the suburban services of the main line railways. It had both British and local capital and the Anglo-Argentine Company was the main constituent. A subsidiary company, known from its initials as Catita, which had been set up by that operator in 1927 to build rolling stock (rather along the lines of the UCC of the London Underground group), was acquired at the same time. Its manager, Sr R.F. Apeseche, had been rolling stock superintendent of the Anglo-Argentine.

In 1942 Catita built three double-deckers for the Corporation. The first, numbered 371, was formally inaugurated at a ceremony on 13 August by Dr R. Segura, President of the Corporation, in the presence of the Lord Mayor of Buenos Aires. The official party then took a short trip in the car, this arousing great public interest, since the new vehicle was totally different to anything else in the existing fleet. It was then placed in operation on service 1,

The poem telling of the horrors of the electric trams. (Courtesy Alberto Centurion)

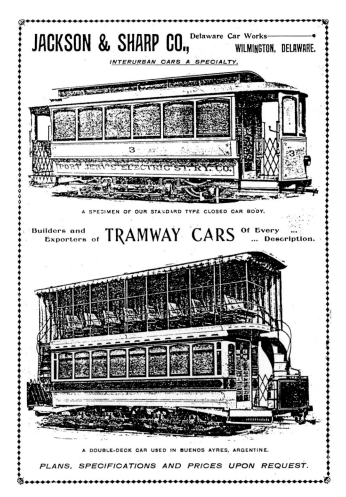

An advertisement for the products of Jackson and Sharp, showing one of the double-deckers built for the Belgrano company.

which acted as a feeder to line A of the Subte at Primera Junta. Two other cars, 372 and 373, followed soon after.

The trams, some of the very few second-generation double-deckers to be placed in service by overseas operators, were of a handsome streamlined design, with front exits, folding doors enclosing the platforms and straight stairs. Both staircases were on the nearside – Argentina still drove on the left at this time – and as only a single trolley was fitted to 371, it would seem that they were single-ended, at least initially, though this cannot be confirmed. However, photographs of 372 and 373 show them with two trolleys, one at each end, and it would seem that they were definitely double-ended cars. Very few single-ended trams operated in the city. There was some resemblance to contemporary British designs, such as the Liverpool streamliners, and there were no bulkheads on either deck. As far as possible, Argentine materials were used throughout, the only imported wood used in the bodywork being oak. In accordance with local preferences, the side windows on both decks were arranged to open upwards.

Dimensions were 36ft 4in. x 8ft 1in. and the height to the trolley base was 15ft 6in. Unladen weight was 19.5 tons. Seating accommodation was for 72 passengers, although the actual layout is not known, and the seats were upholstered in prime Argentine leather. Four GE247 motors of 37hp were fitted, along with Westinghouse air, electric and hand brakes. The cars rode on Brill 27G bogies, which were second-hand from hopper cars originally supplied to the Buenos Aires Puerto (port) system by Dick Kerr.

Car 373 working on line 1 picks up passengers at Primera Junta station of the Subte (Underground) in 1949. The passenger shelter in the photograph still exists and the location is very close to the tracks used today by the Buenos Aires tramway museum line. (David Packer collection)

No series production followed. The cars were later used on a suburban line and were scrapped in 1950.

Total number of double-deck electric trams operated:	
Two-axle	69
Bogie	?25
Total	?94

BRASIL

Although many tramway systems operated in this country, double-deckers ran on only two of these and then only in small numbers. Double-deck trams were known in Brasil as "imperiais".

PORTO ALEGRE

This city had the second tramway in Brasil, opened in 1864, and it may have been the first to use horse-drawn double-deckers. The electric system opened with two double-deckers, 36 and 37, on 10 March 1908. These were open-top cross-bench cars supplied by the United Electric Car Company of Preston, almost identical to the cars supplied to Lourenço Marques (qv). Two further cars followed in 1909, but these had roofed upper decks, apparently without bulkheads. The central part of the upper deck could be sheltered by canvas blinds, as could the lower deck. All these cars were cut down to single-deck form by the operator in 1921.

These were the only double-deck electric trams built in Britain for use in South America.

PELOTAS

Electric operation began on 20 October 1915 and in the following year the operator, the Rio Grandense Light and Power Syndicate Ltd of London, placed five bogie double-deckers in service. These were probably the largest trams to run in Brasil. Their origin is uncertain but the lower saloons resembled those of the double-deckers built by Jackson and Sharp for Buenos Aires in 1899. The Pelotas system was electrified by an Argentinian firm, and it may be that this firm purchased the cars and rebuilt them with roofed upper decks which were open at the sides but had enclosed end balconies, rather like some South African trams.

They were double-ended and, unusually, had front platforms only. Their career as double-deckers in Pelotas was

A builder's photo of two-axle car 36. (UEC, courtesy A.K. Terry)

An interior view of the lower deck on car 36. (UEC, courtesy A.K. Terry)

short, as they were cut down to single-deck form in 1922.

Both these systems used left hand running and both were of standard gauge.

Total number of double-deck electric trams operated: 9

Bibliography:
The Tramways of Brazil. Allen Morrison. Bonde Press, New York, 1989

CHILE

CHILLAN

This city is 250 miles south of Santiago. It had a horse car line from either 1877 or 1884 and this used Stephenson double-deckers, designed for left hand running. The CGEI (Compañia General de Electricidad Industrial) opened an electric line in 1921, quite independently of the horse car system, though it later acquired and electrified one line of the latter. Total route length was about 2 miles.

Details of the rolling stock are scarce, but there were double-deckers, said to have come from the capital. One view shows a Herbrand-type car, fitted with platform vestibules but another view shows a six-window car also with vestibules but quite unlike anything which ran in Santiago. Possibly it was a rebuild. The electric system closed in 1936 and was outlived by the horse cars, whose service was still operating when the city experienced its third severe earthquake in 1939.

CONCEPCION

Chile's third largest city lies 350 miles south of Santiago. It had horse trams from 1886, with double-deck Stephenson cars. In 1906 a franchise for an electric line between the city and Talcahuano, and local lines in both places, was secured by the Compania Electrica de Concepcion. This was an offshoot of the General Electric Company of the USA, whose franchise in Chile was held by the steamship line of W.R. Grace and Co. Their ships served Talcahuano. Services began on 4 July 1908, using single-deckers. Between 1911 and 1913, 20 double-deck two axle cars were bought from Brill. The main reason for the adoption of double-deckers was to obviate the need for trailers except during peak periods.

The 15 cars of the first batch were shipped to Chile in the early months of 1911. These were open-top cars of Brill's standard short canopy design, with five full-drop windows in the saloons. They were strongly built, steel alternating with wood for the rafters of the ceiling of the saloon, to support the trolley tower and to allow the carriage of heavy loads on the upper deck without placing too much of a strain on the body members. Presumably this meant that passengers were allowed to stand on the upper deck. The trolley was mounted on a small tower. Longitudinal seats, made of cherry wood covered with Wilton carpet, were provided in the saloon, which was finished in ash with bronze fittings. A knifeboard seat was fitted on top, to give a total seating capacity of 40. The cars were 28ft long overall by 6ft 7in. wide and height to the trolley tower was 12ft 11in. Two GE 54 motors were fitted and the cars rode on Brill 21E trucks and air brakes were provided. Total weight without electrical equipment was 5.4 tons.

The cars must have been successful since a repeat order for five more was shipped to Chile in the summer of 1913. These were broadly similar to the cars of the first delivery but were slightly shorter, at 26ft, the platforms being only 5ft long, as opposed to the 6ft of the first batch. The canopies were also rather longer and the staircases were displaced to the extreme ends of the car. This ensured a free flow of passengers boarding or alighting on either side of the car. Perhaps there was little other traffic on the streets at that time! These changes allowed a seating capacity of 20/24. The trolley tower was also given additional support in the form of a metal framework fixed to the body sides.

CEC also rebuilt its original twelve single-deck cars to double-deck configuration. The double-deckers were numbered 20-82, using even numbers only. The exact sequence is not known, but it is likely that the first batch of Brill cars were 32-60 and the second 62-70, with rebuilds taking the lower and higher numbers.

The system passed to Chilean control during the First World War. Around 1917 one single-ended open top double-deck car seems to have been rebuilt from a horse car and numbered 23. A photograph shows it with twin trolley poles, as used in Cincinnati, but no explanation for this has been found and other views show only conventional single wire overhead. By 1927 there were apparently 38 double-deckers. A photograph shows a six window car rather like the rebuilt Herbrand cars of Santiago and it is possible that the additional five cars came from there, as no order for new cars has been traced. However, there is also extant a photograph of a double-ended open top car numbered 33 in Talcahuano and it may be that there were also rebuilds of horse cars. It seems that latterly the city's double-deckers received platform vestibules and roofs.

Concepcion was badly damaged by the earthquake of 1939, but the tramway was rebuilt and finally closed in 1941. It is not known how long the double-deckers actually lasted in service.

RANCAGUA

An unusual feature of the tramway history of Chile was the number of small electric systems which opened during the period of the first world war, in which the country was not directly involved. The fourth such system to be opened was in the town of Rancagua, 52 miles south of Santiago. On 8 July 1918 a group of local businessmen, trading as the Compania de Tranvias Eléctricos de Rancagua, began electric service over about 600yd of track connecting the railway station with the town centre. This was extended by about 500yd in 1919. The line was bought by the Chilean Compania General de Electricidad Industrial in 1920 and was closed in 1930. The four trams were second-hand from Santiago and some are reported to have been double-deckers. The livery was red. No surviving pictures of this little line have been found.

SANTIAGO

The capital city of Chile had the first tramway in South America and one of the first in the world. Service began on 10 June 1858, using single-deck horse cars. Double-deckers, of conventional design with knifeboard seating, made their first appearance in 1873. These were built by Stephenson in New York.

In 1896 the city authorities invited tenders for the electrification of the city's tramways and the contract went to Alfred Parrish and Company of London. This firm was then working on the conversion to electric traction of the horse tramways in Cape Town and Port Elizabeth, in what was then Cape Colony. On 3 May 1898 this company registered the Chilian (sic) Electric Light and Power Company in London to adopt an agreement made by AEG of Berlin and the Chilean authorities to construct, purchase or otherwise acquire and work by electric power tramways in Chile and elsewhere in America. It drew most of its capital from Germany and most of the directors seem to have been German. Two, Col. Sir C. Euan Smith KCB, and L. Breitmeyer were also on the board of Cape Electric Tramways. The company shared a registered office (55-56 Bishopsgate Street Within, London EC) and a secretary (L.W. Jameson) with both Cape Electric Tramways and Mexico Electric Tramways Ltd. It also used the same bank as CET and the same auditors as the other two companies. The secretary was the brother of L.S. Jameson who was a figure at that time very much in the public eye, having led a rather farcical and unsuccessful invasion of the South African Republic in December 1895, in one of the less-edifying episodes in British imperial history.

It duly took over the various horse car companies and gave a contract for the electrification of the system to AEG of Berlin. The track was regauged from 5ft 6in. to standard gauge and electric operation began on 2 September 1900.

The initial fleet came from the works of Herbrand of Köln. All the 235 passenger cars had AEG motors, trucks and equipment. Of the total, 115 were two-axle double-deckers numbered 101-215. These were of a short canopy design, the upper deck seating extending only as far as the end of the lower saloon. The lower saloon had five side windows and there were quarter turn stairs. As built, a roof was fitted but the upper deck was open at the sides and

An early view of car 214 working with a trailer on line 6. (Allen Morrison collection)

Car 200 is seen here in as-built condition (Allen Morrison collection)

It is not clear exactly what is happening here, but the young man does not look especially pleased to meet his fashionably-dressed lady friend alighting from car 11 in 1909. The conductor, as Cupid, has a quiver of arrows in his money bag. The car number is, of course, incorrect. (Allen Morrison collection)

ends. However, photographs of the cars in service in early days show them in open top condition and the roofs may have been removable. Later views show a different type of roof. The basic livery was blue with light yellow lining and current collection was by trolley pole. Originally Providence type lifeguards were fitted but these seem to have been replaced by wooden trays at a very early date. Although traffic in Santiago drove on the right, the cars were laid out for left hand traffic and it must be assumed that the small opening under the stairs was used as the main entrance.

One hundred horse cars were rebuilt for use as trailers with the new electric cars but it is not known if this total included any double-deckers. Only single-deck trailers appear in contemporary photographs.

In 1904 ten more double-deckers were ordered from van der Zypen and Charlier (216-225), having trucks by the builder, and in the following year ten more were bought from Brill (226-235). These latter cars, which were the first electric cars built by a US car builder for the Chilean market and were of that builder's standard design, having four side windows, short canopies and quarter turn stairs. They were 31ft long by 7ft 10in. wide and rode on Brill trucks of 6ft wheelbase. They had two 37hp motors. The lower saloon had six pairs of fixed facing seats and there was a knifeboard on the upper deck, seating being (?)24/24. It was stated that the seats on the upper deck were removable. (SRJ 7.4.06). The windows of the lower saloon had double sashes, the lower of which could drop into pockets in the side panels. Interior finish was in cherry

A builder's photograph of Falkenried bogie car 240. (Allen Morrison collection)

At a later date, car 198 has acquired a rebuilt lower saloon and platform vestibules. (Allen Morrison collection)

wood, with the seats being of cherry and ash slats. There were openings on either side of the platforms, those facing the stairs being twice the width of the others. Again this gave the cars the appearance of being designed to operate in left hand traffic. The canopy was extended out to give some protection to the platform and also to carry the headlight. It is said that the van der Zypen cars were identical to these.

There were also some double-deck trailers from the batch 601-650 but it is not clear how many. These were very similar to the cars supplied to Valparaiso but were roofed. Car 621 was a double-decker while 626 was a single-decker and possibly there were 25 of each. They had eight side windows to the lower saloon and full-length canopies, but again the knifeboard seating on the upper deck extended only over the lower saloon. Seating was for 24 passengers in the saloon, arranged entirely in 2+1 transversal form, while the knifeboard probably seated 20. Overall length was 32ft 3in.

Late in 1905 the company became German in law as well as in practice, when it was acquired by the DUEG concern. In 1907-08 20 bogie double-deckers were bought from Falkenried of Hamburg and assigned to the Parque service, which no doubt carried heavy excursion traffic. These were both the only double-deck bogie trams built in Germany and also the largest trams in Chile at that time. They carried the numbers 236-255. These cars had very short platforms with canopies and again the upper deck seating extended

only as far as the bulkheads. Twin trolleys were fitted and the cars had roofs, but the upper decks were open at the sides. There were transverse 2+1 seats in the lower saloon and it is estimated that they could carry about 87 seated passengers. The cars had Böcker maximum traction bogies.

As part of the same order, there were also 15 two-axle double-deck cars, numbered 256-270. These had four-window saloons and by 1915 had platform vestibules, with entrances front and rear. Seating was 20/28, with 2+2 transverse seats in the saloon and again a knifeboard on the upper deck.

Finally 31 two-axle double-deckers arrived from Falkenried in 1914. These were numbered 340-370. They had four large side windows in the lower saloon and vestibuled platforms to the firm's standard design, the upper deck extending over most of the platform. If Hamburg had ever had electric double-deckers, they would have looked like these trams!

The remainder of the company's history is as for Valparaiso, but no more double-deckers were bought. The original Herbrand cars were modified by 1920. Some appear to have been lengthened and some gained vestibuled platforms. New windows, with flat tops, replaced the original arched pattern. However, soon after the sale to CCE in 1921, all the double-deckers were cut down to single-deck form and as such many survived until the 1950s. Final closure came on 21 February 1959.

CET&L was not the only operator in Santiago, as there were several suburban tramways owned by other companies and one of these, the Ferrocarril Eléctrico de Santiago a San Bernardo, which began operation in 1907, later in that year bought five double-deckers from the Saint Louis Car Company. This was presumably St Louis order 716A of 28 June 1907, which recorded five single-truck double-deckers for Sr Horatio Valdes, these being the only such cars built by this firm for export. These were operated over the urban part of the line to Cisterna, the present southern terminus of the city's metro. Unfortunately no illustrations have survived. This line was bought by CCE in 1937 and all its cars were rebuilt; presumably in the case of the double-deckers, this involved being cut down to single-deck form.

It should be noted that single-deckers always formed a much higher proportion of the total fleet than they did in Valparaiso.

The total number of double-deckers operated in Santiago was:	
Urban system	
Two-axle cars	181
Bogie cars	20
Trailers	25*
FESSB	
Two-axle cars	5
Total	
Motor cars	206
Trailers	25*
* Subject to correction	

TEMUCO

This was the most southerly electric tramway on the American continent. Horse cars began operation in 1881 and there was at least one double-decker. The Tranvias Eléctricos de Temuco inaugurated electric service in March 1919, using single-deckers acquired from Buenos Aires. A postcard view also shows a double-decker, which was probably added after the system was taken over by the CGEI in 1920. The line closed in 1936.

TRAIGUEN

This town lies 405 miles south of Santiago.

In 1903 a grain milling company, the Compania Molinera el Globo, built an electric line of 2ft gauge to connect its mill to the railway station via the town's streets. A small locomotive, built in 1900 by AEG for another firm which in the event did not use it, was used to pull goods trains. It has been reported that there was also a double-deck passenger trailer. Unfortunately no illustrations of this have come to light, but in view of the gauge it must have been an unusual vehicle. The line closed around 1930 but the locomotive has been preserved, as the first electric locomotive to run in Chile.

VALPARAISO

The Chilean port was a pioneer in tramway development and its first line was inaugurated on 4 March 1863 by the Ferrocaril Urban de Valparaiso. It used initially 25 double-deckers supplied by Stephenson of New York, to an unusual design. The cars were single-ended and had twin staircases at the rear, arranged in the manner of those on the Blackpool Dreadnought cars with a cross platform. This may have been the first use of double-deckers in South America. It is not known why this design was chosen, but the proprietor was David Thomas, a local banker, who came originally from Britain. Five similar cars were ordered in 1868 and a further 15 two years later. By 1880 the fleet numbered 63. Another operator, the Ferrocaril de Playa Ancha, began service in 1897 using more conventional double-deckers, and a third company, the Empresa de Tranvias Cardonal, opened a line towards Vina del Mar in 1899, again with conventional double-deckers with knifeboard seating on the open upper deck. All these lines were built to a gauge of 5ft 6in. (1676mm).

The German AEG company gained a concession for the operation of electric tramways in 1902 and acquired the three horse car companies. In 1903 the Elektrische Strassenbahnen Valparaiso (known locally as the Empresa de Tranvias Eléctricos de Valparaiso) was registered to build and operate the system. In 1906 this passed to the control of the Deutsch-Uberseeische-Elektrizitäts-Gesellschaft of Berlin, who substituted Compaña for Empresa in the local title. This company also owned the tramways in Santiago and other Chilean cities, as well as in other countries in South America.

The system was converted to standard gauge and electric operation began on Christmas Day 1904 using 60 double-deck cars built by van der Zypen and Charlier of Köln. These cars were numbered 1-60 and were originally open top with canopies over the stairs. They were arranged for right hand running. There were knifeboard seats on the upper deck, but only over the saloon, which had seven side windows. Bow collectors were suspended on small trolley towers. Some cars were damaged in the severe earthquake which struck the city in 1906, but fortunately none were lost. Around 1915 they briefly received rather strange canvas windscreens, into which two windows were cut. Whether these were meant to protect the drivers against the Chilean climate or against rioting commuters is not now clear.

Further cars were ordered at the end of 1907. These had eight windows in the lower saloon, but were otherwise identical to the first batch. They initially took the numbers 161-180, but later became 71-90. Thirty-two of the double-deck Stephenson horse cars were retained for use as trailers with the electric cars, numbered 101-132, and at least two of these, 102 and another car, were later motorised. They retained the twin stairs but a conventional platform with side entrance was fitted in place of the steps at the end

Two of the original cars (23 on left, 10 on right) in as-built condition, pass at Plaza Sotomayor, Calle Bianco. (Allen Morrison collection)

of the car. It is not clear if they became double-ended or used loops at termini.

The German company had become unpopular even before the first world war and, possibly because of its isolation during that conflict, allowed its fleet to deteriorate, to the point where the city council felt obliged to pass a bye-law restricting the number of standing passengers per car. In an attempt to remedy the situation, 25 of the oldest double-deckers were rebuilt in 1920, being fitted with roofs and enclosed platforms with doors and painted in a new red livery. These were then renumbered 201-225. However, despite a publicity parade which was staged when they entered service, they could not save the situation, and on 10 March 1920 a riot occurred when an inspector attempted to remove passengers from an overcrowded car. In the ensuing chaos, 21 cars were destroyed and DUEG lost all interest in the undertaking, selling it shortly afterwards to the Spanish Compania Hispano-American de Electricidad, which had financial links with Belgium.

The new owners rebuilt the double-deckers in various forms within two years of acquiring the system. This may have been done in stages or certain cars may have been more heavily rebuilt than others. Some appear to have been given platform vestibules, roofs (but no side windows) to the upper deck and modified trucks which lowered the body, while others were lengthened, given roofs as above and also enclosed platforms fitted with doors.

A more striking departure was the order in 1922 for 23 very large bogie double-deckers with central entrances from La Brugeoise, Nicaise and Delculve of Belgium, for use on the interurban line to Vina del Mar. These trams carried the numbers 501-523 and were double-ended. They appear to have been painted cream. The design owed something to the "Broadway Battleship" in New York (qv), but the cars were not built to a low height design, although the entrance involved only two steps from street level to platform. The lower saloon had accommodation for 50 or 52 passengers, on comfortable leather upholstered transverse seats with a rearward-facing bench seat for five or six at the bulkhead separating the driver's cab from the saloon, while the upper deck probably provided seating for 48 or 52, again entirely on upholstered transverse seats. The stairs rose from the left hand side of the platform in the normal direction of travel, though at certain points on the line passengers boarded from a central reservation. The entrances were actually two single-width doorways, with sliding doors. It is not known if these were manually or automatically operated. There were separate cabs for the driver, with side doors. One of these trams featured on a commemorative stamp issued by Chile in 1978. These appear to have been attractive and well-finished cars, the only weak point in the design being the shallow windows of the upper deck which made the saloon rather dark. They were the predecessors of MET 331 of 1930 and thus of the many central entrance cars built for service in Britain and India in the '30s and '40s. It is interesting to note that the MET had actually begun preparation of a design for a central entrance car in 1922 and it would be quite possible that they were aware of the contemporary construction of cars for Chile in Belgium; unfortunately the plans which accompanied the MET proposal have not survived.

Before these bogie cars actually arrived, the undertaking was again sold, this time to a British firm which renamed it Compania de Electricidad de Valparaiso and in turn this firm sold it on to the US-owned Electric Bond and Share. This company rebuilt all the German double-deckers and one of the Belgian cars (504) to single-deck form, although the latter was subsequently re-converted to its original layout. However, in 1943 the mayor of Vina del Mar complained that the heavy double-deck cars were damaging the streets of the town and all were then rebuilt as single-deckers. The system closed on 30 December 1952, the last car being 504. No cars were preserved.

As two of the routes in Valparaiso included severe gradients, some double-deckers were fitted with an extra brake, which operated on plates fitted in a slot between the running rails, rather in the manner of the slot brake on a cable tram.

One of the cars rebuilt in 1920, car 217, is seen on Avenida Espana while working on service 10 (Allen Morrison collection)

The total number of double-deck motor cars operated was probably 105, made up of 80 German cars, 23 Belgian bogie cars and two ex-horse cars. There were also 32 ex-horse cars used as trailers, from which these two had been further rebuilt.

Summary

Chile had, after France and South Africa, the third-largest total of double-deck electric trams to operate outwith the British Isles. It would appear that at least 349 motor cars served its cities, though the total could have been slightly greater. Of this total, some cars served in both Santiago and a provincial city. There were also double-deck trailers in the two main cities, a type of tram not commonly found elsewhere.

The reason for the large number of double-deckers is not easy to ascertain. There was substantial British influence in the commercial life of Chile in the 19th century and this may have led to the choice of double-deckers for many of the horse car lines. Apart from the systems mentioned above, double-deck horse cars also operated in Quillota, Limache, Cartagena, and Talca. Those for Limache were built by Stephenson and were double-ended vehicles of very British appearance, while those for Talca were single-ended cars from Brill. Some of these may later have gone to Cartagena.

However, the driving force behind the use of double-deckers in Santiago seems to have been the very close financial and personal links between the Chilian Electric Tramway and Light Company and the by-then established systems in Cape Town and Port Elizabeth, which had just been constructed by A. Parrish and Company at the time

Belgian bogie car 510 is outbound from the city to Vina del Mar, at the point on Avenida Espana where the central island was used for boarding and alighting. (Allen Morrison collection)

electrification was being discussed in Santiago. In addition, Charles Butters, brother of A.H. Butters, the driving force behind these electrifications, was involved in mining and had links with both Santiago and Valparaiso. An electric railway had opened in a coal mine in the city of Lota in 1894 and C. Butters would certainly have been aware of this, if not actually involved. The exact reason for the involvement of AEG cannot now be ascertained, but the situation in the electricity industry was at that time extremely fluid, with regard to both capital and personnel. (Globalisation is not a new concept!) Many of the entrepreneurs concerned were also active in moving capital into and out of the South African Republic, with a view to destabilising it. The Cape company used double-deckers and it would therefore be natural for its sister company in Chile to do likewise. There appears to have been a strong family resemblance between the five-window cars built by Brill in 1895/6 for Cape Town, and the original double-deck cars built by Herbrand for Santiago, even although the latter were intended to operate in right hand traffic.

Ironically, when a purely British company did obtain control of a large Chilean system – Santiago in 1921 – it cut all double-deckers down to single-deck form.

Most Chilean electric systems observed right hand running, but some did not and there were even variations within a city, as on the Avenida Brasil in Valparaiso, where tracks crossed over to allow left hand running.

URUGUAY

MONTEVIDEO

The capital city of Uruguay was initially served by two electric tramway companies, one British and one German. In 1916 the latter, La Transatlantice, rebuilt two of its single-deckers, 156 and 158, as double-deckers. This conversion was carried out in the company's own workshops. The reason for this experiment is not known. They formed part of a batch of ten cars built by the Saint Louis Car Company in 1908 and were the largest on the system, having ten side windows to the lower saloon. The cars entered service as double-deckers in November 1916, running on lines 13 and 17. These lines ran on a common course from the docks through the city centre, from where line 13 continued to the racecourse, while line 17 branched off to serve the nearby terminus of Piedras Blancas. Heavy traffic on race days may well have been the reason for the experiment with double-deckers. Later they also ran on line 16. They were reconverted to their original form in 1924/5 and, as no further conversions were made, it must be assumed that they were unsuccessful.

As converted they had a top deck which extended over

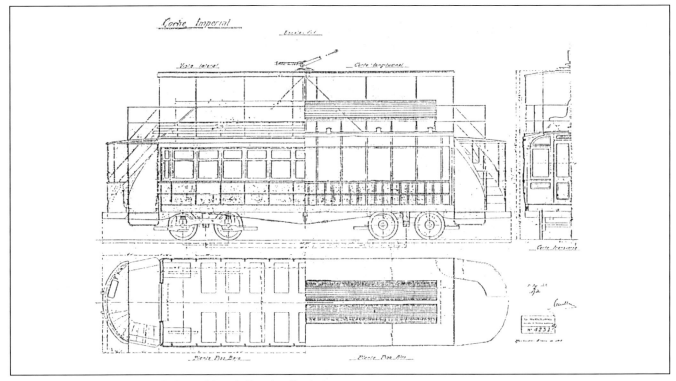

A diagram of one of the double-deckers. (Marcelo Benoit collection)

the length of the lower saloon but not over the platform, which was covered only by a canopy. The upper deck had a light roof but was open at the sides. Quarter turn stairs were fitted and there were front exits on each platform. Seating capacity of the lower saloon was 40, mostly on transverse 2x2 seats and the knifeboard seats on the upper deck would have held at least the same number, giving a high overall capacity. The cars ran on equal wheel bogies and were fitted with Providence type lifeguards. As Uruguay drove on the left, the cars were laid out accordingly.

> **Total number of double-deck electric trams operated: 2**

VENEZUELA

CARACAS

In 1926 this city obtained two double-deckers second-hand from West Hartlepool Corporation, which was then converting its system to trolleybus operation. These were cars 29 and 32 and had been built by Brush in 1920. For that date, they were rather old-fashioned open top cars, mounted on Brill 22E bogies and having two DK 30B 40hp motors and DK K3 controllers. In Britain, seating capacity was 34/39. They were actually sold by West Hartlepool to Messrs Thomas and Company of Liverpool for the Ferrocarril Central de Venezuela and shipped by them from Liverpool to La Guaira. Despite its rather lofty title, this was in fact a fairly short radial line running out of Caracas.

The first six miles had been electrified in 1910 and in 1930 it was taken over by the British-owned Tranvias Electricos de Caracas and merged with the city system. The imported cars were probably used on this line. No pictures showing them in use in South America have come to light and nothing is known of their fate. As both systems used a track gauge of 3ft 6in., the trams would not have had to be regauged for use in Caracas, but as traffic in Venezuela drove on the right, they may have been altered to suit this. This was the only example of British double-deckers being sold for further service abroad, other than the later export of museum cars to North America.

Bibliography

The Tramways of Chile, Allen Morrison, Bonde Press, New York, 1992

Tracks and Trackless, Peter Coates, C. Struik, Cape Town, 1976

E. Garcke, Manual of Electrical Undertakings, various numbers

Metropolitan Electric Tramways vol. II. C. S. Smeeton. Light Rail Transit Association, London, 1986

Brill Magazine

Street Railway Journal, various issues

Tramway and Railway World, May 1899

Modern Transport, 19 September 1942

Modern Tramway, no.59, November 1942

Los Tranvias de Buenos Aires. A.G. Podesta, Buenos Aires, 1986

Latin America by Streetcar. Allen Morrison, Bonde Press, New York, 1996

The Tramways of North-East England. W. H. Bett and J. C. Gillham, ed by J.H. Price. Light Railway Transport League, London, 1978

EXPORT OF DOUBLE-DECK TRAMS FROM THE UNITED KINGDOM

Total	System	Date
Dick, Kerr/ ER&TCW/UEC/ English Electric		
	Two-axle cars	
6	East London	1904
4	Lourenço Marques	1904
17	Cape Town	1901/2
3	Wellington	1905
10	Durban	1906
100	Johannesburg	1906/7
4	Porto Alegre	1908/9
4	Malta	1909
	Bogie Cars	
3	Kimberley	1900
9	Cape Town	1901/2
10	Johannesburg	1907
13*	Alexandria	1909
1	Bombay	1932
184*		
Brush		
	Two-axle cars	
10	Pietermaritzburg	1904
5	Malta	(?)1905
15	Johannesburg	1915
2*	Bombay	1920
	Bogie cars	
6	Auckland	1902
6	Pietermaritzburg	1904
10	Johannesburg	1913
6	Cape Town	1924
60*		
British Electric Car Company		
	Two-axle cars	
32*	Alexandria	1903
12	Wellington	1904
16	Malta	1904
60*		

Total	System	Date
Metropolitan-Cammell		
	Two-axle cars	
1	Johannesburg	1933
	Bogie cars	
1	Johannesburg	1933
50	Johannesburg	1936
52		
G F Milnes		
	Two-axle cars	
9	East London	1900/01
22	Durban	1902
6	Durban (trailers, later converted to motor cars)	1902
8	Lourenço Marques	1904
45		
Lancaster Railway Carriage and Wagon Company		
	Two-axle cars	
20	Hobart	1893
Hurst Nelson		
	Two-axle cars	
1*	Copenhagen (car probably built 1898)	1902
16	Durban	1903
	Bogie cars	
1	Hobart	1904
18*		
Mather and Platt		
1	Kimberley (battery car)	1890

Grand total 440* (* number subject to correction)

It is also quite possible that the 14 accumulator cars used in Dunkerque were built in the UK, but this cannot be confirmed and they are not included in the above figures.

The total number of double-deck electric cars exported was therefore about 440, over half of which (229) were accounted for by deliveries to Durban and Johannesburg alone. It is a small percentage both of the number of trams exported from the UK – Dick, Kerr and associated companies alone exported over 8,000 cars – and also of the total number of double-deckers used world-wide. Moreover, of this total, a considerable number, probably 63 trams, were delivered after 1919, rather than in the peak years of tramcar building between 1900 and 1909. There was also of course the supply of equipment to operators who wished to build their own cars and both Brush (to Johannesburg) and English Electric (to Bombay) did considerable business in this way, though again most of this was after 1919.

It might have been expected that, given the preponderance of the double-decker in the British Isles and the strength of the UK's rolling stock industry in the early part of the 20th century, many double-deck trams would have been built in the UK for export. The ties which bound the then empire were strong in both the economic and engineering fields. But as far as tramcar technology was concerned, this did not translate into a wish to copy the mother country's preference for the double-decker. Some other systems were clearly willing to use double-deckers, but preferred to buy from other countries, as the tables given below will show. It is therefore clear that there was either a failure of will on the part of the manufacturers or that overseas operators were simply not interested in copying British practice, no matter how close they were to the mother country in other respects. The exact reason cannot now be ascertained, but there is certainly sufficient evidence to disprove the theory that the double-decker appeared abroad as a result of the spread of British influence in both the engineering and economic fields.

Exports of double-deck trams from the USA to:

New Zealand	3
Argentina	*61
Chile	25
Mexico	8
S Africa	81
France	42
Total	***220**

Exports from Germany to:

Japan	3
Chile	271
Total	**274**

It would appear therefore that Germany and the USA combined succeeded in out-selling Britain in overseas markets for what has always been regarded as a distinctly British type of tramcar. It is ironic too that the most recent export of double-deckers, from Japan to Egypt, has been from a country which had scarcely any experience of the type to a country which was once a destination for exports from Britain!

THE ROLE OF THE DOUBLE-DECKER

From the table below it can be seen that double-decker trams operated in electric service in up to 72 cities outwith the British Isles. In some of these cities, such as Paris and Buenos Aires, these were operated by more than one company and the total number of operators is therefore slightly greater than this. Nevertheless, when set against the total number of systems which have at one time or another run in places throughout the world, this represents a very tiny percentage of the total. But in only 19 of the 73 cities were there more than 20 trams in service, and in only

WORLD TOTALS OF DOUBLE-DECK TRAMS OPERATED IN ELECTRIC SERVICE

City	Motor trams	Trailers	City	Motor trams	Trailers
1 Hong Kong	433 (R)	(See separate table for details)	28 Auckland	6	
			29 Pelotas	5 (B)	
2 Paris area	404	16*	30 Porte Alegre	4	
3 Johannesburg	264		31 Kimberley	4 (1A)	
4 Santiago	206	25*	32 Christchurch	3	54
5 Bombay	141*		33 Osaka	3	
6 Durban	120		34 Vienna	3	
7 Valparaiso	105	30	35 Sydney	3 (1A)	
8 Berlin		100	36 Caracas	2	
9 Buenos Aires	93		37 Montevideo	2	
10 Cape Town	91*		38 Guadalajara	2	
11 Copenhagen	74		39 Versailles	2	
12 Alexandria – Ramleh	67*		40 Metz		1
13 Hobart	67		41 Adelaide	1 (A)	
14 Barcelona	50		42 Traiguen		1*
15 Concepcion	38				
16 Lyon	38		27 North American cities	58*	14 (See separate table for details)
17 Malta	26				
18 Wellington	21		3 Chilean cities		?* (Cars second-hand from Santiago and Buenos Aires)
19 Milan	20	?*			
20 Port Elizabeth	17				
21 Pietermaritzburg	16				
22 East London	15				
23 Vevey-Montreux	15		* Figure subject to correction		
24 Dunkerque	14 (A)		(A) Accumulator cars		
25 Rome	13		(B) Cars may have been second-hand from Buenos Aires		
26 Lourenco Marques	12		(R) Includes rebuildings		
27 Hamburg		10	*NB Not all cars were necessarily in service at the same time*		

TOTAL OF DOUBLE-DECK TRAMS OPERATED BY COMPRESSED AIR

Paris area:	208	229*

TOTAL OF DOUBLE-DECK TRAMS OPERATED BY STEAM POWER

Paris area:	138	60*
Sydney	7	

(Double-deck trailers operated behind steam tram engines are not included, as it would be impossible to give even a rough estimate of the total number)

eight were there one hundred or more double-deckers. Many cities only ever had one or two double-deckers. In only three large cities – Hong Kong, Johannesburg and Durban – have double-deckers formed over 90% of the total fleet, though in three smaller systems – East London, Pietermaritzburg and Malta – the double-deckers represented 100% of all trams operated. In many cases, such as those of Sydney and Lourenço Marques, the cars had only a brief period of operation.

These systems employed a total of more than 2458 motor trams and over 250 trailer cars. To this total may be added 208 compressed air motor trams, 145 self-contained steam trams and one gas tram (borrowed from Britain) plus their associated 229* and 60* trailers respectively. This gives a total of over 2809 mechanically-powered double-deckers and 539* trailers. When set against the total number of trams which have ever run anywhere, these figures are insignificant and it is clear that the double-decker has played only a limited role in tramway history.

The British tradition certainly influenced the choice of double-deckers for use on the municipal systems of Southern Africa. With some modifications to the cars themselves, Johannesburg and Durban were essentially British systems transported 6,000 miles from the mother country, and the smaller systems such as East London were typical of smaller British systems developed before the motor bus had become a practical proposition for urban transport. However, Pretoria, the former capital of the South African Republic, and the sole Afrikaaner city to have an electric tramway system, would have nothing to do with the concept. The company systems in Cape Colony showed very marked traces of North American influence in their use of double-deckers. In later days, some operators preferred to build their own cars, often, it is true, using British components.

In Australasia, apart from Hobart, the double-decker made little headway, despite the then close ties between New Zealand, Australia and Britain. Even in Hobart the double-deckers were gradually outnumbered and then totally replaced by single-deckers. Both New Zealand and Australia went on to develop their own very characteristic designs of single-decker before reverting, in the case of Australia in recent times, to designs from mainland Europe. Perhaps the double-deck idea would have been accepted in New Zealand if it had not been for the Christmas Eve accident in Auckland.

The four Indian cities which had electric tram systems in the days of the British Raj – Bombay, Delhi, Madras and Kanpur – preferred the single-decker, as did Rangoon in Burma and Colombo in what was then Ceylon. Of the smaller colonies, only Malta and Hong Kong had double-deckers, the others, such as Kingston (Jamaica) using single-deckers only.

Hong Kong, of course, went on to be the world's second largest user of double-deck trams and to-day still runs a fleet of these. The original inspiration was certainly British, but the concept was soon refined locally to produce designs which had little in common with those operated in Britain. Ironically, when new double-deckers were required in recent years for the heritage line opened in Birkenhead, the operator bought two purpose-built cars from Hong Kong, the only difference from the local version being the fitting of standard gauge trucks. The prospect of these vehicles running in the streets of an English city struck horror into the hearts of those now responsible for health and safety matters in transport, and they have been allowed into service only under very strict conditions, and with a limited number of passengers. Presumably those responsible for the restrictions placed on the running of these double-deckers have not seen them running in Hong Kong and carrying passenger loads unlikely to be encountered in Birkenhead!

In South America, where Britain had large investments in railways and tramways, it might have been expected that there would have been widespread adoption of double-deckers. Yet where this was the case, the reasons for the choice of these appear to have stemmed from the influence of the USA, based on practice on US systems in southern Africa, rather than from Britain itself. Germany and, to a lesser extent, the USA far out-sold Britain, and only four of all the trams exported from Britain to the countries concerned were double-deckers.

The concept did find a toe-hold in Egypt, one of Britain's other "economic" colonies, which it has retained to this day, but it did not spread beyond Alexandria, and both French and Belgian single-deck trams far out-numbered those built in Britain in both that city and Cairo.

However, in Paris, the city which used most double-deck trams, the practice had nothing at all to do with Britain and stemmed directly from horse car days, when the only means of achieving anything approaching an economic payload was to put seats on the roof of the car. In turn this probably derived from stage coach practice, copied in the early days of street railways in the USA and introduced into France with the original "American" line. The particular arrangements under which tramways operated in the French capital in the late 19th century did not favour capital investment on any large scale, and thus militated against conventional methods of electrification. In place of this, a variety of forms of motive power were developed and grafted on to vehicle design derived directly from the horse tram. As soon as the legal and financial position of the companies, especially the CGO, was put on to a more rational footing, these forms of traction disappeared very quickly and, with them, the double-decker. Only the conventional electrification and rolling stock of the CFN system had anything approaching a normal life span.

Where used in North America, the double-decker was very much a local product. In many early cases, it followed on directly from horse car design and in some cases from the actual rebuilding of horse cars. Some years later, attempts were made to develop the double-decker into a high capacity vehicle for city use, but these were without lasting result. Street railway technology and vehicle design were advancing rapidly in the USA between 1895 and

1905, the period in which electrification of most British systems was carried out, and by the latter date high capacity bogie single-deckers were available for urban use, making the double-decker superfluous. Very soon afterwards, changes in fare collection methods reinforced the advantages of the single-decker, in many cities because they allowed the introduction of one-person operation. The double-decker saw its greatest use in the USA for pleasure traffic, where there was a demand for high seating capacity for passengers who were riding for a relatively long distance. Canada, though still flying the Union Jack at this time, followed US practice in all transport matters without even making the limited experiments with double-deckers which were made south of the border, other than two cars in Toronto. However, one aspect of US technology did ultimately feed back into British design. That was the concept of the central-entrance double-decker, with only one step up to its platform, as developed in the USA about 1912. Perhaps coming via Chile, the design had some success in the UK in the 1930s, and the surviving "Balloon" cars in Blackpool are the direct descendants of the cars built for New York and other cities almost ninety years ago.

It may therefore be concluded that the idea that the double-deck tram when used overseas was an essentially British concept had at best a limited application. Britain was not in any case a pioneer in tramway technology, lagging in such matters well behind the USA and Germany, and it had already lost any lead it might have had by the time electrification was becoming commonplace. The various dominions seem in transport matters to have preferred to go their own ways. There also seems to have been some failure to succeed with the double-decker in exports. It may also be noted that in the post-1930 period, there was no attempt to sell surplus but still sound cars for further service overseas, apart from the cars which went to Caracas.

The double-deck tram was easily adapted for the operation of a two-class fare structure and as such it was used in many places, such as Paris, Rome and Alexandria. It may have been thought that it could also become an instrument of racial segregation, but, apart from Lourenço Marques, this does not seem to have been the case. Johannesburg, the only city in South Africa which enforced racial segregation in tramway days, did so by the operation of separate cars, most of which had been adapted to give a higher capacity, running at cheaper fares. There is however evidence that in Bombay the tram was viewed as a proletarian form of transport, as was often the case in Britain, and this possibly applied in Hong Kong in the days before mass tourism. In the novel "The Monkey King" the tram is referred to as the lowest form of public transport, only to be used as a last resort. The wheel has now certainly turned full circle, since no self-respecting tourist would now visit the city without having at least one tram ride and the trams have also become a publicity symbol for it.

In summary, it may be said that, where it did appear, the double-deck tram, though limited in application, took on some interesting forms and designs. Its use was by no means always inspired by British practice. It is good to be able to conclude its history in the knowledge that, after more than a century of use, it is still playing a very active role in meeting the transport needs of two important cities, Alexandria and Hong Kong.

INDEX

First page reference numbers to countries and towns

continued on page 179

VIDEO PRODUCTIONS

about the history of the tramway and trolley bus systems of Tasmania, the island state of Australia

---

"The Wonderful Tramways of Mr Parker & Mr Jinks"

running time 2 hours, VHS PAL

Making use of old film footage and photographic material never before seen in a video presentation, The Wonderful Tramways of Mr Parker and Mr Jinks tells the story of the Hobert and Launceston tramways from their very beginnings right to the end of trolley bus operation in 1968. See film of the 1893 Siemens tramcars with their primitive bow collectors. Watch double-deck trams arriving and departing at the busy Hobart GPO terminus. Learn how trolley buses were daily towed out of the Hobart depot by trams to take up running under the wires. Attend the 1911 official opening ceremony of the Launceston Municipal Tramways through the movie camera of the English Amusement Company! Know why Hobart trams used bow collectors, and Launceston trams used swivel-head trolley poles. Learn why the two Tasmanian tramways were different to all of the Australian mainland systems. And of course, find out the answer to... Who were Mr Parker and Mr Jinks?

"Trolley Buses in Hobart"

running time 90 minutes, VHS PAL

For 33 years trolley buses provided a reliable and comfortable form of public transport for the citizens of Hobart. Commencing with one Leyland trolley bus running to Huon Road, these quiet electric vehicles eventually operated over eight routes in Hobart, displacing many of the tram services. Six Australian cities had trolley bus systems, but only in Hobart and Launceston did the trolley bus become the dominant form of public street transport, and with just 3% of the population, Tasmania operated 28% of Australia's trolley buses. All of the Australian trolley bus systems are reviewed in this video production, but the main focus is on Hobart. Extensive use is made of old film footage to explain the history of the system from its opening in 1935 to its closure in 1968. Many engineering and operational features are described, together with details of the Leyland and BUT vehicles. All routes are detailed, and a route map is enclosed so that viewers can navigate their way around the Hobart trolley bus system.

- Price per each including airmail to UK AUD61.00 (Around £22)
- Price if both videos ordered together AUD110.00 (around £40)
- Visa, Mastercard or bank draft, payable only in Australian Dollars

Available from Efftech Pty Ltd
PO Box 4043 Doncaster Heights, Victoria 3109, Australia
Fax: +613 9842 0859
E-mail: efftech@bigpond.com

INDEX

A SELECTION OF OTHER BOOKS PUBLISHED BY ADAM GORDON

My fifty years in Transport – H.Grundy, s/b, 54 pages, 26 illustrations, covers tramways of North Staffordshire, Blackburn, Potteries, Wrexham, and Stalybridge, Hyde, Mossley & Dukinfield, £10

The Cable System of Tramway Traction – 1896, contemporary look at cable systems at home and abroad, 56pp, 1994, 8 illustrations, s/b, £10

Clippie – Z. Katin, a few months in the life of a tram and bus conductress in the war in Sheffield, s/b, 124pp, £7

The Definitive Guide to Trams (including Funiculars) in The British Isles – D. Voice, s/b, 184pp, £15

Double Century – S. Basnett & K. Pearson, h/b, 144pp including 8 in colour, £15

The Douglas Horse Tramway – K. Pearson, s/b, 96pp, over 135 illustrations, £14.50

Edinburgh's Transport, Volume 2, The Corporation Years, 1919-1975 – D. Hunter, s/b, 192pp, £20

Edinburgh Street Tramways Company Rules and Regulations, reprint of 1883 publication, 56pp, s/b, £8

The Feltham Car of the Metropolitan Electric and London United Tramways, reprint of 1931 pub., s/b, 18pp, £5

Glasgow Subway Album – G. Watson, s/b, 64pp, all colour, £10

History of the Steam Tram – H. Whitcombe, h/b, over 70pp, well illustrated, £12

How to go Tram and Tramway Modelling – D. Voice, s/b, 168pp, 184 illustrations, £15

Kidderminster and Stourport Electric Tramway Co Rules and Regulations, 58pp, s/b, reprint of 1899 pub., £7

London County Council Tramways Guide to Reopening of Kingsway Subway – reprint, s/b, 32pp, £6

London County Council Tramways Motorman's Handbook, s/b, 32pp, limited edition, reprint of 1928 pub., £6

London Transport Bus Routes, Central Area No.2 1943, s/b reprint, folds out into c.11" x 17", limited ed., £5

The Modern Tramway, volumes 1 & 2, 1938-9, reprint of first 24 issues, h/b, 214pp, £38

My Life in Many States and in Foreign Lands, G. Train, s/b, reprint of 1902 pub., over 350pp, £12

The Overhaul of Tramcars, London Transport, s/b reprint of 1935 publication, 26pp, £6

Source Book of Literature Relating to Scottish Tramways – D. Croft and A. Gordon, s/b, 48pp, £5

Source Book of Literature Relating to Welsh Tramways – D. Croft & A. Gordon, s/b, 28pp, £4

Source Book of Literature Relating to North East Tramways – D. Croft & A. Gordon, s/b, 32pp, £4

Toy and Model Trams of the World, volume 1 – G. Kure & D. Voice, 128pp, all colour, £25

The Training of Drivers and Conductors of Buses, Trams & Trolleybuses, s/b reprint of 1936 pub., 20pp, £6

Tramways and Electric Railways in the Nineteenth Century (Electric Railway Number of Cassier's Magazine of 1899), h/b, over 250pp, £23

Tramways – Their Construction and Working – D. Clark, reprint of second edition of 1894, 12 plates and over 400 line drawings, h/b, over 750pp, £32

Tramways of Reading – H. Jordan, second edition, h/b, 96pp, 30 illustrations and 1 map, £12

Tramway Review, volumes 1 & 2, h/b reprint of issues 1-16, 1950-1954, includes articles on tramways in East Ham, Nottingham, Luton, Huddersfield, Barking, Sheffield, Oldham, Chester, Ilford, Wallasey, Leyton, Darlington, Cork, Lytham, Walthamstow, Isle of Man and Ireland, numerous illustrations and maps, £23

The Twilight Years of the Glasgow Tram, s/b, 144pp, over 250 coloured pictures, £25

The Twilight Years of the Edinburgh Tram – A. Brotchie, s/b, 194 photographs including 152 in colour, £25

The Wearing of the Green – W. Tollan, s/b, 96pp, 64pp in mono, 16pp in colour, £12

From Death Into Life – W. Haslam, s/b, 250pp, the dramatic autobiography of a clergyman who was converted by, or at least during his own sermon! £8

The Chateau Story – E. Varley, s/b, 64pp, all colour, a mainly animal 'fairy-tale', set in France long ago in the reign of a King Louis, described as "a children's story for grown-ups, or a grown-up's story for children", £10

The Wantage Tramway – S. H. Pearce Higgins, h/b reprint, 208pp, dust-wrapper, with an Introduction by John Betjeman, £28

Omnibus and Cabs – Their Origin and History, H.C. Moore, h/b reprint, 304pp, dust-wrapper, £25

Postage and Packing, UK Retail: please add 10% of the value of the order up to £4.90 maximum. Orders £50 and over post free. Overseas postage extra, at cost. Overseas payments must please be by cheque payable in sterling drawn on a British Bank.

Adam Gordon, Kintradwell Farmhouse, Brora, Sutherland KW9 6LU.   Tel: 01408 622660.
E-mail: adam@adamgordon.freewire.co.uk